Telemarketing in action

Telemarketing in action

A handbook of marketing and sales applications

Michael Stevens

McGRAW-HILL BOOK COMPANY

London · New York · St Louis · San Francisco · Auckland
Bogotá · Caracas · Lisbon · Madrid · Mexico · Milan
Montreal · New Delhi · Panama · Paris · San Juan
São Paulo · Singapore · Sydney · Tokyo · Toronto

Published by
McGRAW–HILL Book Company Europe
Shoppenhangers Road, Maidenhead, Berkshire SL6 2QL, England
Telephone 01628 23432
Fax 01628 770224

British Library Cataloguing in Publication Data
Stevens, Michael
    Telemarketing in Action: Handbook of
    Marketing and Sales Applications.–
    (McGraw-Hill Marketing for Professionals Series)
    I. Title II. Series
    658.8

    ISBN 0-07-707863-2

Library of Congress Cataloging-in-Publication Data
Stevens, Michael
    Telemarketing in action: a handbook of marketing and sales
    appplications / Michael Stevens.
        p. cm.
    Includes index.
    ISBN 0-07-707863-2
    1. Telemarketing. 2. Telephone selling. 3. Database marketing.
    I. Title.
    HF5415.1265.S743   1995
    658.8'4–dc20   95-7968
                                                                 CIP

2345 BL 98765

Typeset by BookEns Ltd, Royston, Herts.
and printed and bound in Great Britain by Biddles Ltd., Guildford.

Printed on permanent paper in compliance with the ISO Standard 9706.

To Margaret Bennett, for her continual support – including the friendly brickbats

Contents

Series foreword

The series title, Marketing for Professionals, was not chosen lightly, and it carries with it certain clear responsibilities for publisher, authors and series advisers alike.

First, the books must actually be intended and written for marketing practitioners. Most, if not all, will undoubtedly serve a valuable purpose for students of marketing. However, from the outset the primary objective of this series is to to help the professional hands-on marketer to do his or her job that little (but important) bit better.

In turn, this commitment has helped to establish some basic ground rules: no 'Janet-and-John' first steps for toddlers; no lessons in egg-sucking for grandmothers (who these days may have a Business Studies degree); and equally, no withdrawal into the more esoteric and abstruse realms of academe.

It follows that the subject matter of the books must be practical and of topical value to marketers operating—indeed, battling—in today's rapidly evolving and violently competitive business environment. Cases and case material must be relevant and valid for today; where authors deal with familiar marketing tools and techniques, these must be in terms which, again, update and adapt them, bringing them as close as possible to what, in the current idiom, we call the leading edge.

This has set demanding standards but, such is the calibre of authors contributing to the series, perfectly acceptable ones. The authors are either senior marketers or leading consultants and marketing academics with a strong practical background in management. Indeed, a number in both categories (and as the series extends, it is to be hoped, a growing proportion) are themselves members of The Marketing Society, with the prerequisite level of seniority and experience that implies.

McGraw-Hill Book Company Europe, as professional in its field as the target marketers are in theirs, has consulted The Marketing Society extensively in the search for suitable topics and authors, and in the evaluation and, if necessary, revision of proposals and manuscripts for new additions to the series.

The result is a well-presented and growing library of modern, thoughtful and extremely useful handbooks covering eventually all aspects of marketing. It is a library that every marketing professional will want to have on his or her bookshelf. It is also a series with which The Marketing Society is very pleased to be associated, and is equally happy to endorse.

Gordon Medcalf
Director General
The Marketing Society

THE MARKETING SOCIETY

THE MARKETING SOCIETY

The Marketing Society is the professional UK body for senior practising marketing people. It was founded in 1959 and currently has 2300 members.

The aim of the Society is to provide a forum for senior marketers through which the exchange of experience and opinion will advance marketing as the core of successful business growth. To this end it mounts a large and varied programme of events, and provides an increasing range of member services.

Foreword

by Alan Bigg, Chairman, Brann

For many years the focus of much marketing and advertising has been on building awareness and image. The heroes have been those who produced great advertising campaigns, the Heinekens, Volvos and Persils of this world. Product plans talked of conquest, of winning new customers. The big image-building launch was the pinnacle of achievement.

In the nineties there has been a new focus. Companies have been building their success on customer relationships. Retention, loyalty and commitment have become the watchwords. Building customer lifetime value has become the marketing grail.

Relationship building, however, is a two-way process. Before the customer will deliver commitment, the advertiser must show enthusiasm and responsiveness. In this context, the first human contact between supplier and customer has proved crucial time and time again. Increasingly this contact is being established through the telephone and increasingly the customer is using the telephone as the main means of communication. We only have to look at the growth of direct banking and insurance for evidence of this.

While the use of the telephone is becoming more central to the marketing activity of many companies, its scope is still less understood than it should be. That is why this book, with its concentration on the many and varied ways that companies can use the telephone, will be so valuable.

At the moment we are only skimming the surface of this medium's potential. As technology helps us deliver more support to the operator and more information to the marketer, the prizes will go to those who understand and harness this most powerful personal communication tool.

Foreword

by Roger Gilbert, Head of BT *Tele*marketing Services

In 1980, *The Times* commented that 'the most powerful marketing tool ever invented lies unused on desks up and down the country.'

In 1994, in the UK alone, telemarketing spend was more than £10 billion in an industry growing at 20 per cent a year and similar developments can be seen emerging across the whole of Europe. Telemarketing has come-of-age and is helping companies, large and small, to build their businesses and enhance their relationships with customers.

The telemarketing industry has undergone a technological revolution in the past decade. Step change improvements in call management flexibility provided by intelligent public networks, when integrated with powerful computer databases, are transforming the way companies do business with their customers. The technology of power diallers, automated voice response and caller line identification are all part of a solution that is offering the opportunity to do better business on the telephone.

A marriage of this technology and new business practice has made it possible for even the largest company to treat its customers with the same individuality, intimacy and immediacy as once found in the traditional corner shop. The telephone has become the latter day equivalent of the corner shop counter and the call centre the heart of the 'Cornershop Corporation'.

The vast majority of consumers now appreciate the benefits of doing business by phone. In addition, the growth of freephone and local call rate numbers with their inherent message of 'we value the business we do with you' has opened up a dialogue between businesses and their customers with benefits to both parties in terms of loyalty, accessibility and enhanced relationships.

The impact on companies has been profound with many early adopters reaping rewards by transforming the way business is done in areas from financial services to catalogue sales. This book will be invaluable in enabling businesses who are considering using telemarketing, perhaps for the first time, to emulate their success. 'Welcome to the Cornershop Corporation'.

Acknowledgements

Brann, and in particular their telemarketing operation, Brann Contact 24, supported this book from the outset and made the project possible by their subsidy of the research costs. BT's sponsorship has enabled more comprehensive coverage of the subject and at a reasonable cover price. I am indebted to both organizations for helping to make this information available to a wider audience.

The views expressed here are those of the author, but many individuals and organizations have contributed information. In particular, I would like to thank the following organizations for their help with specific chapters: *Cal*com Associates (the application of telemarketing), Direct TV and Quantum International (direct response—television), Research International (market research—international), Telelab (crisis management), Fleishman-Hillard, Chicago (investor relations), and Facter Fox International and the Chapter One Group (campaigning and fund raising).

I am grateful to all the organizations who agreed to the publication of material, especially the Henley Centre, BT and Channel 4 Television for their contribution to the appendices.

The following were especially helpful in gathering case study material: Aspect Telecommunications, B's Management Services, Berkeley Public Relations, BPS Téléperformance, Brann Contact 24, Datapoint UK, De Visscher & Van Nevel, The Decisions Group, The Editorial Consultancy, EIS Limited, Gray Associates, Infoplan, Merit Direct, Ogilvy & Mather Teleservices, Periphonics, Procter & Procter, Programmes, and TDS.

My thanks go also to Handel Communications for their early involvement in the project.

Introduction

My fascination with telemarketing was sparked by a chance meeting, in 1986, with the co-founder of one of the UK's first telemarketing agencies. The details of that meeting are long forgotten, but not the experience. It continues to amaze me that something as seemingly ordinary and spontaneous as a telephone conversation can assume such a powerful role in marketing and sales.

Those were early days. The intervening years have seen incredible advances, particularly in supporting technologies. Telemarketing is now accepted as a vital ingredient in the marketing mix, for companies of all sizes in every business sector. For an increasing number of organizations it is the principal channel to the marketplace.

Even so, telemarketing is still in its adolescence and has all the youthful vigour associated with that age of discovery. Aided and abetted by infant technologies such as digital telecommunications, it is bounding headlong into the twenty-first century. It is an exciting period for the telemarketing industry, with expanding horizons yet to be explored.

Digital telecommunications are set to revolutionize world economics and many aspects of our lives before the end of the century. Telecommunication is the medium of telemarketing. It enables direct, personal communication with individuals in the marketplace. More than that, it provides a global infrastructure – for voice, data and visual communication – which enables the largest multinational corporations, and the most remotely situated suppliers, to deliver first-class 'corner shop' service to people, wherever they are, on a one-to-one basis. These advances in telecommunication mean that global village commerce is becoming a reality, and telemarketing is at the forefront of exploiting the opportunities being created.

However, the medium is only one part of the system. The content, timing and delivery of the message are the aspects that build profitable relationships to achieve long-term business growth and stability. Computer systems technology is increasingly providing more accurate targeting and instant access to more wide-ranging information, so that telemarketers can respond in a timely, knowledgeable and personal way to the needs of individuals. But while advancing technology is helping businesses to become more sophisticated, quicker and more cost-efficient in their response, it is only an enabler. It is the *live interaction* that gives real power to telemarketing.

Telemarketing is, above all, a people business, both through direct contact with individuals in the marketplace and in the thought processes that give rise to effective campaigns. The best telemarketing arises from a regard for the kaleidoscope of individual needs, combined with an appreciation of business objectives and processes. A telemarketer on the telephone is a caring partner who is dedicated to using available resources to help another person. The telemarketing planner, on the other hand, has the task of devising ways of creating and using contact opportunities with diverse audiences to deliver maximum value to the company and each of its contacts.

Building sustainable profitable relationships – with both external and internal audiences – is the most pressing need in business today. An attitude of cooperation for mutual benefit is beginning to pervade business planning and market strategy. The aim is to win and keep the trust of members of influential audiences so that the organization becomes their preferred partner in business. Telemarketing – with its unique blend of qualities for one-to-one communication – has a key role to play in building and sustaining these partnerships. Most importantly, it has both tactical and strategic significance. Live interaction with a marketplace means that telemarketing is a highly responsive and dynamic medium. It is sensitive not only to the changing needs of individuals but also to the needs of whole market segments. Response times can therefore be reduced to a minimum without jeopardizing the quality of those responses. As a barometer of market needs and concerns, it is also a seeding ground for new ways to view and relate to a company's influential audiences. Capitalizing on this unique position – the only controlled, potentially large-scale live interface between an organization and its markets – requires a creative and innovative response, through campaigns or applications which break new ground. Telemarketing is, after all, one of the youngest marketing disciplines. It should offer businesses opportunities to leap ahead of the competition by creating partnerships of greater value to both the company and its influential audiences. That is the challenge of telemarketing into the next century.

About this book

First and foremost, this book is about the applications of telemarketing. It examines the many ways of building value into planned and controlled telephone contact with members of influential audiences, such as customers, prospects, dealers, retailers, suppliers, charity donors and investors. However, the book is not comprehensive. Telemarketing has become a very sophisticated and complex discipline and the current pace of advance is astounding. A single book does not offer the scope to cover all aspects in detail, nor does the gestation period permit inclusion of the very latest developments. Instead, the aim here is to set the scene. By illustrating the diversity of telemarketing applications, and by showing how they relate to the challenges facing businesses today, we hope the book will provide an understanding of the current and future potential of this vital business tool.

Examining telemarketing applications one by one has the advantage of providing easy access to information, but it also creates a number of problems. Telemarketing campaigns are never undertaken in isolation, even when they are undertaken as discrete activities. They are designed, ultimately, to fulfil a business need and therefore represent a part of a broader plan. This often includes other marketing and sales activities with which telemarketing must be integrated. Telemarketing is also highly flexible; as flexible as a conversation. So a campaign designed to *generate leads*, for example, can also serve a *sales promotion* function. It may also employ *direct response* techniques, and in most situations will ultimately be aimed at *selling*. In this book, all of these topics are covered in separate chapters. If you want information on how organizations can service customer accounts by telephone, for example, you can find it in the chapter on account servicing, but the case studies there are broader than that subject. On most occasions case studies have been used to illustrate specific points about an application. Additional detail, which may appear more applicable to another chapter, is provided so that campaigns can be understood in their entirety, in the context of their role in fulfilling particular business needs.

Most of the application areas are interrelated and interdependent. A framework is needed to give an overview of what different applications can achieve and to show how decisions are made about which types of campaign are most appropriate in particular situations. Part One of the book is designed to provide this framework.

In Part Two, covering applications, all but the final two chapters ('Campaigning and fund raising' and 'Investor relations') are relevant to most types of business. Together they provide a detailed view of the potential for using telemarketing. Each chapter is designed to provide:

- an understanding of the specific business needs which telemarketing can help to fulfil;
- an appreciation of why telemarketing may be the preferred solution;
- practical guidelines on how telemarketing is used and the benefits it can deliver;
- insight into the flexibility of telemarketing in a given application;
- proof, by example, of the results that can be achieved; and
- food for thought about how a business could implement telemarketing to boost performance and profitability.

Telemarketing uses a commonplace technology, often taken for granted by businesses and consumers, and yet it is one of the most powerful and significant of the marketing disciplines. It is a tool which empowers whole organizations, enabling them to learn, adapt and respond more quickly to market needs, to improve market coverage, and to give added value. It enables them to measure costs accurately, to rationalize expenditure, and to stabilize overheads while improving service levels. These are opportunities which businesses wanting to survive in the competitive nineties and beyond must exploit to the full.

PART ONE
FRAMEWORK FOR APPLICATIONS

1
The principles of telemarketing

Telemarketing is the planned and controlled use of telephone communication to build profitable long-term relationships with members of influential audiences who impact on an organization's success.

1.1 Key elements

Breaking the above definition into its constituent parts gives some idea of the principles and scope of telemarketing. The key elements are:

1. *Planned.* Every telemarketing call is designed to achieve a specific objective. This objective is defined within the context of a current marketing plan and with regard to the profile of the target audience. Secondary objectives, perhaps gathering useful information from contacts, can be achieved during the same call. The structure and content of calls is planned to help telemarketers respond to each contact personally, while remaining true to their objectives.
2. *Controlled.* The cost and outcome of each call is known immediately the call ends, so the cost-efficiency of a telemarketing campaign can be monitored continuously. Targets can be set for the number of calls to be made per hour, the number of decision makers to be contacted, and the proportion of calls where the objective is achieved. All aspects of a campaign can be manipulated (targeting, call content, timing, delivery, etc.) until the lowest cost per positive result is achieved. Calling can be initiated, increased, decreased or stopped, depending upon need and the results being achieved.
3. *Communication.* Although telemarketers are aiming to achieve specific objectives during calls, they are in a dialogue with another person. Every conversation allows a free interchange to impart and obtain information.
4. *Profitable long-term relationships.* The aim of all telemarketing calls, irrespective of their particular objective, is to progress the relationship with each contact. A typical path for this relationship is from suspect

(you think they want what you offer), to prospect (you know they want it), to customer (they have bought it), to client or account customer (if you supply it and they need it, they will buy from you), to advocate (they will recommend you to others). A relationship can also be defined in terms of its longevity and its monetary value. In general, the longer the relationship lasts, the greater its value. Because it costs less to market to loyal customers, the longer the relationship the more profitable it becomes. The telephone is a flexible, cost-efficient way of maintaining regular contact which is so important in developing relationships.

5. *Influential audiences.* The focus in business today is not only on finding, winning and keeping customers. Most businesses also have relationships with other audiences which can influence their performance and profitability. Dealers, for example, may play a crucial role, as do suppliers and, in many instances, shareholders and legislators. Every business has a number of influential audiences (see Table 1.1) and the telephone can play a role in building relationships with all of them.

Table 1.1   Influential audiences

Suspects, prospects, customers, clients, advocates
Retailers, dealers, wholesalers
Suppliers
Shareholders/investors, financial advisers
Legislators
Lobby groups
Donors, supporters, campaigners

When these facets of telemarketing are considered in the light of its flexibility and key features – to be examined in the next two sections – its importance in marketing communications becomes clear.

1.2   A multitude of options

Telemarketing utilizes inbound and outbound calls, each of which can be used to impart and to gather information. Inbound calls are generated by publicizing or advertising a telephone number, either for a specific purpose, such as to obtain a brochure, or for general purpose use, such as a customer information centre. Any medium that can convey a telephone number, visually or aurally, can be used to encourage people to call. The generic term for promoting a number in this way is 'direct response advertising'.

According to the telemarketing consultancy *Cal*com Associates, whatever the reason people have for calling, inbound calls should be handled in a way that:

- satisfies the caller;
- sets a platform for future dialogue;
- delivers the company image and brand values;
- complements approaches made through other media.

People making inbound calls want to make contact with the company, and have a reason for calling. The more accurate the targeting (i.e. promoting the number to the people the company wants to make contact) the better the quality and number of responses.

Outbound calls are made to people selected as appropriate for receiving a particular type of call. An outbound call, irrespective of its purpose, should also satisfy the four criteria mentioned above. Since the recipients of outbound calls are not usually expecting the call, accurate targeting (i.e. making the call appropriate to the individual) is vitally important. The more accurate the targeting the more positively will contacts respond. The call content should also be interesting and skilfully presented.

Telemarketing is rarely undertaken as an isolated activity. It is most effective when integrated with other media. There are many options for integration with media, such as mail, print and broadcast advertising, exhibitions, on-pack advertising, events, personal visits, etc., and some examples are shown in Figure 1.1. The synergy between two well-integrated media produces results greater than their sum. A mailing, for example, might encourage 2 to 3 per cent of recipients to respond. An outbound call might produce a positive response of perhaps 2 to 8 per cent. Combining the two – for example, by calling those who do not respond to a mailing – can often lift response rates to well above 15 per cent.

Each marketing communications medium has a different mix of qualities (including cost, precision of targeting, penetration, etc.) which makes it more appropriate than others for certain purposes. A direct response television commercial for a car, for example, can be used to target a large population among which the company knows there are prospects but for whom it does not have individual details. Those people are offered a telephone response number because that is a quick and convenient way by which they can obtain further information. When they call, their details are taken and they are sent a brochure together with the offer of a free test drive at their local dealership. A week later they are called to determine their interest and possibly book a test drive. A short time after the test drive they might be called again to discuss a possible purchase and payment options. This sequence of events is a contact strategy. Contact strategies are simply a set of integrated marketing communications designed to move members of a target audience forward in their relationship with the company. Media and methods (such as the offer) are mixed and combined in a way that achieves the objective most cost-effectively. This is integrated marketing.

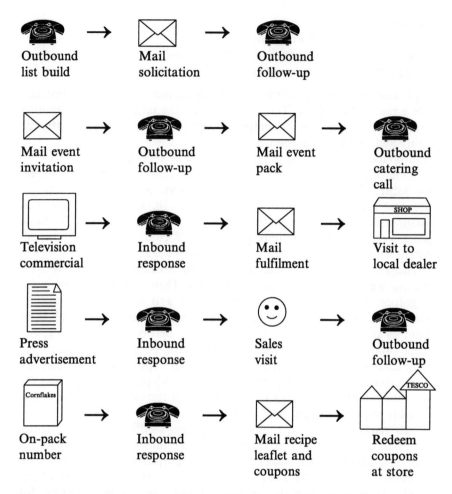

Figure 1.1 Integrating the telephone with other media (Courtesy of *Cal*com Associates)

Telemarketing can be used in a wide range of applications because of the flexibility of live communication. However, its power comes from a mix of features which deliver wide-ranging benefits when used appropriately.

1.3 Powerful features and benefits

A telephone conversation might seem ordinary, but in the hands of professionals it becomes a sophisticated, incisive marketing tool. First and foremost, the telephone offers the opportunity for a live, personal dialogue.

Table 1.2 Two sides of telemarketing

Strengths	Weaknesses
Precision targeting	Intangible
Interactive dialogue	Comparatively low volume
Personal contact	Relatively high unit cost
Fast response	Sometimes unacceptably intrusive
Accessibility	Ease of misuse and abuse
Accuracy and honesty	
Measurable activity	
Accountable costs/benefits	
Easy testing	
Flexible application	
Cost-efficiency	
Discretion	

Nothing is more influential in building relationships and the only similar opportunity is an expensive face-to-face meeting. But telephone communication has much broader significance due to its unique blend of characteristics. These are listed in Table 1.2 and are described briefly below.

1. *Precision targeting.* Each party to a telephone conversation can identify the other. A company can ensure that it reaches the right decision maker, or can tailor the message when talking with someone else. Customers can ensure that requests or instructions are given to the appropriate people within a company when talking with them.

2. *Interactive dialogue.* An answered call gets a guaranteed response, whether 'yes' or 'no'. Because a conversation is two-way, a call can be progressed according to the needs of either party. A company's response can be tailored precisely to satisfy the customer's needs while pursuing its own objectives. A conversation is also a valuable opportunity to exchange information; a telemarketer can ask as well as answer questions and also capture contacts' *ad hoc* comments relating to their specific needs and preferences.

3. *Personal contact.* The parties in a telephone conversation can relate to each other at a human level. A customer can express delight or dissatisfaction and know that these feelings are recognized. Similarly, a company can respond quickly with a human voice interested in the individual. The company's response, if it has prior knowledge of the individual, can be truly personal.

4. *Fast response.* The telephone is not subject to geographical barriers. A company and its customers can initiate contact and be in conversation almost immediately, so the company's response to its markets is fast. It

can start, increase, decrease or stop outbound telephone activity, according to need, almost at a moment's notice. Even inbound calls can be generated within a day or two, if required.

5. *Accessibility.* The telephone enables a company to penetrate all business markets, nationally and internationally, and a growing number of consumers. At the same time there is growing expectation in the marketplace for organizations to be open and easily accessible. The telephone provides individuals with an immediate, direct line of communication with them.

6. *Accuracy and honesty.* Accurate data are vital to effective marketing. Telephone contact is the fastest and most reliable way of gathering, verifying and updating information about individual or corporate contacts. When combined with other marketing tasks, this can also be highly cost-effective. It is known that people are inclined to be more honest and accurate in the information they disclose during a personal conversation than when filling in a printed form. It is also probably true, in many circumstances, that people feel more confident about believing what they are told personally than what they read, provided that a rapport has been established between the two parties.

7. *Measurable activity.* Every aspect of telephone activity can be measured, including call rates, decision-maker contacts and those unavailable, positive and negative responses, with reasons for both. This information is available immediately and continually.

8. *Accountable costs/benefits.* The costs of telephone activity are easily calculated. By comparing these with the measured results, which are known immediately for each call, it is possible continually to monitor cost-effectiveness. Customer value, and the cost of developing each relationship, can be monitored and tracked over time.

9. *Easy testing.* Because the results and cost-effectiveness of telephone activity are known quickly, a company can test different approaches to identify those that work, and those that do not and why, before committing itself to a large investment. By monitoring results closely it is also possible to continually modify the telemarketing activity to achieve optimum results.

10. *Flexible application.* A telephone conversation can be used for an almost limitless number of purposes.

11. *Cost-efficiency.* The unique blend of characteristics of telephone communication make it a highly cost-effective tool in many marketing and sales applications. Because it is accountable, it can be used in those areas where it is most cost-efficient. Also, because applications are easily tested, the way in which it is used can be designed to achieve maximum return on investment.

12. *Discretion.* Competitors will not know the details of another company's

outbound telemarketing activity, and they can only sample (by calling) how it handles inbound calls. Inbound calls can be screened to help identify possible competitor prying.

On the downside, the telephone has some weaknesses which, at first sight, seem to limit its usefulness quite seriously.

1. *Intangible.* A telemarketing conversation is not like a chat with a friend. The visual cues might be lacking when talking with a friend on the telephone but there is extensive prior knowledge which supplements what is said and facilitates communication. Telemarketing conversations are generally blind in that respect, and it requires excellent communication skills to build a rapport with customers and prospects. There is also a more practical drawback in not being able to share visual information directly. Currently this has to be done by some other means, such as mail, fax or computer screen. Nor is there an opportunity for either party to make a written undertaking. Technology will soon overcome these problems with better communication links, such as fax and video, becoming more commonplace in consumer as well as business-to-business markets.

2. *Comparatively low volume.* A telemarketer might make 30 to 40 contacts a day, perhaps double that in some situations. Compare this with a single mailshot to many thousands of contacts and telemarketing contact rates appear very low. However, telephone contact is high-quality communication tailored to the individual. It has many of the benefits of a face-to-face meeting but at a much lower cost and generally at least ten times the contact rate.

3. *Relatively high cost.* Telemarketing is labour intensive and excellent communicators deserve salaries to match their skills (although they do not always receive this recognition). Add telephone charges, overheads, equipment, etc., and the cost per contact can be many times more than direct mail. There are some economies of scale for large organizations which invest in centralized telemarketing operations (such as not duplicating resources and making more efficient use of staff), but it is still an expensive means of communication. It has to be used where it offers benefits over other methods, either in terms of what it can achieve or for reasons of cost. Providing telemarketing support for a field salesforce, for example, can increase their productivity by more than a third.

4. *Unacceptable intrusion.* While the telephone provides a door that is almost always open, no one likes trespassers. In consumer markets, especially, to call uninvited without good reason is almost guaranteed to cause annoyance and do damage to the company's image. Calls should be targeted accurately (with the needs of the contact in mind), made at a

reasonable time, only continued with the individual's permission, and conducted politely and professionally.

5. *Easily misused and abused.* The ease of picking up a telephone, dialling a number and being able to speak to a customer or prospect creates a false sense of security. Even more likely to be mishandled are inbound calls, where individual needs are less easy to predict and suitable responses less easy to plan. Some business people – probably too many – think they know how to use telemarketing because it is 'just making or answering calls'. Yes, it is easy to establish contact, but success lies in the ability to select appropriate contacts and knowing what to do when contact has been made. It takes very little to get it wrong, but it requires a wealth of experience to get it right!

The features of telemarketing combine to make it a powerful, cost-effective medium when used appropriately. Integrated in the marketing mix, it has become a vital tool in the process of identifying, recruiting and retaining customers to maximize their lifetime value, as well as influencing other important audiences. It is a marketing tool for the nineties, helping businesses to address their most pressing concerns arising from increasing competition, the faster pace of change and the globalization of markets. At the same time, technology is enhancing the flexibility and efficiency of the medium.

2
The application of telemarketing

With a technique as flexible as telemarketing, how does an organization decide on the best way to use it? What applications will help it to achieve its business objectives? How does it design campaigns that will strengthen its overall marketing strategy? There are three broad areas to consider:

1. The different telemarketing applications available and the functions they can serve.
2. The tasks an organization needs to undertake to establish and progress its business relationships.
3. Matching needs to the telemarketing options available to provide the most cost-effective business solution.

This book is not the place to detail how business plans lead to marketing strategies and subsequent campaigns. However, it is vital that telemarketing is considered at the outset. The success of direct insurance and direct banking operations provides clear evidence of the strategic significance of telemarketing. The potential role of the telephone should be considered in the planning of how an organization will operate in the marketplace – interacting with its various audiences to help achieve its mission. That is not to say that companies have to rebuild from the ground up, but they should reappraise the channels they use to keep in touch with members of key audiences. By going back to basics and examining the processes through which the business satisfies the needs of these audiences, a company can identify the channels that are best suited to supporting the processes.

2.1 What are the options?

Telemarketing can operate and contribute at many levels within an organization, as summarized in Table 2.1. Their relevance is described briefly below.

Table 2.1   The multi-layered nature of telemarketing

Learning, adapting, responding to market conditions

Accessibility <——> Market penetration and coverage

Finding, acquiring, retaining customers

Building relationships

Marketing tasks/generic applications

Specific campaigns

---

1. The speed and accuracy with which organizations learn, adapt and respond in a changing marketplace is becoming more important with the accelerating rate of change and growing turbulence in the business world. As a channel for live interaction with the marketplace, the telephone offers a window on what is happening, in real-time, and allows a business to respond quickly.
2. People want suppliers to be accessible – quickly and easily. At the same time, competitive pressures mean that companies need to protect their market share by increasing market penetration and coverage. The telephone delivers in both areas.
3. The telephone offers a broad range of opportunities to help companies become more cost-efficient in finding, winning and keeping customers, as well as influencing other important audiences. The end result is greater profitability and business stability.
4. The key to business success today is stable relationships with members of key audiences. Direct personal contact is the most powerful way to build such relationships.
5. Any business typically must undertake a number of generic tasks to build a profitable customer base, such as gathering intelligence about the marketplace, generating and collecting information about leads, promoting and selling the company's goods and services and taking care of its customers. The telemarketing applications which help to achieve these tasks are described later in this chapter.
6. Telemarketing is a creative and flexible medium. Individual campaigns can be engineered to deliver a specific mix of benefits according to current business needs. Any one campaign can not only achieve defined objectives but can also convey corporate and brand values and create a unique 'aura' for the business.

So many options are available that it is difficult to classify them for the purpose of explaining how telemarketing can best be used. In this book they are grouped according to generic application, such as account servicing, sales promotion and traffic generation. The scope of these applications can be extremely wide and the boundaries are fluid and flexible. The brief descriptions below define how they are covered in this book.

List building, cleaning and testing. (a) Building a contact list by phoning contacts and asking for any relevant information required for the intended purpose of the list; (b) cleaning a list by calling contacts to verify and update information already known, so that the list is currently accurate; and (c) testing a list by calling a proportion of contacts to determine its accuracy and/or its fitness for the intended purpose.

Database building and maintenance. The term 'database' implies storing more data and greater depth of information about contacts than is held on a list. Database building and maintenance consists of building lists, enhancing them with useful information on individual contacts, and keeping that information up-to-date. This can be carried out as a dedicated campaign or, more commonly, as a by-product of other forms of telephone contact.

Lead generation, screening and qualification. (a) Identifying leads (suspects, prospects, and even customers for cross-selling or up-selling) through inbound or outbound calling; (b) asking screening questions to learn about their needs and preferences; and (c) using that information to determine their potential value (or qualification) for appropriate follow-up. A variety of telemarketing applications can help in these processes.

Market evaluation and test marketing. When little is known about a market, a list of prospects can be contacted and asked a series of questions designed to provide information about themselves or their business. Collectively, this evaluates the market with information such as its size, structure, potential value and decision-making processes. At the same time it delivers information on individual prospects in that market. A market test can be used for a variety of purposes, such as to identify whether a particular segment of the market will be interested in a new product, or to determine which type of approach yields the best results.

Appointment making and diary management. The process of securing and/or arranging appointments on behalf of salespeople or other specialists and, if required, managing their diary time to fulfil those appointments. Telemarketers can also secure appointments for which each specialist subsequently arranges a date, time and venue.

Account servicing. Using the telephone as a channel for servicing customers' needs. It can be used to support a field salesforce, or to replace them, for all customers or specific customer groups. When customers are serviced only by telephone it is often referred to as telephone account management.

Selling. Securing sales over the telephone on either inbound or outbound calls, including maximizing sales potential through cross-selling and up-selling. Inbound calls may arise from advertising and promotional materials such as catalogues, or from a regular customer base. Outbound calls are made to contacts who have expressed an interest in the company's offering, or have been identified as probably being interested.

Sales promotion. The use of telephone contact to enhance the likelihood of a subsequent sale can take many forms, from describing product benefits and fulfilling sample requests to offering technical advice and product usage information.

Traffic generation. Generating attendance at promotional events or visits to retail outlets or dealerships, often using the telephone in combination with advertising and/or direct mail.

Dealer, distributor and retailer relations. Using the telephone to manage or support the business relationship with intermediaries. It can encompass a wide range of applications, including account servicing, sales promotion, selling, 'customer' service, and lead and traffic generation.

Direct response. Using the telephone as a channel for people to respond to advertising and other promotional activities, and to contact a company for any other reason.

Customer service. The offering and provision of information, help or advice at any stage – before, during and after the buying process – designed to facilitate the purchaser in making appropriate choices and gaining maximum benefit from the products or service offered or supplied.

Customer care. In the context of this book, *care* refers to any activity which adds value to a relationship beyond that which a customer can expect as a 'right' in the current market.

Intelligence gathering and market research. The telephone enables qualitative and quantitative research to be undertaken quickly and often less expensively than other methods. It also provides an opportunity to capture *ad hoc*, non-specific 'intelligence' on the marketplace through regular contact with members of key audiences.

Credit management. Two aspects of credit management are particularly relevant to telemarketing: credit approval and cash (or debt) collection. Credit approval is the process by which a company checks credit worthiness of potential purchasers and makes a decision about granting delayed payment terms. Cash collection is the process of securing payment of monies overdue.

Crisis management. Because of its speed and flexibility, the telephone can play a key role in the management of situations that could lead to commercial damage – for example, by providing direct access to advice during a consumer scare over product tampering. Outbound calling also may be used, for example, to reassure major retailers or key account customers.

Investor relations. As with customer communications, the telephone is a powerful channel for building relationships with investors and investment advisers.

Campaigning and fund raising. The use of the telephone to build profitable relationships with donors, sponsors and supporters of charitable, educational, political and other non-profit organizations.

2.2   Building relationships

The predominant focus for businesses today is building long-term, profitable relationships with members of its key audiences in the most cost-efficient manner. Each of these relationships progresses along a similar path – from suspect to prospect to 'customer'. From another viewpoint, building relationships can be divided into three activities: finding, acquiring and retaining. How a company approaches these three activities depends largely on the business sector, particularly the margins on its goods or services and the scale and nature of its market. Fast-moving consumer good (FMCG) manufacturers, for example, with low margins and a large market, will find and acquire customers with the help of activities such as market research, media advertising and product sampling. Mass targeting and a low cost per contact are a necessity. A supplier of industrial presses, on the other hand, with high margins and a small market, is more likely to use activities such as lead generation, appointment making for field sales visits, and customer service, where the cost is less prohibitive and the higher level of personal contact is merited by the expected customer investment and return. In the middle ground are such companies as car manufacturers, which use a mix of low and higher unit cost activities such as direct response media advertising combined with dealer support for free test drives. Although these broad distinctions generally hold true, there is some blurring of those activities that are considered cost-effective in any given industry. For example, many FMCG companies now use customer carelines to support their marketing effort. And there will always be companies that push forward the boundaries of accepted practice to gain competitive advantage – by developing innovative telemarketing campaigns. The computer software company which offered free telephone support, despite its cost, during free product trials is an example.

Each type of business has its own needs and problems – and there is a suite of telemarketing applications to help. The options for using it to help find, win and keep customers are summarized in Table 2.2. There are no rules which limit the manner in which any particular business can use telemarketing. It is simply a matter of whether it is or is not cost-effective in a given situation.

Table 2.2   Telemarketing applications in finding, acquiring and retaining customers. (Courtesy of *Cal*com Associates)

Finding	Acquiring	Retaining
Market research	Market research	Market research
List building, cleaning, testing	Warm-up (pre-mail)	Welcome call
		Account servicing
Lead generation, screening, qualification		Satisfaction survey
Market evaluation (contact and profile)	Market evaluation (promotion)	Market evaluation (further potential)
Database building (identifying)	Database building (targeting)	Database building (tracking)
Sales promotion (direct response)	Sales promotion (trials, sampling)	Sales promotion (loyalty offers)
Appointment making (contact and agree)	Appointment making (promotion)	Appointment making (servicing)
Selling (direct response)	Selling	Selling (renew, add or upgrade)
Traffic generation (direct response and outbound)	Traffic generation (event and retail visits)	Traffic generation (special customer events)
	Credit approval	Cash collection
Customer service (customer referrals)	Customer service (information/advice)	Customer service
	Crisis management (maintaining image)	Crisis management (customer support)

2.3 Cost-effective business solutions

The perpetual challenge of marketing is to find the most effective strategies and cost-efficient mix of techniques and campaigns to help achieve current business objectives. In making choices about short- and long-term objectives, target markets, product ranges, pricing structures, distribution channels and so on, a company should consider what resources could be employed and their cost/benefit implications. Considering all the options at this early stage means that opportunities will not be occluded by either accepted ways of doing things or simple oversight. Most businesses do not have the luxury of starting anew, but all can benefit from taking a step back and considering the options. The wave of radical business restructuring which began in the early 1990s is proof that even the most traditional of businesses, such as life assurance, can do things in a more efficient *and* customer-friendly way.

So, what are the situations in which telemarketing provides the best solution? It actually depends upon many factors. Cost is obviously a consideration. Telemarketing alone, or in combination with other techniques, can often provide the most cost-effective method of achieving a particular objective – for example, generating good quality leads. It can also help to reduce overheads by supporting a salesforce and making their time more productive (see Table 2.3). Telemarketing can also help a company to increase its market coverage by servicing areas in which it does not have a local presence. Telemarketing can also penetrate markets that otherwise might be inaccessible or too costly to reach effectively. The speed of telephone contact may be especially important in some situations – such as filling excess capacity in the travel industry, or defending market share after a competitor's price cut. Easier access to information and advice, and convenience for ordering, helps to meet customers' expectations of easier accessibility and better service. Some other performance and profit benefits of telemarketing are included in Table 2.4. And, of course, with all telemarketing applications comes the benefit of personal contact to build relationships.

Using telemarketing might actually increase costs, but the benefits can be such that a company may feel the investment is worth while. Carelines operated by FMCG companies are generally cost centres but are nonetheless cost-efficient in delivering certain benefits. A product information line operated by a computer company, on the other hand, could become a profit centre by creating high-grade leads for marketing and sales.

When deciding whether telemarketing might have a role within a company, existing operations can be examined to identify potential opportunities to improve performance on parameters such as cost, efficiency, productivity, market penetration and service levels. Those

Table 2.3   Field sales support applications

Any organization which employs field sales or marketing staff knows the heavy burden of escalating costs. If the field force is indispensable, it makes sense to ensure that their specialized skills are utilized in the most productive, cost-efficient way. Analysis of the routine of field personnel can reveal many time-consuming tasks for which the organization is paying a high premium but which could be conducted by others for less cost, and sometimes more effectively. Traditionally, these tasks have included prospecting (lead generation, screening and qualification), appointment making and diary management, and account servicing.

The cost of a sales visit, which is when salespeople's skills are put to best use, varies widely from country to country. The value gained from providing telemarketing support, which comes from maximizing 'selling' time, also varies. In the UK it has been calculated that telemarketing support can increase field salesforce productivity by more than one-third.

The introduction of telemarketing support requires careful planning and management. Field sales personnel, and sales management, often resist any changes that appear to encroach on their turf. There must be close liaison and two-way feedback between telemarketing and field operations if the full benefit is to be gained. The willing acceptance and cooperation of field personnel is therefore essential. The benefits to them of telemarketing support are clear: it reduces the amount of cold calling they have to do; appointments will be planned and managed efficiently through direct liaison with them; they will have more detailed information on prospects prior to any meeting; they can spend more of their time with people who are ready to make a commitment; and, overall, their efficiency and productivity will increase.

Another way in which the telephone can support a field salesforce is as a back-up resource. When there is a gap in field representation, perhaps due to sickness, holidays or resignation, the service delivered to some customers could be affected adversely. Regular telephone calls to these customers ensures that service levels are maintained and minimizes the risk of their becoming dissatisfied and perhaps considering other suppliers.

apparently offering the greatest potential benefits can then be explored further. The best way to prove what can be achieved with telemarketing, and at what cost, is by testing an application or campaign. This can be done at minimal cost even by companies that have no telemarketing resources. Many agencies are experienced in testing campaigns and offer the added benefit of expert advice on how to get the best out of the medium. Testing and some of the many other issues involved in using telemarketing successfully are summarized in the next chapter.

Table 2.4 Some performance and profit benefits of telemarketing

Improved service	Cost savings
Faster access to information and product/service, cutting time to purchase and increasing customer satisfaction	More accurate data, leading to better targeting and less wastage in communications
More accurate matching of product to customer needs, increasing satisfaction and reducing product failures and returns	Less wastage of field sales resources with lead generation and qualified appointments
Speedier transactions improving cashflow	More accurate prediction of market conditions to help in planning e.g. new products/ services, alternative marketing/sales strategies
Immediate information on stock position, increasing sales	
Quick feedback on problems leading to quicker resolution and improved customer loyalty	Telephone fault diagnosis to reduce call-outs and improve parts delivery
Immediate resolution of problems, or accurate identification to ensure on-site resolution	Less wastage at promotional events by optimizing attendance numbers and profile
Rapid feedback on product/ service performance, reducing time to refinement	Reduction in bad debts by quick, accurate credit checking; more rapid debt collection
Competitive pricing strategies through direct supply	Relocation to less expensive sites while remaining 'close' to markets
	Damage limitation in crises

Added value services	Removed costs
24-hour access to information, help and advice	Direct sell, cutting out intermediaries in supply chain
Direct sales and supply with telephone transactions	Direct account servicing, cutting field support costs

3
Practical issues

There are many practical aspects to running successful telemarketing campaigns or applications, ranging from designing effective contact strategies to ensuring that feedback on calls is used effectively. Other published sources provide detailed information on planning, implementing and managing campaigns. This chapter gives an overview of some of the key issues, while examples of their practical importance can be found throughout the book.

3.1 Staff selection, training, development and motivation

High-quality staff and their sustained effort are crucial to the success of telemarketing. Every call has to be handled with professionalism, no matter what the circumstances. It can be a monotonous, frustrating and stressful job and yet the highest standards are demanded continuously. The key to success lies in recruiting staff with high ability and providing them with all the support needed to achieve and maintain these standards.

The type of qualities and abilities required by telephone staff include a positive attitude and professional telephone manner; they should be outgoing and confident, self-motivated and able to deal with rejection. Above all they must be good communicators. Once recruited, their skills must be developed and honed so that the company can have confidence in this first line of customer contact. The nature of telemarketing means that regular refresher training is required to help sustain each individual's motivation and performance. There should be continuous development of staff expertise to provide a resource of growing value. A good training programme also helps to attract staff of a better calibre, it improves job satisfaction and increases commitment to high standards.

A package of motivators is required to encourage staff to aim to achieve their best at all times. Basic requirements include a good working environment (with the necessary resources), good management and supervision, a comprehensive training and development programme with a clear career path, good corporate communications, goal setting for individuals, teams and the department, good feedback on performance, visible recognition and praise when merited, and active involvement with accountability. Different types of financial reward may be employed, such as basic salary plus commission, bonuses or cash incentives. Non-cash incentives may also be used.

The value of highly skilled teams committed to giving their best at all times cannot be underestimated. It merits the company's continuous effort and investment.

3.2   Legal and ethical constraints

Telemarketing, generally, is subject to few legal constraints, although restrictions are increasing (e.g. to control the misuse of technology) as the medium is used more widely and becomes more sophisticated. Legislation varies from country to country, which can present an obstacle for companies undertaking cross-border or international telemarketing. Germany, of all European countries, has the most restrictive legislation. Calling consumers without invitation, or where there is no prior business relationship, is forbidden. Telephone selling to consumers in Denmark has been limited to a few areas, while in Sweden there has been a ban on payment by credit card for telephone sales. A new EC Directive on distance selling, due to be implemented in 1995, could bring some unification.

Data protection laws are obviously a major consideration with the growing emphasis on data-driven marketing. One of the stipulations of the UK Data Protection Act 1984 is that personal information must be obtained and processed fairly and lawfully. The implications of this include the necessity to forewarn contacts, if it is not obvious from the circumstances, of the purposes for which the information will be used and that it will be kept. Contacts will often be made aware of this by the circumstances, or through the nature of an existing business relationship. Again, a proposed EC Directive on the collection and storage of personal data will end some of the confusion arising from differing national legislation.

A range of other legislation impacts on telemarketing, insofar as it is designed to protect individuals and businesses from, for example, fraudulent or negligent action. In some countries a Telephone Preference Service (TPS) exists to protect consumers who have registered that they do not want to receive unsolicited calls. Telemarketers are asked to check their contact lists against a TPS database to ensure that they do not make such calls to the consumers registered. Adherence to TPS rules is usually voluntary. In the UK, for example, joining the scheme and adherence to its rules is encouraged variously by the efforts of the self-regulatory bodies, regulatory agencies where relevant, peer pressure and public embarrassment at the adverse publicity for breaches of the rules. Providing a TPS is likely to be a requirement of a future Directive from the European Commission.

One reason for the lack of telemarketing legislation is the strenuous self-policing of the industry, largely through codes of practice developed and published by national trade associations. These guidelines are updated regularly to accommodate expansion in the scope of telemarketing applications and any relevant legislation and related codes of practice (such as on advertising, sales promotion and market research). They are designed to promote the professional and ethical use of telemarketing which, after all, uses a highly intrusive medium. Some of these guidelines are presented in Table 3.1.

Table 3.1   Some guidelines on ethical and professional conduct in telemarketing, based on the DMA (UK) Code of Practice for Members. (Courtesey of The Direct Marketing Association (UK))

Organizations using the telephone for marketing, sales or service purposes should comply with any relevant legislation; in addition, they should comply with this code of practice in respect of activities not covered by specific law, or where legal requirements are less restrictive than this code.

Disclosure

The name of the organization on whose behalf a call is made or received will be disclosed promptly and this information repeated on request at any time during the conversation.

The purpose of the call should be stated clearly early in the conversation and the content of the call should be restricted to matters directly relevant to its purpose.

The name, address and telephone number of the organization on whose behalf the call is being made or received should be available upon request at any time during the conversation.

When a person is telephoned as the consequence of a referral by a third party, the telemarketer should, at the beginning of the call, tell the person called of this fact, identify the third party and give the person called the opportunity to ask for the call to be discontinued.

Honesty

Telemarketers must not evade the truth or deliberately mislead. Any questions should be answered honestly and fully to the best of the knowledge available.

Sales, marketing or service calls should not be made in the guise of market research or a survey. Where the words 'research' or 'survey' are used, the information obtained shall not be used as the basis of a sales approach either during or after the call.

Reasonable hours

Organizations should avoid making sales, marketing or service calls during hours which are unreasonable to the recipients; and they should recognize that what is regarded as unreasonable can vary in different locations and in different types of households, businesses or other organizations. Calls should normally be made between the hours of 8 a.m. and 9 p.m., unless otherwise invited by the recipient of the call.

Telemarketers should ask whether the call is convenient; if it is not, they should offer to call again at a more convenient time.

Courtesy and procedures

Normal rules of telephone courtesy should be observed. Telemarketers should avoid the use of high-pressure tactics which could be construed as harassment.

Telemarketers should always recognize the right of the other party to terminate the conversation at any stage, and must accept such termination promptly and courteously.

If, as a result of a call, an appointment is made for a representative to visit a consumer, business or other organization, a clearly identified point of contact should be provided in advance of the appointment to enable the individual to cancel or alter the appointment if desired.

Confirmation of any order placed should be sent to the customer and any relevant documents forwarded in accordance with the prevailing legislation.

Telemarketers should take particular care not to solicit information, orders or appointments from minors.

When consumer sales calls are made or received, there should be a cooling-off period of at least 7 days for oral contracts resulting from such calls, and the consumer should be so informed (unless the consumer has had use of the goods during that 7-day period or the terms of business specifically exclude a cooling-off period, in which cases consumers should be so informed).

Restriction of contacts

Sales, marketing or service calls should not be generated by random number or sequential number dialling, manually or by computer.

Calls should not knowingly be made to unlisted or ex-directory numbers unless the number has been provided by the consumer concerned.

Consumer calls should not be made to individuals at their place of work unless expressly invited.

Telemarketers should abide by the rules of the Telephone Preference Service.

Organizations should block from their telephone contact lists those persons who have specifically requested not to be contacted by telephone for marketing, sales or service purposes; they should maintain a record of these people and have documented procedures to ensure that all such names have been blocked from telephone contact.

When calls are made using automatic message and recording equipment it is necessary either to:

(a)   use an immediate introduction on the lines of 'This is a computer call on behalf of . . .' or
(b)   have a live operator introduce the call in those circumstances where the call is of a personal or sensitive nature.

Additionally, the recipients of such calls should be free to terminate the call at any time and the equipment should, immediately upon termination, release the telephone line.

Use of power and predictive dialling equipment

For the purposes of these guidelines, a Power Dialler is an automated dialler which can store, access and automatically dial telephone numbers and a Predictive Dialler is an automated dialler which will adjust the rate at which it dials, and deliver answered calls automatically to match operator availability.

If a live operator is unavailable to take the call generated by the Dialler, the equipment must abandon the call and release the line in not more than one second.

The Dialler should at all times be adjusted to ensure that the rate of calls abandoned is no more than 5 per cent.

Members shall maintain an up-to-date archive of abandoned call statistics and make that archive available for inspection on reasonable notice from the appropriate authorities.

3.3   Cultural differences

Cultural differences must be considered when conducting international campaigns and when targeting multi-race populations in a single country. The two key considerations are contacts' willingness to accept or make a call for the intended purpose, and the possible variation in response to the messages being conveyed. People are well accustomed to doing business by telephone in the USA but much less so in Europe and the Far East. And certain topics are more sensitive in some countries than in others. The Germans and the Dutch, for example, are generally unwilling to answer questions about personal financial matters. Business culture can also be important; in Japan a personal introduction is often essential. The diversity of population in, for example, the USA means that a different approach might be required for individual states or even within a single state.

Research by the Henley Centre in the UK (see page 277) also identified the existence of distinct groups of people – telephiles, telephobes, functionals, protectionists – who have different attitudes to, and propensity for, using the telephone for sales, marketing and customer service purposes.

3.4 Number availability

Contact telephone numbers are obviously a prerequisite for outbound calls. One of the problems with consumer campaigns is obtaining telephone numbers if they are not already available. An increasing number of subscribers are requesting ex-directory listings, so their numbers are not available in printed or computerized directories. In the UK, in 1991, the proportion of unlisted residential numbers was estimated to be 25 per cent and rising. In some parts of the country it was over 40 per cent in 1993. Obviously the problem is more severe when targeting sectors of the population who are more likely to be ex-directory, such as single women and some groups of professionals. It is important when buying or renting consumer lists to know whether they contain telephone numbers; if not, the size of the list will be reduced substantially and the number search will add to campaign costs.

3.5 Operational systems

Telemarketing is a very controlled discipline despite the flexibility and apparent spontaneity of a telephone conversation. The operational systems help to ensure that telephone activity is carried out in a planned and controlled manner. For example, systems are needed to collect, record and monitor information from calls, and to monitor and measure performance and analyse results, as well as to provide quality control procedures.

Ongoing monitoring of individual, team and overall performance provides the basis for supervision and management of telephone activity. For example, a supervisor could identify whether an individual operator is in difficulty and offer the appropriate help, or recognize that additional operators should come on line to reduce the call queue.

Many small telemarketing operations are run effectively using paper-based systems for recording and analysing information. Today, however, computerization is inexpensive, flexible and delivers many benefits in improved efficiency, productivity and analysis of call activity. Some features of computerized systems are described in the next chapter. Perhaps the most important, operationally, is the ability to monitor activity and results in real time, which provides the basis for quickly testing and fine-tuning campaigns to obtain optimum results. Some of the measurement criteria that may be used in this analysis are described below.

3.6   Monitoring and control

There are many measures that can be used to monitor telephone activity to provide an indicator of control actions required. With outbound calls, for example, these include call rate, decision-maker contact rate, unobtainable numbers/gone-aways, call duration and call outcome/conversion rate. For inbound calls they include response type, media source, respondent profile, time to answer, calls waiting and abandoned calls. The collection of data to provide these measures is achieved through the operational systems. Live monitoring of calls by a supervisor provides more subjective data on call-handling technique, etc.

There are many ways in which such measures can be used to control telephone activity, including quality checking (e.g. of call records for accuracy and completeness of information gathered), monitoring individual and team performance against targets, resource monitoring (e.g. to step up/down the number of operators, or revise schedules), and media planning (e.g. for maximum cost-efficiency in response generation). Optimum results can only be achieved if the campaign is closely monitored and controlled.

3.7   Timing

The timing of telephone activity can be important at four levels: the appeal of the offer (e.g. is the contact ready to make a commitment?); when the contact will be available or most readily accessible; where in the contact strategy the telephone is positioned; and the timing between different communications (e.g. telephone follow-up to mail).

Each communication in the contact strategy should be timely, which can vary according to the profile of the target market, the product/service offered, the contact's position in the product lifecycle, corporate budgeting procedures, and so on.

The main influences on contacts' accessibility by phone are the target market, the time of the day, and the month of the year. In business-to-business markets there can be periods during the day when contacts are not easily accessible, or prefer not to be contacted (such as doctors during surgery hours). Peak holiday periods are also a problem. Consumer markets present a different set of problems. Contact rates during the day, in particular, can be low.

The timing between successive communications can affect response and conversion rates – for example, when mail and the telephone are combined. Unless there is a specific reason for doing otherwise, the optimum time for telephone follow-up to a mailing is generally after three to five days. However, follow-up to a telephone call, such as despatching a brochure or confirming an appointment, should be actioned as soon as possible.

3.8 Testing

Testing is the process of evaluating the effect on results of different variables within a campaign. It takes the form of a mini-campaign upon which a full launch (or roll-out) may be conditional. The immediacy of response with telephone contact, and the flexibility for capturing feedback, provide an ideal environment for testing. This is a staple activity in telemarketing and testing is usually conducted immediately prior to the planned roll-out. Basically it allows a company to:

- plan strategy and tactics to achieve optimum results
- determine the cost-effectiveness of the campaign or application, committing minimum resources until this is known
- obtain benchmark results to use as targets for the campaign
- gain an accurate picture of what resources will be required and deploy them efficiently, and
- fine-tune the operational systems.

Testing can be used at different levels: for example, it can reveal whether the telephone provides a more cost-effective alternative to other channels, such as telephone account servicing vs field visits or lead generation vs mail; it can be used to determine how well different media, such as mail and telephone, work together; and it can also be used to find the optimum set of variables within a single activity (such as telephone script, call timing, approach) or combination of activities.

There is an element of testing in all telemarketing activity, in that feedback can always be used to make adjustments to a campaign. Because response is immediate, changes to improve results can often be made 'on the fly'. The overall cost of finding the optimum approach, and the chance of losing sales in the process, is then minimized. Feedback from telephone staff is extremely important in this process (see Section 3.10).

There is an enormous range of variables that can be tested (some examples from direct marketing are shown in Table 3.2), and experience helps in deciding which should be tested.

Calculating the real value of a particular strategy from test results is not always straightforward. For example, a holiday company may use one strategy to target prospects and make 950 sales, while another strategy, costing slightly more, brings in only 600 new customers. Initially, the more expensive strategy appears far less cost-effective. Over a period of five years, however, the company finds that the customers that cost more to recruit have made a far higher proportion of repeat bookings, with minimal prompting. The more expensive original strategy has now proved to be more cost-effective. Database technology enables highly sophisticated testing, across large numbers of variables, and comparatively easy analysis of

Table 3.2 Some variables for testing in direct marketing

Contact strategy	– Mix and order of media, e.g. mail/phone/visit – Timing of successive communications – Non-respondee follow-up – Segmentation of leads, e.g. by source, order value, stage of buying cycle, level of usage, previous contact
The offer	– Standard, toll-free or local charge number – Fulfilment materials – Promised speed of fulfilment – Pricing, e.g. discounts, bundling, payment terms and period – Guarantees, service provisions
Telephone	– Inbound or outbound – Lead sources – Operator or automated – Script approach – Timing – Length of call
Mail	– List sources – Design/approach: letter, enclosures, envelope/packaging – Call to action – Timing
Direct response advertising	– Media and timing – Objectives, e.g. brand vs response – Call to action – Creative approach, e.g. positioning (page, inside cover), length and positioning of coupon, prominence of telephone number

results. It allows a company not only to analyse the short-term return with a particular strategy but also to track the impact on customers' long-term value.

3.9 Targets

Targets are important as a measure of how well a campaign is performing against expectations and as a means to motivate telephone staff. They also play a key role in monitoring and controlling telephone activity. A variety of targets can be set, such as call rate, decision-maker contact rate, conversion rate, calls answered, time to answer, calls waiting, and number of 'orders' (e.g. sales, appointments, literature requests). Targets may be finite (such as the number of appointments required to fill available salesforce time) or a variable guideline (such as conversion rates and time to answer). The level at which variable targets are set depends on previous similar campaigns, the results of testing, or both. Targets must be realistic (so as not to demotivate staff if they fail to attain them) but should stretch staff to give their best performance. Results generally rise during the first few days of a campaign as staff become more familiar with the campaign and, sometimes, as a result of fine adjustments. Targets and the results being achieved are often displayed in the call-handling area to form the basis of motivation and reward systems.

3.10 Briefing and debriefing staff

Immediately prior to the start of telephone activity staff are briefed on the campaign. This involves telephone staff and any support personnel and can be viewed as a training session designed to help them apply their skills to achieve optimum results. It gives them a full understanding of the campaign and any supporting information they might require. Their feedback is often encouraged to give practical input on final adjustments to the campaign. Generating commitment and motivating staff are key elements.

Debriefing sessions, where telephone and other staff share their experiences with the supervisor or manager, are held in the first couple of days of a campaign. Feedback is encouraged, such as contacts' reactions to call content. This information, combined with the results already recorded, can bring to light ways to improve a campaign, perhaps by amending the script, providing additional guidance on objection handling, or changing the hours of calling to improve decision-maker contact rates.

3.11 'Hoax' calls

Non-legitimate calls, whether intended as a prank or otherwise, can be a problem in direct response campaigns. A number of steps can be taken to minimize the number of time-wasting calls, such as careful selection of the call tariff to suit the application, and possible avoidance of times when such calls might be encouraged (such as school holidays). These issues are examined in Chapter 15 (page 158).

There are two other important issues that can be easily overlooked. One is the question of quality of communication – the message and its delivery. No one would question the importance of this aspect in a face-to-face meeting, and it also applies to telephone conversations, with the added requirement that the communication has to compensate for lack of visual cues. Consider the effort and money expended in TV commercial production to ensure that the right messages are conveyed in the right way. The fact that telephone conversations are commonplace does not mean that any less care should be taken. There is also the question of timescales and management commitment to telemarketing. It can and often does achieve a quick return, but one of its chief benefits is the personal contact which helps to build sustainable, profitable relationships. This takes time. Companies must make the long-term commitment, and provide the necessary investment, to build one-to-one relationships. Direct marketing guru Drayton Bird has written: 'Since 6 to 8 years is how long the average customer remains with you, to learn what direct marketing can really achieve you have to start thinking in decades not years.'

4
Supporting technologies

Technology is having a profound effect on telemarketing – expanding the opportunities for using it, making the medium more effective, and improving efficiency and productivity. This chapter outlines the scope of technological support available for telemarketing operations. However, the pace of advance is such that state-of-the-art at any time may be superseded, though not made redundant, a few months later. Development work is intense and new or improved products are being launched continually. The utilization of technology for telemarketing is an area where expert advice is essential, both in making the right purchasing decisions and in implementing and managing systems successfully. Technology is only an enabler. It offers excellent opportunities, particularly when it is innovatively applied; but equally it can detract from the basic values of telemarketing as a means of direct, personal communication.

Costs are spiralling downwards while the power and sophistication of systems is rising. Already, even small businesses can afford technology that brings sophisticated telemarketing within their reach. Some of this technology is only suitable for organizations with large-scale operations, basically because it requires high capital investment and large volume activity to deliver the justifying cost benefits. But the opportunities for all businesses are expanding rapidly.

The following sections provide an overview of some of the main areas of supporting technologies. Examples of how some are being used can be found in various case studies throughout the book.

4.1 Network services

Telecommunications is obviously central to telemarketing. Telephone networks vary in sophistication, and features, from country to country. Most telemarketing traffic is carried over the public networks which, generally, are of a very high standard. Private leased networks may be used by large corporations to carry internal voice and data traffic that can support telemarketing activities. Increasingly, however, the public networks are offering excellent opportunities for creating information networks, linking all of a company's sites.

Digitalization of networks is bringing an avalanche of new features and services, many of which offer benefits for telemarketing. Some of the more common examples are outlined below, generally using UK terminology, although they may not all be available in every country.

Direct dialling in (DDI)

When a call is delivered, the telephone exchange can inform the receiving company's telephone system of the number being called, and a suitably equipped system can recognize the number and route the call accordingly. Using a different DDI number for different applications – service, order hotline, direct response, for example – calls can be routed automatically to the correct department or operator. Similar services are available in other countries with digital networks. In the USA, for example, it is called 'Dialed number identification service'.

Being able to identify the number being called has many applications. It means that calls can be routed automatically to the people best able to handle them without first having to be screened by an operator (see Holiday Inn, page 111, for example). Callers get a quicker response appropriate to their needs. Linking the telephone system with a computer system (see Section 4.5) enables the DDI number to be used to retrieve appropriate information automatically and deliver it to the operator's screen as the call is connected. It might be the script for capturing information in a direct response campaign. Different DDI numbers could be used for different media, or different advertisements, obviating the need to ask the caller where the offer was seen. The computer system can identify this automatically. Or, if key account customers are each given a personal DDI number, account details can be displayed on screen and the operator can greet customers personally, by name.

Overall, DDI helps companies to make better use of their resources and improve the efficiency of call handling.

Calling line identity (CLI)

This is a service in which the recipient of a call is notified of the caller's telephone number. In the USA, where it is used widely, the service is called 'Automatic number identification' (see World Vision U.S., on page 256). A barring system, enabling callers to block transmission of their numbers, is a feature of the UK service launched in November 1994.

When the telephone system is linked to a computer, CLI can be used to search databases to identify known customers and prospects from their telephone numbers, and automatically deliver the appropriate record to the operator's screen. Callers can be answered personally and their needs met more quickly. By referring to a telephone subscriber database, it can also be used to identify the subscriber to the number from where the call is being made. Name and address details can be displayed on the operator's screen or recorded automatically on a database (see Ross Perot, page 257). This application, however, is subject to restrictions under data protection law in some countries. Another application of CLI is the creation of secure networks, which can only be accessed from specified telephone numbers.

Integrated services digital network (ISDN)

This provides businesses with the means of sending and receiving high volumes of voice and data traffic (including image files) over a single digital exchange line. It provides better quality transmission and lines can simultaneously carry voice calls with other transmissions. For example, if a call is transferred to another site, any relevant data about the caller can be transferred with the call.

The significance of ISDN is that it provides a national and global infrastructure to link all of a company's sites, thus enabling information to be shared dynamically. Details of an order despatch, for example, can be made available instantly at a customer service centre located hundreds of miles away. It gives companies the ability to organize their resources in the most efficient way while improving the speed and efficiency with which they can meet customers' needs.

Preplanned call routeing

Digital network technology provides the ability to preplan the distribution of inbound calls to different answering sites according to the time of day, day of the week, by predetermined percentage of total calls, and the geographical area in which calls originate. Alternative routeing plans can be defined, e.g. to be put in force in emergencies. Companies can also change the routeing of calls between predetermined alternative plans using a dual tone multi-frequency (DTMF) telephone.

Conditional call diversion

A suitably equipped telephone system can signal to the network exchange that subsequent calls should be diverted temporarily to another site. For example, this may be used between certain hours, or when the call load at one site reaches a certain level, or if calls are not answered within a specified time, diverting subsequent calls to an 'overflow' facility (perhaps for automated call handling). This is especially valuable in coping effectively with a highly variable call volume.

Mid-call transfer

Where a company has different service functions located at different sites, or has a central service operation which sometimes has to call on expertise located elsewhere, the ability to transfer calls 'seamlessly' can improve service significantly. When callers are connected to the wrong site, or their enquiries prove too complex to answer without referral, they can be transferred immediately to an appropriate person elsewhere. Their call is simply rerouted, perhaps over hundreds miles, thus avoiding the inconvenience of having to redial. When calls have to be transferred mid-conversation, relevant computer files can be transferred instantly with the call (see page 144, for example). This means that a company could have one site – a central 'switchboard' – filtering calls and transferring them seamlessly to that part of the country in which the appropriate expertise is located.

Call tariffs

The introduction of different call tariffs, signified by special dialling codes, opened up enormous opportunities for inbound telemarketing. The ability to offer toll-free calls has been the single most powerful driving force in the growth of inbound telemarketing. There are three basic tariff groups: free, local charge and premium rate. Many countries have multiple, or flexible, premium rate tariffs, which can be useful in setting a charge appropriate to the service being accessed. The different options are examined in more detail in Chapter 15 (page 158).

Call queuing

Some network providers offer the facility to hold a company's calls in a queue, within the network, when answering sites are busy. A network-based recorded announcement alerts callers that they are being held in a queue. Company-specific recorded announcements can also be used.

Call management information

For companies which rely upon network services to route their calls (i.e. they do not have sophisticated switching systems), the network providers can now supply detailed call statistics of the type available from automatic call distributors (see below). Some network providers even supply live statistics via a PC terminal.

The current pace of change in telecommunications is such that even the largest corporations may find it too expensive to maintain state-of-the-art systems. Many network providers have found a market in supplying managed services which enable companies to deploy the latest resources, whenever needed, without a major investment in equipment or people.

4.2 Automatic call distribution

Automatic call distributors (ACDs) are telephone 'switches' offering a variety of features to improve the efficiency of inbound call handling. Call queuing, for example, ensures that every caller waits the minimum time by sending calls to the next available operator in the order that the calls have been received. Another useful feature is the ability to trip a switch at the network exchange to signal that subsequent calls should be diverted temporarily to another site (see 'Conditional call diversion' above). Some ACDs offer interactive voice response features (see below), which can give information to callers, ask them to leave a message, or take instructions from them via a DTMF phone. Some ACDs can 'talk' with a host computer, notifying it of the data that is required to handle an incoming call (recognized via DDI or CLI, described above) so that it can be delivered to the operator's screen as the call is connected.

Statistical data available from ACDs about call traffic and call-handling efficiency is invaluable for supervision and management of inbound telemarketing activity. Sophisticated management reporting of real-time and historic activity is available for each application, operator group and individual. Real-time information covers such areas as the number of calls waiting, operators busy/free, number of abandoned calls and how well preset service targets are being met (i.e. speed of answering and proportion of answered versus abandoned calls). A supervisor can see instantly how efficiently calls are being handled across different applications, and by different operators, and dynamically alter the number of workstations assigned to a particular application. The data also helps to identify individual and group training needs, or the requirement for additional briefing. Historic reporting provides management information such as average call length, average wait time, and call traffic over time showing any peaks and troughs. This data helps to plan staffing levels, schedule work and identify trends and influences on call volumes. Recent advances are bringing these reporting features to less expensive switches used by relatively small companies. And some digital network operators are now offering similar statistics either in real-time via PC connection or, for example, via a report faxed to the company every 24 hours.

Monitoring call traffic at an ACD can also be used to integrate inbound and outbound activities, so that when particular operators are not required for inbound call handling they can be switched automatically to outbound work (and vice versa). The technology enabling this integration is described at the end of Section 4.6.

4.3 Interactive voice response

The ability to automate all or some aspects of inbound call handling has obvious uses in dealing cost-effectively with very high volume call traffic, or dealing with call peaks without over-staffing. But it has much greater significance, as described below.

Interactive voice response (IVR) is a generic term applied to automated systems which generate voice messages or prompt directing callers to respond in an appropriate way using a DTMF phone or speech. IVR systems are available as stand-alone units, although, increasingly, many of their features are being incorporated into telephone switches such as PABXs and ACDs.

A basic function of the IVR facility on some telephone switches (often called a voice response unit – VRU), is the ability to play a digitally recorded message as calls are received. This can be played to all callers, selected callers (only on specified DDI numbers), or only those calls that cannot be answered immediately. The message can be used to advise callers of the number of people already waiting in the queue, as well as to give information, such as new product lines or special offers (to give callers some value while they are waiting for an answer), or to invite them to leave a voice message after a predetermined waiting period. The overall aim is to minimize the risk of people abandoning their call.

Voice messaging has several uses. Callers can be invited to leave their name and number, enabling an operator to return their call at some later time; and these can be passed automatically to operators when they are less busy. Callers can also be given the option to request brochures, leaving their name and address details, or to place verbal orders. A VRU can also recognize and respond to dial tones to offer callers self-selection of different services using a DTMF telephone, and can be linked to computers for transaction processing. Dedicated IVR systems employ various types of speech recognition, as well as DTMF tone recognition, to accommodate callers who are not using a DTMF telephone.

In fully automated call handling the ability to divert to a live operator can be very important. Callers can be given the option of speaking to a live operator (for example, if they require specialized help or would prefer to speak to a person), or diversion may be triggered automatically if they are experiencing difficulty in responding appropriately to prompts.

IVR systems can be linked to local and remote host computers. Information from databases can be voiced to callers (such as their available credit) and the information they give (perhaps an order) used to update multiple data files (their credit balance, stock levels and order processing). A simpler application might involve giving details of a local stockist, having asked for the caller's postcode or telephone area code. A feature of some systems is the ability to fax information automatically to callers when they input their fax number (see below).

IVR systems can support multiple simultaneous applications and can be networked to handle many hundreds of calls simultaneously. Real-time monitoring and sophisticated management reporting are also available. The potential applications are wide ranging, from providing information, such as product availability and freight delivery status, through the reporting of service problems and research data capture, to credit authorizations and order entry. The design of the interaction with callers is very important, not only to ensure that a service can be used effectively but also to make it customer-friendly. This and other issues are examined in Chapter 15 (page 164).

The use of IVR technology is increasing rapidly in Europe, following the lead of the USA. There is a trend towards the use of PCs for IVR rather than dedicated technology, which means that these facilities are becoming much more accessible.

4.4 Software

Software available to support telemarketing comes in many forms, but basically it provides a user-friendly interface with powerful computing facilities. Some of the major areas of support are described below.

Database

Databases are employed for many purposes – for example, maintaining stock inventories and supplying information on the status of deliveries – in addition to managing customer and prospect data. Today's database technology enables relationships to be managed in very sophisticated ways. By tracking responsiveness it can help to identify the timing, frequency, offer and creative treatment that will yield the best results from particular customer groups. It can also be used to determine the sales channels most suited to individual customers, and help to minimize conflict in multiple channel communications.

Increasingly sophisticated analysis of information on customers and prospects is improving targeting for outbound telemarketing. Calling lists can be generated automatically at appropriate times and delivered directly to operators' screens or to a predictive dialler (see Section 4.6). Selection can be triggered by any pertinent data held, such as reorder cycles, product usage (for selling-in prior to a price rise or during special promotions), lapse of loans, contracts and subscriptions, and so on. Other types of database also help to deliver better service over the telephone. With immediate access to a stock inventory, for example, an operator can reassure a customer that there will be no delay in fulfilling an order or, if out of stock, suggest alternative products. An enquiry about delivery of a parcel can be answered quickly by accessing the appropriate information system. Every piece of information impacting on a customer may be of use during either inbound or outbound calls. Instant, easy access to these systems, and keeping them up to date, is therefore crucial (see Chapter 16).

'Telemarketing'

Computer-assisted telephone interviewing (CATI) software has been available for many years but has advanced tremendously since the late 1980s. There are now many advanced features which improve both the efficiency of operators and the quality of communication, but even the basic features are invaluable. Computerized scripts, for example, can hold a vast amount of information that can be structured in such a way that the operator can easily find the relevant information to answer a particular enquiry. It also provides prompts to gather information. Scripting can reduce the amount of training time required; first, a conversational structure is provided to guide the operator through handling different types of call and, second, the necessary information does not have to be learnt.

Software can be programmed to provide short cuts for entering routine data and to provide gateways into various information systems. Linked to a postcode database file it enables an operator to input a postcode and instantly see on screen the name of the corresponding road and town. It can also provide instant access to customer and prospect records.

Numbers can be dialled automatically from on-screen records at the press of a key. Putting a follow-up time and date in customer records enables the software to generate queues of calls to be made. The length of calls is timed automatically for later analysis. Qualification of individuals for specific types of follow-up can be determined automatically, and many fulfilment activities, such as printing personalized letters, can be automated.

Highly sophisticated reporting gives historic and real-time information on telephone activity, including results, by individual, team and campaign. Some telemarketing software is available as part of a modular family of products which variously support activities such as database marketing, field sales, order processing and customer service, and offer an integrated environment for all these functions.

Resource planning and management

Various specialized software is available to help plan and manage telephone resources. For example, it is possible to analyse historical call traffic flow and predict future staffing requirements, in specified time bands, taking into account any additional factors such as current trends in call traffic. Generally the software works by taking data from the ACD and continually updating its database upon which calculations are based. In addition, it can hold information on hours of operation, shifts, employees, their skill levels and work assignments. It can be used to forecast workloads and calculate staffing requirements, to plan work schedules and assign staff, and to analyse budgeting needs. It can determine optimal patterns of start times, days off, breaks and shifts, as well as assign staff to specific jobs based on their skill level. Other software can help to calculate such things as the number of agents required to achieve a given average speed of answering, or the average speed of answering with a given number of agents. It can also calculate the number of agents required to maintain a given service level, and vice versa. Resource planning and management have an impact not only on the cost-efficiency of the telemarketing operation, but also on the level of service delivered.

Knowledge-based ('expert') systems

Non-specialist operators can deliver expert advice with a consistently high level of accuracy when supported by a computerized knowledge-based system. Basically, this holds expert knowledge in a structured form and has an interface which allows the user to interrogate the 'expert'. This is often done by answering a series of on-screen questions or inputting parameters, from which the system deduces the 'expert' answer. Benefits include a reduction in skill levels required for first-line service and the easy availability of expert advice at any time. Some example applications are described on page 184.

Geogaphic information systems

Sometimes local knowledge can help an operator to handle a situation more effectively. With the move away from local enquiry offices towards centralized customer communication centres, local knowledge has been lost. Geographic information systems replace this knowledge with an on-screen map which can show any data relevant to answering enquiries or providing service. A typical use would be for an emergency breakdown service. With an on-screen map it is easier for the operator to clarify the location of a breakdown, while the apparent local knowledge of the operator inspires customer confidence. Another application is described on page 192.

Other software solutions that can support telemarketing include route planning and delivery tracking. Technology is no longer a limiting factor. It is the ingenuity in the application of technology that makes the difference.

4.5   Computer telephony integration

Businesses increasingly rely on information to respond quickly and appropriately to individual and market needs. This has led to a growing need for company-wide data networks that allow easy access to any relevant data resources. For telemarketing this has meant linking the telephone system to computer systems, or computer telephony integration (CTI). It enables operators, or customers, to access and update whichever corporate information system is appropriate. These are dynamic systems which are often being updated continuously at multiple sites, such as the customer communications centre, distribution points, accounts and billing, and field service centres. When an enquiry or instruction is logged onto one system, all other relevant systems can be updated automatically. An order taken over the telephone, for example, and input by the operator, will be reflected in stock inventory, despatch, delivery, accounts and billing systems. This enables a company to coordinate its resources more efficiently and deliver a better service over the telephone. Because the system is dynamic, it also provides a rich source of management information on company-wide operations.

Another benefit of CTI is the ability automatically to deliver information relevant to each call to the operator's screen. Appropriate customer records, for example, can be delivered as either inbound or outbound calls are connected. CTI also enables automated transaction processing, allowing callers to interact directly with a company database, using either speech or a DTMF telephone.

4.6   Predictive dialling

There are many tasks associated with making a successful outbound call which do not add value, such as identifying who to call, dialling the number and recording data. Many of these tasks can be automated with telemarketing software and/or databases, but operators still often waste a considerable amount of time waiting for an answer, and even then they may be greeted by an answering machine. Predictive dialling systems are designed to maximize the amount of time operators spend productively, i.e. talking to contacts. They are available as stand-alone units or as an integral part of a telemarketing system.

A predictive dialler automatically dials numbers on a list and only delivers answered calls to operators, with the appropriate file on screen; at the same time they aim to have an answered call ready as soon as an operator is available. The dialler monitors calling activity and the percentage of calls answered, to determine how many numbers to dial to keep operators busy without abandoning answered calls. It continuously adjusts the dialling rate as conditions change. The maximum allowable percentage of abandoned calls can be preset. Unanswered and engaged calls are rescheduled and recalled automatically.

Calling lists can be generated by a database or the dialler, with selection based on any data field in customer records. Various types of control terminal are used to manage and provide statistical data on the calling activity (see page 114, for example).

Traditionally, most predictive diallers installed in the UK have been used solely for cash collections (see page 225). Although this remains the application which most clearly justifies the investment, more UK companies have begun using diallers for marketing applications. This is more commonplace in the USA, where Electronic Information Systems (EIS), the market leader, had supplied over 150 clients by 1993, including telemarketing agencies, market researchers, retailers and insurance and service companies.

Predictive dialling typically delivers productivity increases of around 300 per cent, although some users report gains of nearly 400 per cent. Cost per contact is reduced significantly. The technology is most commonly used in consumer calling, because of the high volume of calls. Two increasing applications are follow-up to direct mail and regular renewal of contracts such as insurance.

It is possible for operators to alternate between inbound and outbound work, as inbound traffic fluctuates, without changing their workstations. One example of the technology enabling this integration is the Davox SwingAgent marketed by Datapoint. To ensure that the efficiency of inbound call handling is not compromised, SwingAgent monitors incoming calls at the ACD and gives them priority. When call traffic rises, additional operators are assigned automatically from outbound calling (driven by a predictive dialler) to inbound call handling for as long as they are required.

SwingAgent allows parameters to be set for each ACD call queue (corresponding to calls on a particular number, for example). These parameters include the number of calls on hold, the average time on hold, the number of operators to be moved, which operators are to be moved, and the wait time (after moving operators) before re-evaluating the situation. The status of each call queue is monitored continuously against these parameters. When call traffic for a queue begins to exceed the predetermined number of calls on hold, and/or the time on hold, SwingAgent automatically assigns the prescribed additional operators to handle calls in that queue. As traffic diminishes and the queue falls back towards the preset parameters, SwingAgent begins to transfer operators back to outbound calling. Each operator can be given a priority, determining the first to be allocated to inbound work. Thus operators can be transferred individually or, if they are given the same priority, in groups.

SwingAgent can also be set up to transfer additional operators to inbound call handling between specified times. If a company finds it has a peak of calls during mid-morning, for example, a specific number of operators can be transferred automatically to inbound work to cover the duration of the peak.

4.7 Facsimile

Spoken information lacks permanence. In some situations this can be a drawback. Facsimile can be used in many ways to improve the speed with which individual needs are met. Written or graphical information can be sent quickly, either to help illustrate something under discussion or as part of the fulfilment process (allowing concurrent fulfilment). It can provide hard copy confirmation of what has been discussed, or in-depth information on something covered only in outline, as well as visual images that cannot be described easily.

The whole process of accessing large volumes of hard copy information can be automated with dial-and-receive fax services. Callers use a DTMF phone or voice recognition technology to request the information they require, from either a voiced menu of options or a printed directory supplied by the service provider. Companies can also put customers on a subscriber list and automatically fax them with updated information on a regular basis.

4.8 Adding pictures

By the end of the century it may have become routine for callers to be able to see as well as to hear an operator. Already it is possible to give callers using a videophone access to computerized libraries of photographs – for example, illustrating products or holiday destinations and providing appropriate commentary. The technology used for desk-to-desk videoconferencing can also be employed in telemarketing and will increase in importance as its use becomes more widespread. The advent of interactive television will revolutionize the way companies can establish and maintain a dialogue with consumers and business buyers. Suppliers will be able to offer customers and prospects the opportunity to view product demonstrations, testimonials and detailed product specifications on demand, on their television screens, while talking to a company representative.

As mentioned in the introduction to this chapter, technology is only an enabler. The human element – both operator and customer – must be the prime consideration. If the implementation of any technology detracts from the basic advantage of the telephone for personal communication, then its use must be very carefully justified.

PART TWO
APPLICATIONS

5
List building, cleaning and testing

The starting point for a company wanting to initiate direct contact with people in the marketplace (as opposed to encouraging them to make contact) is in almost all cases a contact list. The cost-effectiveness of making contact is related directly to the availability of relevant, accurate information on that list. The telephone provides the most efficient way to ensure list accuracy prior to making the marketing approach.

5.1 The need for list accuracy

Inaccurate contact details reduce the cost-effectiveness of a direct marketing campaign irrespective of the medium being used. In direct mail, for example, incorrect names, addresses or job titles, duplication, misspelt names or the changing circumstances of individuals can make response rates plummet, increase costs and reflect poorly on the efficiency of the organization. In a telemarketing campaign, highly skilled callers would have to spend valuable time either identifying the relevant contact before they can deliver the marketing message, or calling businesses that are no longer trading. The better the list, the more cost-efficient the marketing activity.

The higher the cost of the planned marketing activity, the more cost-efficient it becomes to build, clean or test a list by telephone first. The benefits of accurate targeting are obvious. With mail, for example, it increases the chances of the mailing being read by the intended person, thereby increasing the response rate. There is reduced wastage in terms of printing and postage costs. The annoyance factor (from poor targeting) is reduced and the company creates a better image with a well-targeted, correctly addressed and personalized letter. Finally, the cost of follow-up is reduced because time is not wasted following up contacts who did not receive the initial message.

Contact lists become out of date very quickly. Business-to-business lists are most susceptible to change (some say around 5 per cent per month), but consumer mobility is increasing, particularly among certain population groups. The more recently a list was built or checked, the more accurate it will be and the more cost-efficient to use.

The telephone is the only practical way to gather or verify information about specific contacts. Response rates of 80–90 per cent can be achieved by telephone compared with, sometimes, less than 5 per cent from mail. The disadvantage of mail is that you will not know why people did not respond. Did they receive the letter? Were they not interested? Did they just not bother to reply? Details of those who failed to respond – the vast majority – cannot be gathered or verified.

The telephone is also quick. In business-to-business markets information can often be gathered at the switchboard, which reduces the length and cost of calls. Also, a wide variety of information can be gathered in addition to basic contact details. Data gathered by telephone is usually very accurate – for example, there is less risk of questions being misunderstood or of incomplete information being given. Given the impact that list accuracy has on campaign results, the telephone can be very cost-efficient for list work.

The one major problem may be the unavailability of contact telephone numbers (see page 25). If numbers are not available from the list source being used, they have to be researched. This adds to the cost and many numbers (those unlisted or 'ex-directory') will still be unavailable. Where numbers are available, the telephone can be used in three main ways: to build (originate or add to) a list, to clean (verify and update) a list, and to test list accuracy. The primary aim in list building is to obtain the information required for targeting, i.e. the decision maker's name, title and full address. In business-to-business markets there may be multiple contacts within the same company, such as a specifier, decision maker and multiple users of a product or service. These may have different addresses and telephone numbers which can be gathered at the same time. A secondary aim might be to gather additional information, such as the number of sites or branches, type of business, name of the parent company or subsidiaries, and so on. At this point list building begins to merge with market evaluation and database building.

The best way to keep lists up-to-date is through regular contact within the marketing programme. But list cleaning is often required when the source is such that data accuracy is unknown or questionable, as with many published sources, some bought-in lists and lapsed customer records. Some service companies offer list cleaning, for example by checking against continually updated databases. One way of finding out whether cleaning is required is to test the accuracy of the list.

List testing consists of calling a proportion of contacts on the list and checking the accuracy of the details listed. A minimum of 5 per cent of contacts is usually used in a test to obtain results which are statistically valid, but the size and type of list may allow a smaller or require a larger proportion to be used. A test will often encompass checking not only contact details but also whether they meet targeting criteria. Are they frequent air travellers, for example, as the list source suggests? The results of the test will give a measure of the list's accuracy and help to determine whether it would be cost-efficient to clean the entire list. It obviously makes sense during the test to update those contact details that are found to be incorrect.

Call rates for list work vary widely depending, for example, on the accuracy of the list, whether information is obtainable at switchboard level or requires contact with a specific department, the ease with which decision makers can be reached (varying according to their seniority and the market), and what additional information, if any, is being gathered. The emphasis, obviously, is on accuracy. List work is monotonous and is best conducted in relatively short bursts, or by rotating callers, so that boredom does not lead to diminishing accuracy.

With advances in database technology and the increasing number of specialized data and list resources, the need for list building, cleaning and testing is diminishing. However, it often forms a part of several other activities, such as market evaluation, database building and maintenance, and lead generation, which are examined in the following chapters.

6
Database building and maintenance

As data-driven marketing strategies become more widespread, every opportunity to gather and maintain the accuracy of pertinent data on contacts becomes more important. The term 'database' implies the computerized storage of more data than is manageable on a simple contact list. Acquiring data obviously has a cost, even when it is gathered as a by-product in other activities. Maintaining its accuracy is even more costly, since it needs to be checked and updated on a regular basis. Every type of contact activity needs to be exploited to gather and maintain accurate information on customers and prospects. The telephone is playing an increasingly important role, both because it is ideal for data gathering/ checking and because of the growth of telemarketing.

The same qualities of telephone contact which make it so useful in list work (Chapter 5) are even more advantageous in database building and maintenance (i.e. maintaining its accuracy and relevancy). It is fast, interactive, penetrative (especially in business-to-business markets) and accurate. It also has the advantage of enabling a company to capture details of prospects attracted through direct response advertising. Examples of this include the sampling promotions described in Chapter 12 (page 118) and the food manufacturer which used direct response television advertising to build a database for research purposes (page 211). Both inbound and outbound calls can be used for data gathering at all stages of database development. It can be used to originate a database, using direct response advertising or outbound calling; it can be used to fill gaps in information on existing databases, or to add new names; and it can be used to verify and update information regularly and enrich the database with new data gathered during the course of normal business contact over the telephone. Observance of prevailing data protection legislation is obviously essential (see page 21).

There are four main considerations in establishing and maintaining a database: deciding what data will be held, how it will be gathered, how its accuracy and relevancy will be maintained, and how it can be enhanced.

6.1 What data?

The key criteria for deciding the data to be included in a marketing database are whether or not it has value in (a) planning and driving marketing and sales activities and (b) fulfilling market needs. The company will want to know, for example:

- the key characteristics of its customers so that prospects with a similar profile can be identified;
- what, when, how often and how much customers buy, so that their needs can be serviced efficiently (and to provide information such as sales forecasts);
- the potential value of each customer (e.g. the number of sites and their product usage) and his or her credit worthiness;
- why some people buy and others do not;
- why people have chosen particular suppliers;
- the competitors from whom people are buying.

The nature of the data required will often vary across different target markets. The information required to identify, for example, the amount of construction materials a farm might use is different to that required to identify the potential value of sales to a factory site. The actual design of a database is a highly specialized field, but the chosen architecture should be appropriate for the types of data analysis the company requires and should also enable easy access to information on an *ad hoc* basis, e.g. when a customer calls with an enquiry.

Once the data requirement is known, it is often beneficial to conduct a data audit to identify the information currently available within the organization, how accessible it is, how accurate it is, and how easily it could be transferred into the new database. The available data may be so patchy or so old that it is more expedient to start from scratch, perhaps using just the basic contact details as a foundation.

Case study 6.1

A leading UK food and drinks company wanted to establish a database to enable more cost-effective targeting of customers and prospects in the catering trade, such as hotels, restaurants, pubs, wine bars and station buffets. Telemarketing agency Merit Direct was appointed to build the database, starting in June 1991, and to develop it as an ongoing project. Contacts were sourced initially from records of current and lapsed customers. Merit called approximately 40 000 establishments, about 30 per cent of them classified as cafés, 30 per cent as pubs and 40 per cent as hotels and restaurants. Information gathered included usage of the client's products, competitive suppliers and why they were used, purchasing criteria and volumes, and ordering procedures and cycles. Using an on-screen script, Merit operators entered this information directly into the database. The decision-maker contact rate during this phase averaged 12 per hour, from 18 dials. The database is updated monthly with information from the client on customer spend, so that a fall in spend or lapses in trading can be identified quickly and appropriate action taken. Profiling the customer base has enabled Merit to purchase similar data to use for prospecting by telephone and thus to extend the scope, and long-term value, of the database. It is also used to calculate the lifetime value of each type of outlet to help determine the appropriate level of marketing spend in each market sector.

6.2   Data gathering and updating

The telephone can be used to gather data basically in two ways: proactively, where the company instigates contact for the purpose of gathering data; and passively or reactively, where data gathering is not the primary aim of the dialogue.

After data which an organization already has within existing records, the next most cost-effective source is new data coming into the organization. All contact opportunities should be exploited, across all communication channels, both to capture data initially and thereafter to ensure that it is kept up to date, for example, by inviting mail recipients to make contact if their name and address details are incorrect. It makes sense to gather information when it is most readily available and can most cost-effectively be captured. Everyone having contact with individuals in the relevant markets should be set a minimum standard of information for each class of contact and each type of contact activity. Thus, for example, when a prospect calls in response to an advert offering a free insurance quotation, it makes sense to ask for the expiry date of any existing insurance policy along with the caller's personal details and any information required to give a quotation. If, in addition, the company sells life policies, then the date of birth of the caller is also relevant.

Providing scripts for both inbound and outbound calls makes it much easier for the operators to capture the data required. The type of data that can be gathered unobtrusively depends on the purpose of the call and data protection law stipulates that only relevant data can be requested.

For known contacts, operators will need direct access to the relevant database(s) so that they can retrieve the customer or prospect record and update or add to it during the conversation. One benefit of this live updating is that everyone with access to the database has available the most recently gathered, up-to-date information. The database should allow rapid searches on relevant data fields, whether it is an account number, customer name, or any other identifier which customers or known prospects will find easy to remember. It is possible, in some circumstances, to have relevant database records delivered to the operator's screen automatically as inbound calls are connected (see page 40). With outbound calling it is obviously much easier to arrange to have the appropriate record on screen prior to the conversation commencing.

Speed is an important benefit of the telephone in some circumstances. For example, changes in the UK credit card retail laws, introduced in early 1989, offered great opportunities to financial institutions to process the Access and Visa transactions previously processed by the Joint Credit Card Company (JCCC).

Case study 6.2

One of the top UK high street banks already processed 19 per cent of the total UK Access business in January 1989. By reacting quickly to the change in the law, it now had an opportunity to steal a lead on competitors and rapidly build its market share.

Programmes, the Northamptonshire-based telemarketing agency, was briefed by the bank to design and implement a campaign, in as short a time as possible, to capture market share by encouraging retailers who currently had their Access transactions processed by the JCCC to transfer their accounts to the bank. The campaign the agency developed incorporated market research, database building, mailing and outbound and inbound calling.

The JCCC provided Programmes with magnetic tapes carrying the basic details of specific companies for whom it processed Access transactions. These included 25 000 retailers who already banked with the client, together with the top 70 000 retailers in the UK (some of which did, and some of which did not, bank with the client). These were de-duplicated, leaving 52 000 retailers who did not bank with the client and the 25 000 retailers who did (77 000 total). Programmes had thus built a database which allowed the client to identify retailers accounting for 90 per cent of the total Access business in the UK.

The campaign was designed to contact all of the larger retailers on this list to let them know that the client bank was now offering the service of processing Access accounts, irrespective of the bank with whom they were already trading. Before mailing this list, in February 1989, Programmes phoned the top 20 000 retailers (defined by turnover) to get up-to-date decision-maker names and addresses. During this process, the telemarketers also spoke to 4000 decision makers from the bank's larger accounts. The purpose of this contact was to let them know personally about the changes (as Programmes' research had shown that the majority were unaware of the changes) and to inform them that they would be sent a letter outlining all the details. The 77 000 retailers were then mailed with a two-page letter, explaining how the changes in Access transactions would be handled, and containing a 'Retailer Registration Form' to be completed and returned. A toll-free number was provided to enable any retailer who had a query while filling in the form to ring for advice or assistance.

Five versions of the mailshot were targeted at different market segments. The mailing achieved an initial response of 2500 signed forms returned over two weeks (3.2 per cent response rate). A team of 48 telemarketers then phoned non-responders in the best market segments (selected by turnover) in order to increase response levels. They found, in the process, that many retailers wished to negotiate their service charge rate. As a result, the telemarketers were given a matrix against which they could negotiate, and were then able to secure agreements to return the forms from 75 per cent of calls. On average, they negotiated one-tenth of the available discount and thus avoided encouraging a price war.

By the end of July 1989, 11 277 completed and signed registration forms had been returned (14.6 per cent of the 77 112 forms mailed). The signed forms represent retailers committed to having their Access account processed by the bank. It would have taken the bank almost a year to obtain the same number of registrations through their salesforce alone. The marketing database for this campaign needed to be, and was, set up in five working days in order to capitalize on the competitive opportunity. It cost the bank approximately £50 in marketing expenditure to obtain each account, which is worth on average £500 a year in service charge revenue. The business generated by the end of the campaign was worth £5.6 million, giving a projected £40 million a year incremental business.

Planning routine data capture

With an increasing proportion of business conducted by telephone, inbound and outbound, this provides an ideal opportunity for gathering and routinely checking data about individuals. Obviously each contact made and each transaction should be recorded, for example, to build up contact and purchase histories, but beyond that a large amount of data can be gathered and checked during conversations which are intended primarily for other purposes. The potential to gather additional, relevant information should always be considered when planning any telemarketing campaign. However, in addition to requested data, very significant information will often be disclosed freely by contacts, without any prompting, during the course of a conversation. This might be the names of competitors a company normally uses, or the fact that the company is about to undergo expansion, or a complaint about late delivery on the last order. Many people enjoy talking about themselves, especially business people, and listening is a key telemarketing skill. Negative as well as positive comments should be captured routinely whenever they are relevant, and a database therefore should accommodate the recording of relevant *ad hoc* 'comments' as well as planned data. The only other contact opportunity which routinely offers the opportunity to capture *ad hoc* comments is an expensive face-to-face meeting.

Inevitably, some data will not be checked regularly through normal business contact. In these circumstances, that data must be identified and a method of 'cleaning' it should be devised. This does not necessarily mean dedicated calling to contacts on the database, but could be incorporated into one or more campaigns designed to fulfil other objectives, such as satisfaction surveys.

Increasingly, direct response campaigns are being designed with the primary objective of gathering customer and prospect information for a database, subject to any restrictions under data protection law. Prospects are not made aware of this objective, they are simply responding to the company's offer of a brochure, free quotation, sample, etc. However, the amount of information that can be gathered at first contact is limited. It should not go much beyond that which is required to fulfil the caller's request. However, careful design of a campaign can help. A good example is the food manufacturer that used direct response television advertising to help build a research database (page 211). The company wanted quite detailed information on aspects of callers' lifestyles and so it created a campaign, offering a health information pack, in the context of which it was relevant to ask callers about these aspects.

The cost of building and maintaining a database can be reduced significantly if all contact opportunities are used wisely. It is important to have a strategic plan of how data will be gathered, regularly checked and updated, and to have procedures which ensure that newly captured data is channelled quickly into the database so that effort is not duplicated. Staff involved in data gathering and checking must be made aware of the importance of the data and its accuracy.

A database, once established, provides the company with a means to identify valuable new sources of data, both to expand the database, by adding new contact records, and to enhance it, by adding new data to existing records.

6.3 Database expansion and data enhancement

A well-designed database with a reasonable number of records (varying according to market size) provides the owner with a range of information on the target market(s). Analysis of this data can reveal some useful things about the market, such as the key characteristics of its customers which can be used both to design campaigns intended to capture details of more prospects with similar characteristics, and to identify suitable external sources of prospect lists.

There is an increasing number of companies offering their services as data resources, either in the form of targeted lists or comprehensive databases. In many instances it is more cost-efficient for a company to use these resources than to gather the data itself. They can be used as sources of new prospect names and for enhancing data on existing contacts.

A company can approach an appropriate data resource with a list of its customers and ask for a profile analysis. The data resource will compare the customer names with those on its database and identify matches. From the detailed descriptions it has of those contacts, it can provide the client with a profile of the distinguishing characteristics of its customers. Armed with this information, the client can then look for the most relevant source of contact lists which match this profile. These lists can be used to target prospects who are most likely to have the same needs and preferences (reflected in their profile characteristics) as the client's existing customers. (Where no customer names are available, the characteristics of likely prospects can be identified through research.) Data enhancement works in a similar way. The client provides a list of contacts on which it wants additional data and this is matched against the supplier's database. This provides the client with the type of data that will enable it to do its own customer profiling. When two or more data sources are to be combined it is vital that they are merged and purged to remove both duplication and any data that is not required.

Whatever data source a company is using, there are three important questions (this applies equally to internal and external sources):

- What was the original source of the data?
- How and when was it gathered?
- When was it last updated?

The following example illustrates how external data resources can be used in building a database, and the impact that accurate telephone-researched data can have on results and marketing planning.

Case study 6.3

To reach its very diverse markets, one of the world's leading air express carriers has developed a multi-targeted marketing communications programme covering a wide range of activities including advertising, direct marketing and field sales visits. As communications with its markets became increasingly complex, problems arose in coordinating and integrating the various elements to achieve maximum benefit.

In the early 1990s, the company's UK division was committed to a strategy that would make its database central to all marketing activities, from sales and marketing planning to customer communications and new business acquisition. The objective was to create a flexible marketing database that would help to increase under-standing of customers, enhance targeting and integrate all marketing programmes.

Database specialists TDS were chosen to create and manage the new resource.

The first step of the four-stage approach recommended by TDS was to merge, de-duplicate and format the courier's two main customer and prospect databases, each of 60 000 files. This provided a 'clean' database, without duplication of company or individual details. In the past, duplication had resulted in some of the courier's customers receiving multiple copies of the same mailing. Formatting ensured that the database would have the flexibility required to drive the company's diverse range of marketing activities.

The resulting database was then enhanced with profiling data from the TDS Business File. This is a comprehensive database, of about one million British businesses, which TDS continuously updates by telephone, researching a minimum of 400 000 company records annually. It contains details such as contact name, company name, address, full postcode and telephone number, business type code and description, number of employees, SIC code, and so on. Data is selectable by geographic area and by 2000 business types. By matching the courier's file against the TDS Business File, new data was added to the records. As well as improving address quality, the profiling data would enable analysis of the current customer and prospect base, such as identifying key business groups, their size and geographic locations.

Control tests, conducted prior to implementing the database project, had proved that using TDS telephone research to update contact details prior to a mailing by the courier could lift response levels from 9 per cent to 27 per cent. Using TDS telephone-researched profiling data to enhance the database cost only about one-quarter of an equivalent bespoke telephone research programme.

The third stage involved the addition of financial information based on customers' spend, with the courier's marketing department working closely with field sales personnel to provide back-up facts and figures. The addition of this data enabled detailed market analysis by territory, including sales revenues and market penetration by comparing the data with the TDS Business File.

Stages one to three of the project were completed over a three-month period. The final stage was an ongoing programme of database development, updating and analysis, supported by direct response advertising, mail and telemarketing campaigns. The impact of the new marketing database was felt immediately, even under the tough trading conditions of the recession, with a 300 per cent increase in mailing response levels. In addition, an estimated £100 000 was saved on mailing costs in the first year alone, as a result of preventing duplication and improving address quality.

For the first time, the courier company had a detailed, scientific analysis of its marketplace within each sales territory, which highlighted a range of new niche markets. Analysis of sales revenue and penetration by territory proved especially useful in identifying possible future site locations and for sales territory planning. Database analysis provided a detailed understanding of the profile of the company's best prospects. Brann Direct Marketing undertook a programme of direct response press advertising and direct mail to encourage response from companies that fitted these profiles. The courier's in-house telemarketing team handled the responses to provide high-quality researched and qualified leads. Niche markets and cross-selling opportunities were addressed by direct mail and by the direct salesforce.

The database now drives a programme of regular communications to build customer relations. It also enables the company to respond immediately to exploit market changes and react to competitive pressures. On one occasion, for example, the company was able to gain market share by making an offer to known customers of a competitor that was the subject of a takeover.

This strategy represents a major long-term commitment by the company, with all direct communications with customers and prospects providing data continuously to enrich the database and build its commercial value. Even so, apart from the increased sales already achieved, the project costs were covered by savings made in the first 12 months.

There is a limit to the usefulness of external data resources. They are meant to serve the needs of a range of clients and therefore have very broad objectives. Every company's data needs are different and the full benefit of a database comes when the data is tailored to a company's operations and markets. This can only be achieved with ongoing development, where data is continually verified, updated and enriched through contact with the marketplace. Telephone contact can play a key role.

7
Lead generation, screening and qualification

Every organization needs to win new customers to fuel growth and to replace those lost, perhaps to competitors or because of their changing needs or financial circumstances. Existing prospects, nurtured through the marketing communications programme, often provide the most immediate source of new customers, but a regular supply of new leads is required to replenish the system. As prospects convert or fall by the wayside they are replaced by new prospects identified from among the supply of leads. Lead generation, screening and qualification are the processes by which this new 'stock' is identified and evaluated to decide what subsequent marketing activity is appropriate to their individual needs and value or priority. The telephone can play a role at all stages. Whether leads are called or they call the company in response to advertising, they can be asked screening questions to determine their needs, their value and what follow-up action they 'qualify' for, which can then be agreed and arranged during the same call. It is a quick and efficient way to grade leads and identify prospects of known probable value who can be prioritized for follow-up. Although the cost can range from approximately £1.50 to £8.00 per contact, it can be cost-efficient.

Lead sources can include lapsed customer records, lists, commercial profiling databases and direct response advertising. When using lists, the telephone can be used in a variety of ways. A list can be tested by telephone to determine the potential yield of good prospects. It can also be used to gather any additional contact details required, or to ensure that targeting information is accurate. The method used to establish contact with leads on a list depends on their potential value, the market, how much information the company wants to obtain, and how it intends to follow up good leads (e.g. with an appointment or information pack). The first approach is usually made by telephone or by mail.

If the telephone is being used to identify or to confirm the details of decision makers, then the same call can be used to screen and qualify the leads. This may be used, for example, where a high value mailing is being sent. Principally, it ensures that the mailing will reach the right person. By screening the leads at the same time the company can grade them according to value or priority, e.g. delete from mailing, mail and follow up at a later date, or mail and follow up immediately. If contact is made directly with the decision maker, the call can also be used to build interest and encourage commitment to reading the mailing, by telling people that they will be recalled, soon after receiving the mailing, for their comments or opinions (at which stage they will be screened again to determine the next follow-up action).

If the company wants to gather a substantial amount of contact information initially, such as for market evaluation, then generally the telephone is the best choice. The same is true if the company is looking to book appointments for a salesforce when it identifies good prospects. However, 'cold' calling is expensive. The alternative is to mail leads.

7.1   Limitations of mail

Leads cannot be screened by simply mailing them; the company needs to ask questions. A coupon or questionnaire can be used effectively, although these can have drawbacks. On a coupon, for example, only a limited number of questions can be asked. With a questionnaire, such as those used to gather information to provide insurance quotations, there is the possibility that some leads will be unable or unwilling to answer all the questions (and consequently may not return it). Most important of all, the company will only learn about those who respond to the mailing. Some people may not respond because the offer is not relevant now, but it will be in, say, six months. By learning about this interest the company could arrange to contact them again at the appropriate time. Encouraging leads to respond by telephone enables the company to gather this vital information (as well as enabling leads to respond spontaneously, while their interest is high). Obviously the offer will still determine who responds, but it can be designed in a way that encourages a response from anyone who, at some stage, *may* be in the market, and not only those with immediate needs. Alternatively the mailing can be followed up with a telephone call.

The disadvantages that apply to written response mechanisms in direct mail also apply to media advertising. Offering a telephone number enables leads to be screened more quickly and accurately and follow-up to be actioned immediately (so leads get a quicker response to their needs). Direct response advertising is an increasingly popular method of lead generation and is examined in more detail in Chapter 15.

Telephone contact is the only way, apart from a face-to-face meeting, to screen leads accurately. In some instances it can supply leads who will be in the market to buy at various times over the next year or two and who need to be kept 'warm' until then. However, the cost-effectiveness of this type of strategy will depend on profit margins and potential customer value. It is important to decide how interest will be generated and to what level, i.e. how far ahead of a potential sale it is viable to generate and have to sustain interest.

The aim of screening and qualification is to identify how to maximize the value of leads with the minimum amount of expenditure (hence 'qualification' – what spend they qualify for). So, for example, a 'warm' lead (i.e. of low value or interested in buying at a later date) might be sent a brochure, while a 'hot' lead (i.e. of high value or wanting to buy soon) could be encouraged to book an appointment to see a salesperson. Similarly, a lead expressing interest in a particular product might be sent a specific leaflet, rather than a full product brochure, and perhaps be directed to a local outlet which supplies the product; the outlets could then be advised of leads that they can follow up.

7.2 What screening information?

The information required for screening largely determines the questions that leads will be asked. However, depending on the circumstances, the company might also want to gather other information. Obviously, lead details need to be captured if this is the first contact, and where they saw or heard of the offer if they are responding to advertising. The amount of information gathered can be substantial, as in market evaluation exercises, and much of it may be sought for its long-term value rather than for deciding the next stage in the contact strategy. But screening does not have to be complex to be effective. In the case of direct response lead generation campaigns in consumer markets, for example, often only a few simple questions are required to provide sufficient information to plan and execute follow-up, as in the following example.

Case study 7.1

The name Bang & Olufsen has high levels of awareness among UK consumers as a manufacturer of premium-priced audio and visual products for the style-conscious connoisseur of quality sound and vision. What is not so widely known is that the Danish company is a leader in the field of computerized system programming and control. This was a major theme in a combined brand and direct response advertising campaign undertaken by the company between October 1992 and March 1993.

Bang & Olufsen has a turnover of around £15m (1992/93) in the UK, supplying products priced from £800 to around £10 000 through a national network of about 200 dealers. The magazine advertising campaign was designed to raise awareness of product capabilities and style and, more importantly, to generate leads for the dealers. It was also used as an opportunity to launch Bang & Olufsen's flagship product, the AV 9000 'surround-sound' system, which has a recommended retail price of £10 000.

Bang & Olufsen's traditional market has been 'B's, concentrated in the thirties age range, although it has now broadened across younger and older age groups. This was reflected in the mix of titles used in the campaign, which encompassed glossy aspirational magazines like *House Beautiful* and *Expression*, as well as *Radio Times*, *Classic CD*, *The Economist* and Sunday newspaper magazines. This was Bang & Olufsen's biggest and broadest ever UK direct response advertising campaign. A series of 13 advertisements featured either a specific product, such as the AV 9000, or concentrated on a feature of the product range, such as ease of system control. Each advertisement displayed a freepost address and a prominent toll-free telephone number to obtain further information.

Telemarketing agency Brann Contact 24 was briefed to handle calls and postal responses, despatch fulfilment packs, forward lead details to the appropriate dealers, and provide daily and weekly feedback to the client. Given the high potential value of each lead, the quality of call handling was the major priority. When prospects called for more information, Contact 24's Aspect CallCenter identified the number dialled, using the direct dialling in (DDI) feature, and brought the script on-screen so that operators could answer in the name of Bang & Olufsen. Callers were then asked for the following information:

1. Name, address and telephone number (daytime and evening).
2. Where they saw the advertisement.
3. Whether they currently used Bang & Olufsen products and, if so, whether it was audio, video or television.
4. Whether there was a particular product they were interested in (the AV 9000, other products, or both).

This final question enabled the Contact 24 operator to identify the most appropriate dealer to recommend to the caller. The computerized script had two built-in location searches, which automatically identified appropriate dealers according to the caller's postcode. Bang & Olufsen dealers that stock the AV 9000 formed a separate list which was accessed when the caller had signalled an interest in this product. Each caller was then given the name and address of up to three dealers in their area. Telephone numbers were given only if requested, since a key aim of the campaign was to encourage callers to visit a dealer showroom.

Fulfilment packs were despatched daily to leads by first-class post. Each pack contained a personalized letter with local dealer details dropped in, a complete list of dealers, a general product brochure and, when appropriate, a leaflet on the AV 9000. Lead details were printed onto custom-designed 'urgent' sales lead forms, printed red on white, and despatched daily. The dealers had been briefed to expect, and to follow up, these leads, although in many cases Bang & Olufsen's marketing department assisted in this as part of the company's dealer package. The dealer network

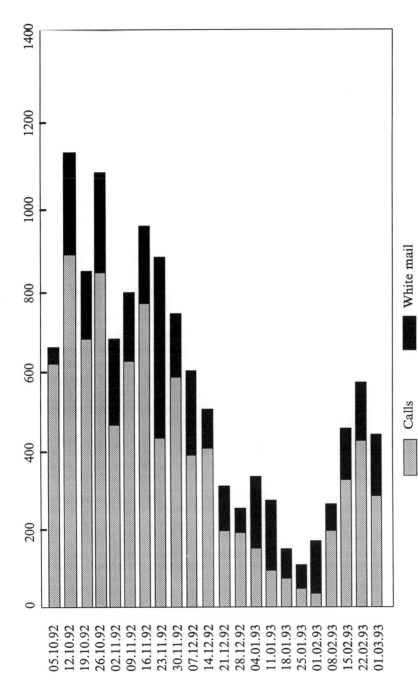

Figure 7.1 Weekly call and mail volumes in a direct response lead generation campaign. (Courtesy of Bang & Olufsen)

incorporates a broad range of outlets, ranging from the small independent retailer dealing exclusively in, and therefore totally committed to, Bang & Olufsen products, up to branches of large high street retail chains which stock a diverse range of electrical goods from many manufacturers.

Brann Contact 24 reported regularly to the company on the volume of leads received, with a breakdown of response by media. By February 1993 more than 12 000 calls and 3000 written requests for information had been received. Most activity took place just before Christmas (see Figure 7.1), when the majority of advertising was placed. The average call length was about 2.5 minutes and eight operators were handling calls during peak activity.

Bang & Olufsen tracked the number of leads sent to each dealer who, in turn, reported at the end of each month the products that had been sold and the reason those customers had visited the showroom. One dealer received 210 leads and all dealers received at least one. At February 1993, over 500 products were known to have been sold to leads generated by the campaign, and some dealers converted as many as 70 per cent of their leads. However, this probably underestimates unit sales because of some delay in feedback from dealers.

The campaign marked the best ever response to marketing activity for Bang & Olufsen in the UK and, additionally, has provided useful marketing information. The breakdown of response by media together with lead tracking, for example, reveal which media provide the highest response levels and which generate the most valuable leads in terms of purchases.

Further information was provided by qualitative research, also conducted by Brann Contact 24, among a sample of 499 leads selected at random from across all the titles used. Because lead details had been captured recently, by telephone, the quality of the list was very good and there were no dead lines, for example, or 'gone away's. Questions were open (as in, 'What do you think of . . .?'), which meant that calls were quite long, with around six or seven decision-maker contacts per hour. The three main areas of interest were (a) what prompted people to respond?, (b) the reasons for not making a purchase, and (c) their level of satisfaction with the service they received at the Bang & Olufsen dealership. The two most common reasons for responding were (a) the qualities of the advertisement (232 respondents) and (b) past experience/knowledge of Bang & Olufsen (134). The most popular reasons stated for not having purchased were (a) that they were still thinking about it (158 good prospects to follow up) and (b) the product was too expensive (109 people, who may be sensitive to price promotions). Ninety-five per cent of respondents were happy with the service received from the dealer, confirming that the company's ongoing dealer training seminar programme still has a vital role. Another finding was that, while the quality of literature was generally well received, a significant percentage of respondents thought that individual, product-specific leaflets would have been more relevant.

The types of screening questions that leads are asked depend on various factors, such as the market, the target audience, the offer, the range of enquiries that may be received (in direct response campaigns), and the types of follow up that are appropriate or available. Screening questions can encompass a huge range of topics but basically serve to answer three questions: What, specifically, is the lead interested in, and in the market for? What value does the lead offer? What is the most cost-efficient way to progress the lead to gain maximum value?

Sometimes the answers to these questions can be determined quite easily. Leads calling for free household insurance quotations, for example, can be asked when their current policies lapse to determine the buying timescale. In a business-to-business situation, however, it may be much more difficult to identify buying timescales or potential value. That could depend upon the size of the organization, for example, including the number of sites and employees, or buying structures and supplier policies, or when budgets are available. A good example of how telephone screening can be used to prioritize follow-up is provided by the Royal Mail market evaluation exercise described in Chapter 8 (page 68).

Screening for recruitment

A more unusual application of telephone screening can be found in recruitment. It is not uncommon, when advertising for telemarketing staff, to ask applicants to phone, initially, rather than to apply in writing. The telephone call is used as an opportunity for a skilled interviewer to assess the telephone skills and manner of the applicant. If callers pass this screening, and appear to have what it takes to make a good telephone communicator, they are sent an application form and/or invited for an interview. Apart from being the quickest and simplest method of identifying whether applicants have some of the essential characteristics required for the job, this early screening reduces the number of application forms that have to be read. The same technique, in a slightly different form, has also been applied successfully to other areas of recruitment advertising in the UK, such as nursing and the armed forces. Major press and direct response television campaigns have been used to attract applicants interested in a career in one of these areas. When telephone and written responses are compared, it has been found that the telephone offers some advantages. Apart from the more rapid receipt of responses (and the larger volumes in at least one instance), those responding by telephone are more likely to meet the qualification criteria, for example in terms of age, than those responding in writing.

In direct response campaigns it is possible to capture lead details and screening information through automated call handling (see pages 119 and 140). One disadvantage is that calls tend to be longer when handled automatically, and this may limit the extent of screening that is practical. Another problem is that automated systems cannot easily accommodate the screening of *ad hoc* needs. Someone might call for a brochure, but may also want to know where they can see a product demonstration.

7.3 Qualification

After screening, the appropriate follow-up action can be selected. In many cases there may be only one type of follow up, such as mailing fulfilment, although this can include several options, such as different types of brochure. Where the choice of follow-up action is more diverse it is often important that operators can identify, during the call, the type of follow up that is appropriate so that it can be agreed with the lead. If there is a choice, for example, between sending a brochure and arranging an appointment, the leads will obviously want to know what happens next; and if a lead qualifies for an appointment, then it makes sense to arrange it during the same call. Even if this is not practical, it will create a better impression if the operator can tell the lead to expect a call shortly from a named representative.

Deciding the appropriate action may be difficult when screening information is quite complex – as it can be in some business-to-business markets. If answers to screening questions are entered directly into a computer, it is possible to automate the matching of screening information against qualification criteria. After operators enter the contacts' responses the system simply informs them of the appropriate follow-up action. But, whatever the situation, it is vital that the qualifying criteria for different types of follow up are clearly established beforehand (in many cases this is necessary to identify the screening questions that will be asked). Even where there are just different types of brochure (e.g. full product, specific product, technical) it is preferable for the operator to know, and be able to inform the lead, what brochure will be sent.

7.4 Consistency adds value

Lead screening and qualification brings consistency to the way a company deals with leads and inevitably results in cost savings (because the company is spending no more than necessary). It also helps to avoid losing business by ensuring that the follow-up of valuable leads is not under-resourced. Large organizations commonly have different lead generation activities running simultaneously, which may be executed by various departments and external agencies. There is a danger, when leads arrive through multiple channels, that they will not be exploited consistently and fully. This is true particularly where leads are followed up on a 'local' basis without any overall control on lead processing. Centralizing lead screening, qualification and tracking can provide a solution. This ensures that adequate lead details are captured consistently, that the correct follow-up action is chosen, that leads are assigned quickly to the appropriate people for follow up, and that the outcome is logged to determine the next action – as in the following example.

Case study 7.2

In 1990, one of the UK's leading parcel carriers had a large regionalized salesforce of approximately 70 people who were fed leads from several sources. In addition to external suppliers undertaking marketing activities, the company's six regional centres handled enquiries and organized their own promotional campaigns. Prospects at a head office in one region could have requirements spreading across several of the company's sales territories. Under this system, coordination of lead activities was difficult, reporting was fragmented and lead tracking from source through follow-up to outcome was incomplete.

The company appointed telemarketing agency Merit Direct to carry out a number of tactical campaigns, which subsequently led to the agency becoming the focal point for lead processing. Merit's role, initially, was to screen and qualify prospects, gather data for a marketing database, and arrange follow-up. Merit set up a special script-on-screen database processing system to enable operators to screen and qualify prospects and arrange appropriate follow-up during the same call. On-screen prompts guided operators to ask prospects profiling questions and they entered this information directly into the computer. The data gathered included the type of packages sent, their typical weight, the type of carrier service used, and whether the traffic was inland or international. As soon as the profiling information was complete, the computer analysed the data, using a point-scoring system, and guided the operator to the next correct action. Depending on the prospect profile, this ranged from sending out fulfilment materials to booking an appointment for the appropriate client salesperson to visit the prospect. Journey-planning software was used to help arrange appointments. This automatically calculated the distance between the prospect and appointments already booked, and identified when the salesperson would be nearest to that location. Operators were thus able to plan the journeys of sales representatives to minimize the amount of travelling time.

In the next phase of the programme, a sales lead tracking and management system was established to be used in conjunction with a centralized marketing database. Information for this database, maintained by a third party, was gleaned from sources such as inbound and outbound telephone contact, coupons, bought-in lists, existing customer data, exhibition leads and salesforce feedback. Merit became the focal point for lead processing in this ongoing programme. All telephone and written enquiries resulting from the client's direct marketing activities – advertising, inserts, and direct mail for upselling, cross-selling and prospecting – fed into Merit.

Centralizing the operation ensured 24-hour turnaround from receipt of enquiry, through screening and qualification, to despatch of literature with a personalized letter and allocation of the lead to an appropriate salesperson. Essential feedback from sales visits, including sales and future interest, was logged, and all data gathered by Merit was downloaded regularly to the main marketing database.

The developing database prompted a series of customer care and audit programmes, conducted mainly by telephone. A proportion of leads were called after sales visits, for example, combining a customer care objective with assessment of salesforce competence. Immediate access to more consistent and comprehensive lead data produced many benefits and was exploited in tactical new business campaigns, for example, when one of the client's competitors withdrew from the UK market. Without centralized lead management, essential data on many leads would have been unavailable, or inaccessible, for this type of campaign. Accurate management reporting became possible in such areas as the overall campaign costs, the cost of each lead, and the cost of sales by product type. Management could also forecast business trends and identify future distribution network requirements – which were seen to be essential for medium- and long-term planning.

These benefits were reflected in the business results. At the beginning of 1993, business gained through the telemarketing programme amounted to 194 per cent of overall campaign costs, as a result of increased spend by existing customers and a substantial new business element. Potential business identified was 861 per cent of overall campaign costs. Sales management reported that the field force was being used much more effectively and salespeople were happy, too, with a very high proportion of valid appointments.

Using telemarketing resources to screen and qualify leads offers many other benefits. Apart from its speed and accuracy, the dialogue provides an opportunity to influence leads positively about the company, both through the quality of call handling and what is said. Because results are known immediately, activity can be increased or decreased quickly according to need to ensure that follow-up resources are available and are used efficiently. In generating qualified leads for a salesforce, for example, a specific number of appointments can be booked. Using a dedicated telemarketing team to generate, screen and qualify leads also enables specialists to spend their time more effectively. When combined with appointment making it can increase salesforce productivity by as much as 20 per cent. The telephone might seem an expensive option, particularly where the qualification criteria are very simple, but in almost all situations the benefits outweigh the costs.

In a sense, all telephone contact should include an element of screening and qualification. The company should be able to determine the appropriate action to continue building the relationship, and both parties should know when and how they will next have contact. The whole purpose of screening and qualification is to help a company decide the most cost-efficient way to deploy its resources to obtain maximum return. When dealing with a constantly changing marketplace this should be an ongoing process, not a one-off exercise.

8

Market evaluation and test marketing

All businesses need to investigate markets for their products or services to identify who will buy what and how best to sell it to them. Market research can provide comprehensive marketing intelligence, but it does not deliver specific data about individual prospects (market research approaches should never be used to identify leads or to sell). Market evaluation is a method of building a detailed picture of a target market and, at the same time, obtaining information on individual prospects that can be used subsequently to exploit their sales potential. It can serve a similar function among existing customers – for example, when a company wants to evaluate the sales potential of new products or services. Test marketing may be used as a follow-up to evaluation or independently. By targeting a sample of the chosen market, minimal investment is required to measure the value of potential new business and to find the most cost-effective way of winning that business.

The telephone is undoubtedly the best medium for market evaluation. It is fast, highly accurate and enables feedback to be gathered from a high proportion of contacts (often more than 90 per cent). Given the long-term value of a market evaluation exercise, it is also very cost-effective. Test marketing also benefits from the speed of telephone contact and the ability to capture information accurately, as well as being immensely flexible. Ease of access to markets, nationally and internationally, can be a major advantage in both evaluation and test marketing exercises.

8.1   Market evaluation

Market evaluation consists of contacting customers or prospects in a given market and asking them questions that will provide information to help the company to sell to them, and often to others. The objectives are to build up a picture of the market according to chosen criteria, to identify individual selling opportunities, and to help determine appropriate follow-up action.

As evaluation calls are normally conducted from an existing list, part of the task is to verify known data. New data, identified as being relevant to selling the product or service in this particular market, can include a wide range of information. In a business-to-business market, for example, it may cover the names of buyers, influencers and specifiers, their buying procedures, the products/services they use currently, their suppliers, why they use those suppliers, how they view the company and its offerings, their spend on different types of product, when budgets are available, the influence of pricing structures, and so on.

Building in more value

Although evaluation calls are not made generally with the intention of making an immediate sale, they are used often to promote the company's offerings and to arrange appropriate follow-up, such as an appointment or a literature mailing. The primary aim, however, is to build knowledge of the contacts, and the market, for long-term use. That knowledge provides the basis for precise targeting of subsequent communications. If only part of a market has been evaluated, either because of its size or lack of appropriate lists, the profile data gathered from those surveyed may be useful to identify others, potentially in the market, from non-specific lists. The best way to illustrate the far-reaching implications of a market evaluation exercise is with an example.

Case study 8.1

When the UK's Royal Mail planned the market launch of its EDIpost service in 1992, there was little information available about the market. The first stage of the launch campaign, planned by Ogilvy & Mather Teleservices (the telemarketing consultancy division of direct marketing agency O&M Direct), was therefore designed to identify potential users and qualify their value (i.e. potential spend on the service). Prospects would then be invited to one of two seminars being held during the EDI '92 exhibition, at which Royal Mail would have a stand. The telephone played a central role in both stages of the launch contact strategy (Figure 8.1), as well as in subsequent follow-up.

EDIpost is a service developed by Royal Mail to help companies which use Electronic Data Interchange (EDI) to communicate data, such as pricing information, internally between sites and with trading partners over the telephone network. Specifically, the service is designed to serve companies using EDI who want to send data to others who cannot receive the data via EDI. The sender would therefore have to use more traditional methods, such as post or fax. EDIpost enables these companies to send the data via EDI to Royal Mail, which then delivers it to the non-EDI users.

As this was a new market, there were no available lists of potential users of

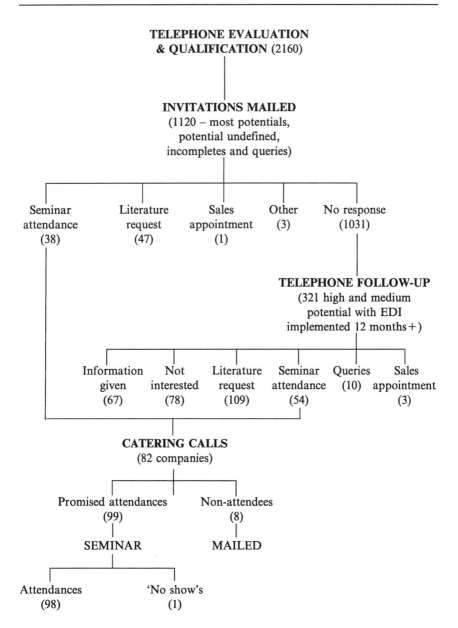

Figure 8.1 First stage contact strategy for the launch of Royal Mail's EDIpost service. (Courtesy of Ogilvy & Mather Teleservices)

EDIpost. Royal Mail and industry estimates suggested that there were about 8000 companies using EDI and, of these, approximately 1000 companies were 'hubs' that drive major EDI decisions through their trading partners and were therefore in the market for EDIpost. This was a small target market, but each company had significant revenue potential.

As with many business-to-business markets, the decision-making process for EDI was known to be lengthy and complicated. A key to the success of the launch would be the ability to define the decision-making unit within each company and to understand who Royal Mail needed to influence and when. In simple terms, there would be two key people: the specifier would be typically an information technology (IT) middle manager responsible day-to-day for EDI issues; the decision maker(s) would be a senior person(s), probably at board level, responsible for IT/productivity issues. Identifying these people, and designing promotions relevant to their needs, would be central to the successful promotion of EDIpost.

Two lists of EDI users were available in August 1992, when the market evaluation was undertaken. These were from the National Computer Centre (numbering 580) and a directory, EDI Spread The Word (numbering 3590).

An agency specializing in the computer industry was contracted to provide telemarketing services. The objectives of the evaluation calls were to identify and qualify potential users of EDIpost, and to identify named individuals, at decision-maker and specifier level, within these companies. The information gathered is shown in Table 8.1.

Table 8.1   Contact and qualification information gathered for the launch of Royal Mail's EDIpost service. (Courtesy of Ogilvy & Mather Teleservices)

INFORMATION COLLECTED AT SPECIFIER LEVEL

Contact
- Contact name
- Contact position
- Company name, address, postcode, telephone number
- EDI decision maker name(s) and position(s) (address if different)

EDI usage
- EDI implemented or planned
- When implemented: 0–6 months, 6–12 months, 12 months +
- Messages sent/received/both
- Number of trading partners 1–25, 26–50, 51–100, 100 +
- Percentage of trading partners linked to EDI
- Document volumes generated via EDI and sent non-EDI, per year < 25 000, 25 000–250 000, 250 000 +
- How these documents are currently sent (%): EDIfax, fax, 1st/2nd-class post, other
- UK/International (%)
- Printing: in-house/bureau
- Comments

A considerable number of contacts sourced from the USA-compiled directory were found to be inaccurate and, after de-duplication of the two lists, the telemarketing agency attempted to contact 2106 companies. The agency made contact with over 87 per cent (1842) of those listed (Table 8.2), the remaining companies (264) either refusing the call, or being unreachable or having a wrong number listed.

The evaluation and qualification process provided a detailed picture of the current market and accurate data to drive the next stage of the launch strategy. There were over 800 companies with immediate potential for EDIpost, plus more than 300 prospects for the longer term, and full contact details had been gathered.

Two seminars were to be held in the first week of October 1992. A promotional pack, targeted at IT project managers (the specifiers), was designed to create

Table 8.2 Summary of qualification data gathered for the launch of Royal Mail's EDIpost service. (Courtesy of Ogilvy & Mather Teleservices)

	Number of contacts	% of Effective calls
Effective calls (named contact spoken to):	1842	100%
EDI implemented for 12 months+	132	7.2
EDI implemented less than 12 months	21	1.1
High potential (250 000+ documents per year)	153	8.3%
EDI implemented for 12 months+	302	16.4
EDI implemented less than 12 months	71	3.9
Medium potential (25 000–250 000 documents per year)	373	20.3%
Low potential (< 25 000 documents per year)	299	16.2%
Total companies with potential for EDIpost	**825**	**44.8%**
EDI not implemented, planned 6 months plus (potential undefined)	249	13.5
Do not use, no plans to implement EDI	175	9.5
Use EDI but all transactions via EDI	24	1.3
Use EDI but only to receive	434	23.6
Individual queries for Royal Mail action	17	0.9
Incomplete call/partial information	118	6.4
Total others	**1017**	**55.2%**
Total non-effective calls	**264**	
Total contacts attempted	**2106**	

awareness of EDIpost and generate interest in attending EDI '92 and the Royal Mail presentations. The pack was mailed to 1120 contacts, selected according to potential value. A proportion of high and medium potential non-responders were followed up by telephone, and catering calls to those booking places were made shortly before the seminars to confirm attendance. The results are summarized in Figure 8.1 and the process is described in more detail on pages 129-31.

While a traditional mail–telephone–telephone strategy was used to generate seminar attendances, the contact opportunities were fully exploited both to build interest in EDIpost and to further segment the prospect base to help determine subsequent contact strategies. These initial follow-up strategies are summarized in Table 8.3.

The intention was to design a sales lead management system that would be of long-term value, driving the communications programme to keep prospects 'warm', build interest and convert to sales. Leads would be prioritized and allocated

Table 8.3 Initial follow-up contact strategy after the launch of Royal Mail's EDIpost service. (Courtesy of Ogilvy & Mather Teleservices)

Segmentation criteria	Potential	Follow-up action*
1. Requested appointment	(High)	Salesforce direct contact
2. Attended seminar	High, medium, low	Thank you letter/brochure with telephone follow-up
	Misc. 'don't know'	Thank you letter/brochure with telephone follow-up to qualify potential
Planned to attend	High, medium, low	Thank you letter/brochure with telephone follow-up
3. Requested information	High	Telephone to follow-up information
	Medium	Call when possible
	Low	No immediate follow-up
4. Non-responders to mailing	High, medium	Thank you letter/brochure with telephone follow-up
	Low	No contact at present
	Future	Keep in touch programme
5. Queries	(Unknown)	Contact to establish if query can be answered
Stand attendees		
– requested appointment	(High)	Salesforce direct contact
– other	(Unknown)	Letter with telephone follow-up

*Groups 2 to 5 screened for appointment request prior to action.

appropriate marketing and sales resources based on resource availability, time sensitivity and budgets available. The outcome of all contact would be fed into the database to drive subsequent communications.

The evaluation exercise had quickly provided Royal Mail with an accurate picture of the size and composition of the market. At the same time, it identified a large number of leads, representing the majority of potential users in the marketplace, and provided the basis for building the EDIpost customer base in the long term.

Applications

Market evaluation by telephone is very flexible, because almost any relevant questions can be asked. As well as product launches, it has applications in product evaluation and new product development, and in database building for identifying and targeting niche markets. It can help companies to penetrate new markets, revitalize neglected markets and, significantly, exploit existing markets more effectively. Evaluation data can be used for sales forecasting, for planning sales territories or after-sales service structures, and to support any other decision making where knowledge of market segments is important. It can also reveal new trends or stimulate different ways of looking at a market.

Market evaluation has obvious value when a company is thinking of entering new overseas markets, particularly if they will be served through intermediaries. Before going to the expense of setting up an international network of agents, for example, it makes sense to ensure that the various markets have a need for the products or services being offered. At the same time, the evaluation calls identify potential customers, determine the extent of their need, how they would prefer to buy, and so on. The exercise therefore not only provides accurate prospect details for sales targeting but also gives an accurate picture of the distribution needs in each market.

Evaluation calls can be time-consuming, with call rates varying from as low as 3 up to perhaps 10 per hour, depending on the volume of data being gathered. Most contacts are generally happy to disclose all but the most sensitive information (which varies from market to market) provided that they are approached correctly (there must be some recognizable benefit for them) and the calls are timed for their convenience. However, not all evaluation has to be conducted as a dedicated campaign. The same process can be undertaken, though less quickly and systematically, during other telemarketing activities. All companies should be evaluating the needs of their markets continuously, through all relevant contact opportunities. Dedicated market evaluation may then be reserved for filling gaps in knowledge, or when a new market is being investigated or a new product is being launched.

8.2   Test marketing

Testing is used traditionally to measure the impact on results of different variables within a marketing campaign. The idea is to make minimal investment, targeting small groups with mini-campaigns, to find the most successful combination of variables to use in the main campaign. A number of test cells (sample groups in the target audience) are established, each of which either differs in one variable (e.g. age range or geographical location) or is targeted in ways that differ by one variable (e.g. communication medium, offer or timing). Generally a control group is also established to provide a base against which other results can be evaluated, and large numbers of variables may be tested simultaneously across different cells. The same principles form the basis of all test marketing. Small groups are targeted to test their value and/or to determine the most profitable way of selling to them.

Tangible benefits

The telephone is highly flexible in the testing environment. It can, for example, be used to determine whether or not a particular product will sell in a specific market or sector. This could involve a new product which the company wants to test before investing in production plant; or it could involve testing the viability of selling an existing product in new markets before setting up appropriate sales channels. In either case a test, perhaps combined with market evaluation, provides hard evidence of the size and potential value of the market, as well as gathering valuable feedback on the best way to penetrate it. An important advantage of the telephone is the ability to capture both planned feedback and *ad hoc* comments. Also, the telephone does not necessarily form part of the strategy that will be used ultimately to reach the market, but may simply be a means to test viability and gather information to help establish appropriate channels. The telephone can also play a peripheral role in testing. An FMCG manufacturer, for example, might use it to help recruit retailers for a regional test and, perhaps, to research consumer reactions to the product.

In addition to providing information, test campaigns deliver tangible benefits, such as leads, appointments or sales, which offset some of the costs even when the proposition being tested proves unviable. The applications of testing are wide-ranging. It can be used to identify niche markets, for example, or to find ways of reactivating lapsed customers, or to explore opportunities for cross-selling and up-selling.

Case study 8.2

A leading UK financial services group recognized that there was enormous sales potential lying in a group of customers it terms 'orphans'. An orphan client is one who has an insurance policy sold by a person who has since left the company or moved to a different area. These clients are no longer serviced by a salesperson and therefore have become 'orphaned'.

Working with telemarketing agency Procter & Procter, it was decided that the best approach to these customers would be a customer care telephone call. There were four main objectives:

1. To test the value of orphans as sales leads.
2. To test the effectiveness of a specialist agency in arranging an initial meeting compared with the financial services group salespeople.
3. To gain sales for the company to validate the method.
4. To improve the customer care service provided by the financial services group.

Procter & Procter worked with the client to develop the customer care campaign. In the long term, the company was looking to speak to orphaned clients on a national basis. Initially, however, a pilot was planned to test the campaign and to ensure that the appropriate systems were in place to coordinate the activity.

Eight branches, spread across the UK, were selected. The company's salespeople at four of these branches would contact orphan clients in their area to sell in meetings, while Procter & Procter would service the remaining branches, acting as a field sales office. A letter was sent to all the orphaned clients being targeted, explaining that as part of a new customer care initiative they would be receiving a telephone call at their home over the next few days. A team of three telemarketers at Procter & Procter called clients, in the evening between 6 p.m. and 9 p.m., to arrange meetings for the salespeople to visit the following week. Once an appointment had been made the relevant branch was notified to obtain confirmation of which salesperson would attend. A confirmation letter, with the name of the salesperson, was then sent to each client.

An inbound helpline had been established to give clients a central point of contact, for example if they wished to raise a query or rearrange their appointment. It also provided a means for clients to give feedback, after their meeting, if they wished.

The pilot test proved very successful. The company's own salespeople arranged meetings with 42 per cent of the clients contacted, while the Procter & Procter team achieved a conversion rate of 68.5 per cent. Most importantly, one in every six meetings resulted in an immediate sale. An additional benefit of the campaign was improved awareness of the financial services group and a boost to their caring image, despite the sales objective of the campaign. Subsequently, the company began to plan how the campaign should be rolled out nationally. In July 1993, the Direct Response Innovation Awards recognized the success of this campaign by awarding Procter & Procter the Gold award in the telemarketing category.

There are broadly three dimensions to testing – the product/service, the end user and the marketing strategy required to bring those two together. The objective is to match the product/service with an end user in the most cost-efficient way. Even when there is a known affinity between a group of prospects and a particular product or service, there are still many variations in the ways they can be brought together (see page 28).

Telemarketing under test

Testing is a staple activity in telemarketing, for both campaign elements and the operational back-up needed to ensure that everything runs smoothly. It puts systems and procedures through their paces and provides feedback for making adjustments to campaigns prior to launch.

Case study 8.3

During the early part of 1993, the Bristol & West Building Society was finalizing plans for the launch of a new telephone financial services operation. Research on the concept, target customer and product offering had already been undertaken. What the society required next was a means of testing all the elements of the plan, in a real-life situation, before committing to launch. It wanted to know, in particular, how potential customers would react to the telephone elements of the new operation so that final adjustments could be undertaken before launch. The specific areas to be investigated included how product information should be communicated, the best way of responding to problems and queries, the tone of voice to be adopted by operators and the best way to address customers.

To answer these and other questions, an inbound telephone research study was planned in conjunction with telemarketing agency Brann Contact 24. A number of test cells were set up to represent potential customer groups. All had over £10 000 in savings and were grouped according to age (35–54, 55+), sex and geographical location (north/south).

One hundred people were recruited for the research panel. Each person was given two sample direct response advertisements (one long, one short copy), bearing a toll-free number, to which they were asked to respond as if they were interested in learning more about, and possibly purchasing, the financial product on offer. They were also given a diary in which they were asked to record all their comments on the simulated response and purchase process. The diary included a mix of open and closed questions to provide both quantitative and qualitative feedback.

Brann Contact 24 had assigned two workstations within its call centre in Bristol to receive calls made by panel members using the dedicated toll-free number. These were staffed by trained Bristol & West personnel so that, as far as the 'customer' was concerned, this represented a real-life interaction.

The Bristol & West staff were asked to test two types of overall response to the calls – one 'hard' and one 'soft' in approach – and note the general reaction and specific comments of callers. At the same time, 'customers' recorded in their diaries comments on how their call was handled, using both open and closed responses. The impact of an outbound follow-up call to one cell was also tested.

Overall, this test enabled the Bristol & West Building Society to explore reactions of different customer groups to different approaches by operators in handling direct response enquiries. The results provided valuable feedback for refining the operation and highlighted key issues for communication as well as staff training.

Despite its speed and flexibility, the telephone is not without its disadvantages in test marketing. Unlike direct mail or advertising, telephone communication is spontaneous. It relies upon individual communicators who, inevitably, will vary slightly in approach even when using scripts. It is important that telemarketers involved in testing different variables are of comparable ability and adhere strictly to any guidelines laid down for call handling, otherwise differences in results cannot be attributed with certainty to the effect of the variables being tested.

Another factor to consider is the duration of a test, which can influence results. In some test situations prospects need to be allowed time to change their normal patterns of behaviour before the true impact of a particular strategy will be revealed in their response. In a similar way, the success of telephone activity, notably with outbound calling, increases to an optimum over time. This is a result of telemarketers' increasing familiarity with the activity, which can increase both the hourly rate of decision-maker contacts and the conversion rate. In appointment setting, for example, 25 hours of outbound calling might result in a call rate of 3 per hour and a conversion rate of 10 per cent. This could rise, in a 100-hour test, to a call rate averaging 5 per hour and a conversion rate averaging 15 per cent. Some other factors to be considered are included in Table 8.4.

One of the benefits of telephone contact that cannot be measured easily in testing is the value of additional prospect or customer information which can be gathered as a by-product of the main objective of a call. As marketing relies increasingly on knowledge of markets, opportunities to gather information become increasingly important and valuable. Market evaluation and test marketing prove the power of telephone dialogue in building market knowledge and point the way to these two activities being used in a continuous process of learning and adaptation.

Table 8.4 Some considerations in test marketing by telephone

Limit tests to the most important variables, remembering that separate test cells will be required to measure the impact of each variable.

Select test cells to give representation, collectively, of the target market, and ensure that the control group is representative.

Make cells of sufficient size to provide significant and meaningful results.

Ensure that test and control cells are insulated from influencing each other but are open to similar outside influences.

Establish targets and success criteria before testing begins.

Design recording systems to capture all the data required for evaluation, including any unexpected outside influences.

Ensure that test duration is long enough for prospects to change their behaviour, if appropriate, and for telemarketers to become accustomed to the application.

Make tests of different variables the same duration.

Where telemarketers are involved in testing different variables, ensure that they are of comparable ability.

If comparing the telephone with other communications channels, consider the value of additional information gathered as a by-product in telephone applications.

9
Appointment making and diary management

9.1 Appointments

Appointment making is commonly associated with a field salesforce, where telemarketing can be used to arrange meetings with prospects, or with customers who are not on representatives' regular routes. However, it is relevant to any situation where company personnel will be meeting with a significant number of prospects or customers on a non-routine basis. It can be useful for field marketing personnel, for example, prior to visiting busy retail outlets to discuss topics such as point of sale display. It can be used to arrange a meeting between a customer and a company adviser at a branch office, or to organize personal product demonstrations, or meetings with individual prospects at company events. The principal is the same irrespective of the situation. The telephone is used to 'sell' an appointment and, if required, to arrange a place, date and time for the meeting.

It is clearly important that the customers or prospects are potentially prepared to make the commitment that will be sought during a meeting, which is why appointment-making calls often incorporate, or are a follow-up to, lead screening and qualification (see Chapter 7). This is essential when little is known about a prospect, so that the time spent subsequently is of benefit to both the company representative and the prospect. The prior knowledge it provides, such as product usage and competitive suppliers, can also make the difference between a positive and negative outcome to the meeting.

Specialist skills

Calling a large number of contacts is time-consuming. Having telemarketers take over this task enables the specialists to spend their time more effectively. Also, company personnel who are specialists in the face-to-face situation will generally not have the same level of telephone skills as a professional telemarketer. In one case, examined on page 75, telemarketers booking appointments with prospects for a salesforce achieved a conversion rate of 68.5 per cent, compared with 42 per cent by the salespeople themselves. In the case of booking appointments with existing customers, salespeople and telemarketers generally achieve comparable conversion rates, but salespeople have other commitments and are subject to distractions which reduce their call rate.

Another use of appointment-making calls is to arrange a time for a longer discussion over the telephone, perhaps with a technical expert or with the telemarketer to complete a market research questionnaire. This is useful where the 'transaction' can be completed over the telephone, but a positive outcome is more likely if contacts are given the option of when it should take place, e.g. when they have more time or have the necessary information at hand.

Diary management is often incorporated with appointment making, although telemarketers can simply gain commitment to an appointment for the specialist then to call to arrange a mutually convenient time. This may be preferable where, for example, the specialists already have heavy diary commitments or are simultaneously making their own appointments, as in the following example.

Case study 9.1

The Training and Enterprise Councils (TECs) in England and Wales have a remit to maximize the success of their local economy by providing a variety of services, including advice, information, consultancy and training programmes, based on sound knowledge of local business conditions. In October 1990, the UK Secretary of State for Employment announced the Investors in People initiative, which is designed to encourage commitment by employers to invest in staff training and development to achieve a national standard of excellence, for which a kitemark will be awarded. The TECs have a responsibility to promote and administer the initiative in their catchment area, and their success in doing this is a major criterion by which their overall effectiveness is measured by the government.

Gloucestershire Training & Enterprise Council faced particular difficulties when it came to marketing the initiative locally in 1992. Within its catchment area there are many small market towns where companies employ perhaps no more than five people. As the Investors in People initiative requires substantial investment, and a high level of management commitment, it was not unreasonable to expect these small companies to dismiss the idea without consideration. The TEC reasoned that it would have a much better chance of recruiting companies, particularly the smaller ones, to the scheme if they were made aware of the full benefits available on an individual basis through a face-to-face meeting. Before the TEC could secure appointments, however, it would have to raise levels of awareness, since the Investors in People initiative had received relatively little publicity.

The strategy chosen was a mailing followed by two waves of outbound

Table 9.1 Immediate telephone follow-up to a mailing to secure appointments for Gloucestershire TEC consultants. (Courtesy of Brann Contract 24)

Stage One: Immediate follow-up to mailing

Number of prospects	400	
Total diallings	1470	
Operator hours	116.25	
Average diallings per hour	12.65	
Unable to contact decision maker	112	
Decision-maker contacts (DMCs)	288	
DMCs per hour	2.5	
	Number/% of prospects	
Decision-maker contacts	288	72%
Appointment required	86	22%
Further information required	70	17%
Not interested	77	19%
Not interested, try later	19	5%
Already contacted by Glos. TEC	13	3%
Head Office decision	23	6%
Decision-maker conversion rate (86/288)	**30%**	
Unable to contact	112	28%
On holiday (including schools)	68	17%
Incorrect telephone number/dead line	4	1%
No reply/not available:	35	9%
Company policy, no information given	1	–
Duplicated records	2	1%
Company closed	1	–
Under 20 staff	1	–
Overall conversion rate (86/400)	**21.5%**	

telemarketing, together designed to inform companies of the initiative, to generate interest in obtaining the prestigious kitemark, and to encourage them to make an appointment for one of the TEC's consultants to visit their premises. On 3 August 1992, 500 companies were mailed with an information pack and a personalized letter inviting them to telephone or write to Gloucestershire TEC to arrange an appointment.

Bristol-based telemarketing agency Brann Contact 24 had been briefed to provide outbound telemarketing in two stages. The idea was to test the impact of telephone contact in parallel with receipt of the mailing, and after a period of two to three weeks. The 500 companies were split into two groups: approximately 80 per cent to be called initially and the remainder at a later date. Prior to the start of calling, test

Table 9.2   Telephone follow-up 2–3 weeks after a mailing to secure appointments for Gloucestershire TEC consultants. (Courtesy of Brann Contact 24)

Stage Two: Follow-up after 2–3 weeks		
Number of prospects	94	
Total diallings	424	
Operator hours	35	
Average diallings per hour	12.11	
Unable to contact decision maker	29	
Decision-maker contacts (DMCs)	65	
DMCs per hour	1.9	
		Number/% of prospects
Decision-maker contacts	65	69%
Appointment required	20	21%
Further information required	6	6%
Not interested	16	17%
Not interested, try later	8	9%
Already contacted by Glos. TEC	3	3%
Head Office decision	12	13%
Decision-maker conversion rate (20/65)	**31%**	
Unable to contact	29	31%
On holiday	7	8%
Incorrect telephone number/dead line	3	3%
No reply/not available	17	18%
Company closed/closing	2	2%
Overall conversion rate (20/94):	**21.3%**	

calls were made by Brann Contact 24 to a Gloucestershire TEC representative who assessed the calls with a view to refining the script.

All calls began with an introduction to Gloucestershire TEC and then outlined the benefits of the initiative. Contacts were asked if they would like a TEC consultant to contact them to arrange a convenient time to visit their premises and discuss the specific benefits that were available. Any 'in-depth' questions – for example, regarding cost – were fielded with the suggestion that a consultant could assess their individual needs. During this period, Gloucestershire TEC consultants were also making calls to companies with which they already had a relationship. This led to some overlap, with a small number of companies being called by both the agency and the TEC.

The first wave of calls by Brann Contact 24 began on 6 August and resulted in a 30 per cent conversion to requests for appointments (Table 9.1). The second stage, starting on 21 August, produced a 31 per cent conversion rate (Table 9.2). Accepted wisdom says that quick telephone follow-up to a mailing (after 3–7 days) produces better results, although in this instance the results are remarkably similar. Details of companies requesting an appointment were faxed to the client daily, or immediately when leads were 'hot', and a summary of the results was provided after each stage. In difficult circumstances the campaign provided Gloucestershire TEC with a good start in raising companies' awareness of the Investors in People initiative and gaining openings to secure subscriptions to the scheme.

The principal objective of appointment-making calls, outbound or inbound, is to sell the appointment and *not* the product or service. However, selling an appointment will often entail promoting the company and what it has to offer. It is important that the call objectives are arrived at in liaison with the people for whom appointments are being made. This ensures that the idea of an appointment can be sold effectively, that the promotional messages delivered during the call are apt, and that any information the company representatives require prior to the meeting is gathered. Close liaison is essential between the telemarketing function and those keeping the appointments. It is obviously essential to know the diary availability of representatives and to inform them of appointment details, but liaison has other important functions. Feedback on the outcome of appointments, for example, gives an indication of the effectiveness of any screening and qualification undertaken and whether the prospects' expectations resulting from the telephone call matched the reality of the meeting. Good lines of communication and reporting are essential. The importance of communication also extends to the individual prospect. When appointments are agreed they should be confirmed in writing within 24 hours. Prospects should also be offered a means to contact the company to cancel or change an appointment if they wish, particularly when consumers are being visited at home.

Appointment making by telephone appears deceptively straightforward, but it requires careful planning to ensure that all the relevant activities are coordinated and the best possible outcome is achieved. Some of the key points in planning are summarized in Table 9.3.

One of the benefits of using the telephone is that activity can be stepped up or down, immediately, depending on needs. A precise number of appointments can be arranged to fill available diary time and to make optimum use of the specialists' time. The number of leads required to book a specific number of appointments will depend on factors such as the proportion of decision-maker contacts (or response rates to mailing or direct response advertising), the proportion meeting qualification criteria, and the conversion rate (which depends largely on the accuracy of targeting). If it is important to book a specific number of appointments

Table 9.3   Key points in appointment making by telephone

What are the call objectives, e.g.:
– book a time, date and place for an appointment?
– gain commitment to an appointment and a call back date/time?
– get further information into the hands of the prospect?
– raise awareness, generate interest, sell benefits?

What time in the salespeople's diaries will be dedicated to the appointments made?

What time will be allowed per appointment?

What is the geography of representatives' territories and how will travelling time between appointments be estimated?

How will leads be sourced and what number will be required to yield the necessary number of appointments?

What information has to be gathered during the call, e.g.:
– to qualify/grade prospects?
– to brief representatives prior to the meeting?
– to gain marketing intelligence, e.g. list or media evaluation, market evaluation?

What follow-up action will be taken for different types of lead, e.g.:
– appointment?
– call back to arrange appointment?
– send further information?
– interest in 3–6 months, etc.?

What systems are required to ensure that appropriate follow-up takes place?

What action will be taken when an appointment is booked, e.g.:
– update representative's diary?
– confirm appointment with prospect?
– send appointment and prospect information to representative?
– update prospect record?

What arrangements will be made to enable prospects to cancel or to change their appointment if they wish to do so?

Will prospects or company personnel need directions to the meeting place? If so, how will this be provided?

If the representatives have individual territories, what arrangements need to be made to enable calling to be stepped up or down if some areas have a lower or higher than expected conversion to appointment?

What feedback will be required (to assess accuracy of the qualification criteria, etc.) from representatives on the outcome of appointments, e.g.: level of interest, sale/sales value, next action required, date/time of future action, etc.?

What type of briefing and ongoing liaison will be required between telemarketers, representatives and their managers?

Table 9.4 Calculating the number of leads required in an appointment-making campaign

Contact, response and conversion rates	Leads required
Qualified appointments required (50)	50
Predicted decision-maker contact rate (72%)	(69)
Proportion likely to meet qualifying criteria (84%)	(82)
Estimated conversion to appointments (22.5%)	(364)
Contingency margin for shortfall in predicted response and conversion rates (+20%)	(+73)
Leads required to generate 50 qualified appointments	437

an additional number of leads should be made available to allow for contingencies. An example calculation is shown in Table 9.4.

9.2 Valuable management information

Maximum value will be gained from the telephone activity if the potential of all prospects is fully exploited. Many of those who reject the offer of an appointment may have potential in the future and that should be identified during the call so that appropriate action can be taken now (perhaps sending a brochure) or at a later date (perhaps calling again in six months). When lead screening and qualification are combined with appointment making, telemarketers should be able to recognize easily those contacts who 'qualify' for an appointment, or other type of follow-up, so that they can arrange the next stage in the communication. If the qualification criteria are complex, it helps if this process is computerized and the decision on future action is made automatically (see page 65).

Computerized telemarketing operations help to ensure that information is communicated quickly and effectively to representatives and their managers. Many telemarketing software packages include an electronic diary management feature and the availability of route planning software has made diary management a much more significant function when making appointments for representatives on the road. Route planning helps telemarketers to ensure that the sequence of visits arranged follows the shortest possible route, thus minimizing the amount of time spent unproductively between appointments. Computerization also makes analysis of results easier. An important by-product of appointment-making activity is valuable sales management information. This provides an insight into regional variations in market response, for example, and allows comparisons to be made between sales territories, as in the following example.

Case study 9.2

As part of a major dealer recruitment campaign by Canon (UK) in 1990, Birmingham-based telemarketing agency BPS Téléperformance (BPS) followed up a mailing to dealers to make appointments for Canon's national salesforce. Of the 1574 decision makers contacted, 40 per cent either booked or committed to an appointment.

The launch of Canon's new FC1 and FC2 personal copiers was being used as an opportunity to extend the dealer network. A mailing to 26 000 existing and potential dealers was supported by advertising, editorial and loose inserts in all the major trade publications. Dealers were being offered an attractive package of incentives and ongoing support.

BPS was briefed to call all dealers who responded to the mailing to convert their interest, and to call a randomly selected group of non-responders to generate interest. The objective in both cases was to book appointments for Canon's seven-strong national salesforce, or at least to arrange a later date at which a salesperson could telephone to arrange one. Each salesperson allocated diary days for these appointments. BPS started by booking up to 30 'week commencing' appointments for each salesperson, although this was amended later to six morning or afternoon appointments per day per salesperson, and then to four appointments.

At the end of each day, BPS sent updated diary pages and call record sheets (with dealers' details) by fax to each salesperson's home. Copies of diary sheets and summaries of daily and cumulative results were faxed daily to the sales manager. As the campaign progressed, however, these procedures were amended, with only the 'urgent' appointments being faxed to salespeople and the remaining information being posted daily and copied to the sales manager. Copies of each call sheet, sorted by sales area and call outcome, were posted weekly to the sales manager. At a late stage, it was decided to send confirmation postcards to all dealers booking appointments. However, as the printers were unable to deliver before calling began, only about 80 per cent of appointments were confirmed.

Call structures differed for existing and prospective dealers. With existing dealers, BPS checked if they had received the FC1/FC2 mailing, whether they required further information, and whether they were interested in an appointment to discuss adding the products to their range. Non-Canon dealers were asked for their opinion of the mailing and questions to qualify both the type of outlet and their level of interest in the products, booking an appointment when appropriate. Call record sheets provided detailed information on dealers, both for the salespeople when they kept appointments and for the Canon database.

The campaign proved very effective, with 24 per cent of decision-maker contacts resulting in a booked appointment and a further 16 per cent gaining commitment to an appointment (Table 9.5). Over 90 per cent of those who responded to the mailing either booked or committed to an appointment. At the end of the campaign BPS provided Canon with a detailed report containing various statistical breakdowns of results, including effective and non-effective calls by mailing responders and non-responders (Table 9.5), effective calls by sales area (Table 9.6) and by business type, and responders and non-responders to the mailing by sales area.

In the report, BPS made recommendations for future improvements in two areas.

Table 9.5 Results of telephone follow-up to a mailing to make appointments in a Canon (UK) dealer recruitment campaign. (Courtesy of BPS Téléperformance)

Total calls attempted:	2360	(100%)
Effective calls (DMCs):	1574	(67%)
Non-effective calls:	642	(27%)
Call-backs (leads not spoken to and to be called back):	144	(6%)

	Responders to mailing	Non-responders to mailing	Total
Effective calls (1574 (67%))	**144 (9%)**	**1430 (91%)**	**1574 (100%)**
Appointment made (existing and prospective dealers)	99 (69%)	283 (20%)	382 (24%)
Interest expressed (salesperson to call later to arrange appointment)	32 (22%)	224 (16%)	256 (16%)
No immediate interest	11 (8%)	411 (29%)	422 (27%)
No interest/sole dealers for competitors	2 (1%)	512 (35%)	514 (33%)
Total effective calls	**144 (100%)**	**1430 (100%)**	**1574 (100%)**
Non-effective calls (642 (27%))	**37 (6%)**	**605 (94%)**	**642 (100%)**
Out of business/no number avail.	21 (57%)	247 (41%)	268 (42%)
No answer after four calls	0 (–)	142 (23%)	142 (22%)
Duplication/already contacted by Canon telesales	16 (43%)	216 (36%)	232 (36%)
Total non-effective calls	**37 (100%)**	**605 (100%)**	**642 (100%)**

The first was on salesforce involvement. The major criticism received from the sales team was that they had not been informed of the call approach and had doubts about the agency's ability to manage their sales territories effectively. BPS therefore recommended one-to-one briefings between the salespeople and the agency staff booking their appointments. This would serve to establish a working relationship and create awareness and understanding of each others' objectives and priorities. BPS also suggested that the system of despatching information to salespeople at the end of the day should be developed, in principle, with the sales manager and then adjusted as necessary for individual salespeople. This would take into account individual requirements and difficulties within their sales territories.

Analysis of the results provided some important insights. For example, calls to 1430 dealers who had not responded to the mailing resulted in a 36 per cent conversion to either an appointment or commitment to appointment. This suggests high awareness resulting from the mailing and media campaign, and highlights the

Table 9.6 Breakdown of effective calls by sales area in Canon (UK) dealer recruitment campaign. (Courtesy of BPS Téléperformance)

Sales area	Appointment booked	Committed to appointment	No immediate interest	Not interested	Total (%)
Area 1	45 (26%)	29 (17%)	46 (27%)	50 (29%)	170 (11%)
Area 2	44 (19%)	34 (15%)	85 (38%)	63 (28%)	226 (14%)
Area 3	64 (27%)	46 (19%)	59 (25%)	70 (29%)	239 (15%)
Area 4	55 (26%)	40 (19%)	48 (23%)	66 (32%)	209 (14%)
Area 5	65 (30%)	27 (12%)	52 (24%)	74 (34%)	218 (14%)
Area 6	51 (16%)	51 (16%)	77 (24%)	142 (44%)	321 (20%)
Area 7	58 (30%)	29 (15%)	55 (29%)	49 (26%)	191 (12%)
Total	382 (24%)	256 (16%)	422 (27%)	514 (33%)	1574 (100%)

importance of telephone follow-up. Similarly, the large number of contacts who were duplicated, or had already been contacted by Canon's in-house team, highlighted the need for both de-duplication of the prospect database and close liaison between the agency and in-house activities. Subsequently, both these issues were addressed.

Analysis of call results by sales area (Table 9.6) highlighted some interesting features of the sales territories. One was the disparity in the amount of prospecting required to secure appointments. Area 6, for example, had the lowest conversion rate (16 per cent) and required the largest volume of calls (20 per cent) to gain a suitable number of appointments. As a consequence, the salesperson for this area had 51 dealers to follow up later, compared with only 27 in Area 5. This type of analysis helps to identify if and where the sales team needs to be strengthened or supported to meet the demands within individual territories. Analysis of call results by business type revealed those dealers and non-typical dealers who were responding to the campaign, and provided valuable information for planning subsequent marketing of the FC1/FC2. Overall, the campaign provided a sound basis for the ongoing dealer recruitment and support programme (see page 140).

Communications with field representatives is improving with developments in portable computing and other mobile technologies such as in-car fax machines and pocket modems. Information on prospects can be sent down the line to representatives' computers prior to their appointments and they can immediately inform their office support staff and management of the outcome of meetings in the same way. They can also request documentation, such as letters, quotations and order confirmations, to be generated centrally. Good communications helps to ensure a slick, seamless operation.

Making appointments is just one way in which field representatives, or even local branch specialists, can be supported (see page 18, for example). In many situations the telephone can provide further support in the form of account servicing, which is examined in the next chapter.

10
Account servicing

Customers have increasingly high expectations of their suppliers. The greater the value of their business with a supplier, the more consideration and individual attention they expect. However, it is not only the large accounts that require attention; *all* customers are expecting better service, and as every account has the potential to increase in value and grow long term, it is important to maximize the value of each order and to nurture the relationship.

The needs of regular customers can be serviced directly in several ways, ranging from head office key account managers, through field sales representatives, to the telephone and mail. In the past, generally the higher the value of the customers the more expensive were the methods used to service their accounts – for example, face-to-face meetings. Now, in an effort to find ways to deliver more personal service to customers while minimizing costs, many organizations are exploiting the telephone as an integral part of their account servicing strategy.

10.1 Lower costs, better service

The potential for using the telephone in account servicing varies from market to market, but increasingly it is seen as a way to improve market coverage and deliver better service at a much lower cost than having more representation in the field. Some sectors, such as courier services, have always relied on the telephone as a method of doing business, while others are recognizing that some or all of their customers can be serviced in this way. The telephone can be used to provide them with a choice of how they do business, or to support or replace other channels. Banking provides a good example of how the telephone can be used profitably while giving the customer added value.

Case study 10.1

First Direct, a subsidiary of Midland Bank plc, was one of the world's first stand-alone telephone banking services. Launched in October 1989, it offers the full range of personal banking services, 24 hours a day, 365 days a year, and is Britain's fastest growing bank. By the end of 1992 it had 350 000 account customers and new customers were joining at the rate of 10 000–12 000 each month.

Customers use a local call charge number, which enables them to transact all their banking needs, whenever they want from wherever they are in the UK, for the price of a local telephone call. Since all business is conducted over the telephone, immediate response to a customer's call is essential. The call can relate to any one of First Direct's many services, from a simple balance request to organizing a personal loan or mortgage. The company handles up to 17 000 calls a day, almost 50 per cent of which arrive outside traditional banking hours, and the systems it uses are essential to delivering high levels of personal service.

To ensure maximum security for transactions by telephone, customers are asked to provide First Direct with a password of their choice. In all subsequent dealings with the bank, customers are asked to verify that password by giving two random characters from it. For additional security, the customer is also asked to provide several memorable pieces of information.

First Direct operates two Aspect CallCenter ACDs and customer calls are automatically routed to banking representatives (BRs) who handle 85 per cent of calls, including statement requests, bill payments, standing orders and direct debits. The most common transactions are balance enquiries, automated bill payments and transfers between accounts. First Direct customers pay 4500 bills a day over the telephone. Calls requiring a more detailed response, such as share dealings, investment, foreign exchange and loans, are passed to a second group of operators, known as financial services advisers, who are skilled in these specialized areas.

The CallCenters enable additional staff to join groups of BRs when call traffic is busiest. Experience has shown that this is likely to be necessary during several daily peaks, including the early evening when customers arrive home from work. The peak times for customers to call are 10.00–11.00 a.m. and 6.00–11.30 p.m. The routeing of inbound calls is determined by the volume of traffic at any one time. Calls could be routed to additional BRs depending, for example, on the time of day or the length of time a customer has been waiting. This ensures that all customer calls are answered in the shortest possible time.

First Direct uses an integrated sales and marketing system to personalize communications with its customers. The system gives BRs immediate access to full details of each customer, including previous dealings. Successive contact builds knowledge of individuals' behaviour and purchasing patterns (which are stored in the database), and helps to develop an understanding of their needs and provides the basis for developing the relationship. The system also offers facilities to analyse customers by different criteria and categorize them into precise, targetable groups. The system is not inert. Automatic analysis of data provides information for decision support. A financial services adviser talking to a customer requesting a loan, for example, need only take details of the request and the system will automatically analyse the customer data to evaluate the request and give a reasoned decision immediately. This type of decision support also extends to targeted marketing activities. Individual customers are flagged automatically to receive a specific marketing communication, by mail or telephone, when there is a change in the information held about them or affecting them. An additional feature of the system is that it helps to increase understanding of the marketplace and its trends. All of this helps the company to give customers what they need when they need it.

First Direct recognizes that lack of face-to-face contact with customers could pose additional problems when the subject matter is as important as money. Consequently, the company has particularly rigorous recruitment and training procedures. All applicants are invited to a three-hour selection session during which they have several ability tests. Those who pass undergo four weeks' training on product and system knowledge, and communication techniques particularly focused on the telephone. This is followed by a further three weeks concentrating on 'role playing' calls, when trainees are coached by experienced staff. Then, to ensure that they are of a sufficiently high standard, the trainees have a further test. Only then are they allowed to take calls without supervision. The BRs are taught to be more than just order takers. Their role is to ensure that what customers ask for is what they really need. The coaching is designed to ensure that all frontline staff listen as well as talk.

The company's investment in information technology and staff training has produced the desired results. First Direct won the UK prize in the 1993 Téléperformance Grand Prix. The Grand Prix survey is conducted each year by the Paris-based Téléperformance Group to measure the quality of telephone customer service provided by leading companies throughout Europe. For 1993, 30 'mystery shopper' calls were made to each of 200 companies asking questions relevant to their business. All calls were graded according to the quality of response, awarding marks for speed of answering, greeting used, warmth of welcome, tone of voice, call control, suggested solution, customer awareness and warmth of call close. First Direct scored higher across these criteria than any other UK company surveyed.

Among the most active users of telephone account servicing are sectors such as fast moving consumer goods, food and drink, stationery and pharmaceuticals. Businesses in these sectors traditionally have serviced their customers through field sales representatives. Today, the cost of maintaining a field salesforce is too high to have them use valuable time in such routine activities as taking orders. A telemarketer can generally make at least several times more selling contacts a day than someone on the road and, with the support of technology, they can often do the job more effectively. Because it is more efficient, and reduces costs, the supplier can afford to make contact more regularly and to suit individual customers. The cost of sales is also more easily quantified.

However, the benefits of telephone account servicing are not all for the supplier. Customers get better service in many ways: business is conducted more easily at times convenient to them; they can get a faster response when they have urgent needs or simply require information; and because there are no geographical barriers, all customers can get the same level of service.

10.2   When is the telephone applicable?

Identifying those customers who can be dealt with effectively by telephone depends not only on profit margins, but also on the channels that are used for selling specific products or services into specific markets. The telephone may be used to support a field salesforce or key account representatives on all or some accounts, or as the sole channel to serve some or all customers. The example of Dental Linkline (page 175) shows how, under the right conditions, it can be used very successfully as the main channel for managing accounts. In this case, it has helped the company to sustain annual growth averaging 49 per cent for seven years. Canon (UK), examined on page 140, uses the telephone to service the majority of its dealers while field representatives service the smaller number of larger accounts. The smaller dealers can request a field visit at any time, but business is routinely conducted over the telephone with Canon's in-house telesales team.

In deciding if, and how, the telephone can improve account servicing, a company should examine how its account base is currently serviced. If a salesforce is used, for example, the company can calculate at what point (in terms of individual account revenues) it is not cost-efficient for salespeople to visit some customers regularly, and research among those customers will reveal whether they are willing (once the benefits are explained) to do business by telephone with, perhaps, occasional visits or visits only when requested. The customer base can generally be divided into bands, by sales revenue or other distinguishing factors like product usage, customer type or distribution channel. A different account servicing strategy can be designed for each of these groups, defining the methods and frequency of communication. Table 10.1 shows how the telephone might support a customer base segmented according to sales revenues. The intention is to allocate resources in the most cost-efficient way while trying to improve service to each customer:

Table 10.1   Telephone account servicing options

Account type	Telephone servicing
Prospects	Lead screening and qualification; building interest and keeping 'warm'; arranging appointments
New accounts	Welcome call – initial order capture or delivery confirmation; confirm account servicing options; capture additional data
Lapsed accounts	Call to identify reason for lapse and try to reactivate; arrange field visit
Declining accounts	Call to identify reason for lower spend; build business; arrange field visit
Marginal accounts	Regular call cycling for order capture, promotional work and to enquire if visit required
Regular low-spending accounts	Telephone support only, unless visit expressly requested
Mid-range accounts	Regular call cycling for order capture and comfort issues; booking appointment times
Key accounts	Customer care-type calls in between sales visits; pre-visit research call; inbound emergency order capture and enquiries

Case study 10.2

Royal Mail, one of the UK's largest businesses, found that telephone account servicing was welcomed immediately by one group of its customers. The business had faced increasingly fierce competition from independent carriers since the early 1980s. Growth in the use of other business and advertising communications media – telephone, fax, TV, radio and electronic mail – compounded competitive pressures. As a result, Royal Mail lost market share worth approximately £1 billion over the decade up to 1993. Analysis of the customer base revealed that there was a significant loss of revenue from one particular group of customers. Telephone account management was introduced in an attempt to reverse this trend and to increase customer satisfaction.

Royal Mail segments its business customers into three main groups: key accounts (the largest businesses and government departments), major accounts (spending over £40 000 a year on postage) and minor accounts (spending £5000 to £40 000). The key and major accounts, which together generate revenues of £1.45 billion, are serviced by a direct salesforce of 120 people. Until 1993, 69 business centres across the UK provided additional *ad hoc* sales support, such as handling enquiries about contracts and delivery. These centres were also the sole source of support for minor account customers, who could call their local centre for information or advice. This group was spending nearly £1 billion annually, representing over 20 per cent of turnover, and yet they received no proactive support and little targeted marketing. There was obvious scope for improving management of these accounts and service to individual customers.

Minor account customers number over 300 000. With a face-to-face sales visit costing around £120–£150, providing full field sales cover was out of the question. Direct mail could play a major role, but it did not offer the flexibility required and, more importantly, the opportunity for personal dialogue. Royal Mail was considering employing telemarketing staff in each of its nine divisions to support existing sales and marketing activities. In August 1992, telemarketing consultancy *Cal*com Associates was contracted to audit the organization's opportunities for telephone marketing and put forward proposals for implementation.

The audit revealed that minor account customers were the least satisfied with their relationship with Royal Mail and offered a number of opportunities to develop business. *Cal*com proposed setting up Telephone Account Management (TAM) units, whose principal objectives would be to:

- build relationships;
- protect the customer base;
- generate incremental business;
- add value for the customer.

Overall, the TAM units would enable the company to sell deeper and wider through planned, frequent contact with this previously neglected group of customers and with prospects. The Royal Mail board agreed, in January 1993, to commence three-month trials at three sites. Leeds, Bolton and London – each representing a different customer base mix – were chosen in order to gain a broad knowledge of the dynamics of TAM and how it could work for Royal Mail. *Cal*com's role was to provide telemarketing expertise to the company's senior project team and to support other areas of the business in developing telephone account management.

Within each trial area the business centres, numbering three or four, were amalgamated onto one site. This had the benefits of combining resources, increasing sales efficiency and streamlining customer communications. Each TAM unit would have an account base of around 10 500 to 14 000 customers, and up to about 40 000 prospects. Over a period of 16 weeks, the following tasks were undertaken:

- Staff selection and recruitment (a manager and 6–9 telephone account executives for each unit).
- Set-up of systems.
- Design of working practices.
- Transfer of telephony from business centres to the TAM unit sites.
- Induction and training of staff.
- Selection of customer data from the main database and downloading to the TAM unit systems.

During the trial period, from May to July 1993, the telephone account executives (TAEs) aimed to speak to all customers and prospects in their catchment area at least once, and to arrange appropriate follow-up such as further telephone contact, sending printed information, or a field sales visit. Each TAE worked the same postcode areas as a member of the area sales team, thus giving a clear line of communication for liaison between the telephone and field sales functions. Telephone calls took a customer care approach, designed to help businesses become more efficient in their use of the postal service. The aim was to:

- introduce Royal Mail and the TAM concept;
- identify business opportunities;
- sell directly, by telephone, to prospects and to customers spending less than £40 000 a year;
- book appointments for the salesforce with customers who had the potential to spend more than £40 000 a year.

Critical success factors had been identified in *Cal*com's proposal and would be used to measure the effectiveness of TAM. Results from the three-month trial were used to project full-year results. Telemarketers had a target of four decision-maker contacts per hour and actually achieved 3.4. The three TAM units together had a target of £8 million annual sales secured by telephone, with a further £5 million sales resulting from the qualified appointments booked for the salesforce. In fact, sales secured by telephone exceed the target by 100 per cent, at a projected £16 million for 12 months, while qualified appointments would result in a further projected £19 million annual sales, 280 per cent above target. Compared with the remaining business centres, used as control sites, telephone account management increased revenues by 12 per cent (direct and indirect sales).

Further evidence of the success of the new telephone account management structure came from research. Contacts were surveyed for their opinions at the end of each telephone call. Only 0.5 per cent claimed to be dissatisfied with this type of approach and 7.5 per cent were indifferent. The majority (92 per cent), however, expressed satisfaction. Further research conducted by an external agency, using focus groups and face-to-face qualitative interviews, gained extremely positive feedback. A key point made by customers was that they did not want a telesales approach, but they understood telephone account management and welcomed the opportunities it presented. The consensus, overall, was 'We didn't know you cared'.

Following the validation of this new style of account management, Royal Mail decided to introduce TAM across the UK. Working with *Cal*com Associates, an additional three units were being set up during January to April 1994, with the balance (giving a probable total of 18) planned to be in place by the end of 1995. Royal Mail also believes that the TAM units will have a role to play in servicing customers in the key and major account groups, releasing the salesforce to spend more time following up qualified new business prospects.

10.3 Building value

Order capture is a basic account servicing function that can be conducted very efficiently by outbound or inbound telephone contact. The objective is to take the order quickly and accurately and try to exploit further sales opportunities, for example, by rounding up quantities to the next discount level, cross-selling related items, encouraging the acceptance of promotional offers, and ensuring that lines normally bought but not requested are offered. Inevitably, telephone staff will become involved in fielding miscellaneous enquiries and complaints, which is all part of the telephone account servicing function. Indeed, 'ownership' of the customers is a key ingredient when this is the primary channel. Some of the ways in which telephone staff can be supported in delivering first-rate service are examined in Chapter 16.

Capturing orders personally, rather than by mail or fax, has two important benefits. Obviously, it offers the opportunity to maximize order value in a way that only dialogue can achieve. But it also enables the order-taker to identify a fall in regular order value. Whatever the reason for the drop – perhaps the customer is buying from a competitor or has been unable to sell as much of the product – direct contact means that the company can identify the cause and quickly take appropriate action to try to rebuild the business.

Case study 10.3

The speed of the telephone as a method of conducting business is increasingly important for Coca-Cola & Schweppes Beverages Ltd (CCSB) in developing customer relationships. The company's Telebusiness Centre at Peterborough, opened in 1992, is a cornerstone of its strategy to provide fast, efficient account servicing, working in conjunction with the company's trade marketing and sales teams. CCSB is responsible for the distribution of Coca-Cola and Schweppes soft drinks in Great Britain, amounting to 60 brands in approximately 220 different pack variations. The Telebusiness Centre services 42 000 direct-delivered account customers in the licensed and retail trades, leisure industry and other outlets such as workplace canteens.

Outbound calling forms the major part of the Centre's activity, with Customer Contact Representatives (CCRs) making about 3200 scheduled calls each day. Most of this is order capture from direct-delivered customers, although there is also a team of cold-callers generating appointments for vending machine sales representatives. A small number of customers prefer to call CCSB rather than be called, for example if their restocking requirements are irregular, and the Centre also handles customer enquiries. About 1200 inbound calls are handled each day, 50 per cent of which are enquiries and 25 per cent of these concern deliveries.

CCSB customers obviously have widely differing ordering requirements and the Telebusiness Centre uses a customer database to ensure that each call is tailored to the individual's needs as well as helping to maximize the selling opportunity. The telephone system and database are integrated through an Aspect CallCenter ACD with Application Bridge (Aspect's intelligent ACD/computer interface), enabling CCRs to dial customers' numbers automatically from the database records.

Information available to CCRs when they talk with customers includes previous order history, approved product listings (i.e. agreed between the customer's head office and CCSB), promotions currently in force (at particular outlets and CCSB's own special promotions), CCSB's sales priorities (such as brands suited to particular outlets or helping to achieve particular financial targets), and the time at which it is most convenient for customers to take calls.

The customer base is divided into two market sectors – Impulse (neighbourhood stores such as garage forecourts, corner stores, off-licences, etc.) and On-premise (licensed premises, restaurants, etc.) – which are assigned a different telephone number for contacting the Telebusiness Centre. The Impulse sector is serviced by two outbound and one inbound team of CCRs, while the On-premise sector has five outbound and two inbound teams. This specialization helps CCRs gain a better knowledge of the needs of their sector and enables some prior sorting of incoming calls at the ACD, according to the number that has been dialled.

Outbound calling lists for each team are generated automatically, using the database, by day, grouped in half-hour timebands allocated to customers according to their requirements. Publicans, for example, generally prefer calls in the morning, between 11 a.m. and midday, or just after closing time; shops prefer calls early in the morning, while workplace canteens prefer 10–11 a.m. or 2–3 p.m.

As outbound-calling CCRs close one call, the computer automatically presents the next customer record on screen. As soon as the representative is ready to talk with that customer, a simple keyboard command dials the number automatically. On inbound calls, the CCRs access a customer's record by keying in the outlet (account) number or, if necessary, by conducting a search on name, address or telephone number.

The Telebusiness Centre aims to answer all inbound calls within 12 seconds (4 rings), after which the caller is welcomed with a recorded message and the current main advertising jingle plays until, after a preset time (decided according to call traffic), the CallCenter invites the customer to leave a voice message to enable the call to be returned. This message is passed automatically to an operator, when available, and CCSB aims to return all calls within one hour.

In addition to taking orders, inbound and outbound calls are both used to inform customers of current promotions and to up-sell and cross-sell according to the outlet's approved product listings. Information in customer records helps the CCRs to gain maximum order value from each call. The average duration of both inbound and outbound calls is about 180 seconds.

Soft drinks sales are affected by seasonal and holiday peaks, so unusually hot summer periods can increase call traffic dramatically. CCSB has been exploring all possible options to help manage these peaks and maintain the stringent service levels it has set.

Avoiding channel conflict

When the telephone is used to support other channels, such as a field salesforce, it is vital that there are clear objectives for the telephone communication. The role of each channel must be clearly defined for each customer group to avoid conflict, for the sake of the customer and cost-efficiency. If a customer is bombarded by sales messages from a salesperson, a telephone agent and, perhaps, mail, or is offered different terms through different channels, it is likely to damage the relationship. If, for example, key accounts are serviced by regular field visits, then any telephone activity should not serve the same functions as the visit but should aim to support and extend it. Calls can be used to identify interim needs, reflect the high priority given to key account customers, and help to ensure that the outcome of visits is mutually beneficial by identifying any special needs beforehand. The telephone serves to add value, increasing the frequency of personal contact and showing that the company is caring and supportive of its customers' needs (but not pressurizing them for more business or apparently charging a premium for goods sold through a particular channel). Every call should also have a clear purpose, perhaps confirming a time for a visit or calling to check on a delivery, so that it is not seen by the customer as unnecessary time-wasting. Within such calls, whatever their stated purpose, a skilful telemarketer can address any number of customer care and service issues.

Reactivating lapsed accounts

The best source of additional sales, after live accounts, is likely to be lapsed customers who know the company and its products or services. Lapses can go unnoticed when there is no regular dialogue with customers, and these accounts may be forgotten. Telephone contact provides an efficient way to identify the reasons for the lapse and to try to reactivate the account. Depending on the recency of the lapse, contact might be re-established by a mailing or immediately by telephone. A mailing could offer former 'valued' customers a special deal, or free trial offer on a new line, and encourage them to call the company to discuss their needs. Once in conversation, the company can establish the reasons for lapses – perhaps a competitor is offering a better deal, or the customer has changed to a central buying policy, or it felt the service offered was inadequate – and discuss the possibility of their valued business being regained. The credit card division of a major UK bank decided to phone customers who said they wanted to close their card account. Eleven per cent of calls resulted in customers reactivating their card.

Growing customer expectations to do business when it suits them has led to increasing pressure on companies in many sectors to extend their hours of service availability. High staffing costs are often a limiting factor, particularly when a company operates from many sites, and centralizing customer service operations is a typical strategic response for large organizations (examined in Chapter 16).

10.4 Delivering automated service

Another option in limiting costs while extending service availability is the automation of some services, although cost reduction may be the sole reason. Automation is especially suited to account servicing, where the customer and service provider have an ongoing relationship (although this means losing the 'personal' touch and requires serious consideration of the consequences). Knowledge of the customer on a database provides the basis for servicing individuals' needs over the telephone network, using either an interactive voice response (IVR) system or dedicated customer terminal as the mediator for exchanging information and instructions. Customers can be identified by account number and, if necessary, verified by a personal identification number (PIN) or voice print (the ability to recognize individuals from their voice, coming soon on IVR systems).

Dedicated terminals in the office or home are used on a limited basis at present, except in France. Télétel, established by France Télécom, enables telephone subscribers to access more than 20 000 independent services using a Minitel videotex terminal, with keyboard and screen, connected to their telephone line. More than 6.3 million terminals were installed by early 1993, 75 per cent of them lent free by France Télécom to any subscriber who requested one, in place of the paper directory. During 1991, nearly 40 per cent of users were placing orders via Télétel services, including making hotel, flight and train reservations, ordering a courier, and buying books, cassettes and records. Nearly 45 per cent were using it to access banking services.

Some companies, independently, have provided customers with some form of terminal that can be used, for example, in home shopping or telephone banking. However, the cost of equipping a large customer base, particularly one that is fluid, can be prohibitive. The growth of cabling networks that carry television and telecommunications data, combined with sophisticated consumer terminals, will eventually provide the necessary infrastructure. Until then, IVR systems are currently the most viable alternative.

IVR systems are already being used widely, particularly in the USA. Customers are ordering goods from catalogues, checking the current value of their personal investment portfolio, obtaining information on the status and whereabouts of parcels and freight, replenishing stocks with a call to their suppliers, and doing their banking all at times convenient to them. Even in Europe, where the use of IVR is not yet widespread, companies are finding that many customers will use an automated service even when they have the option of speaking to a live operator or visiting a local outlet.

Case study 10.4

National Westminster Bank launched its first IVR-based service in July 1988 and now offers comprehensive automated telephone banking services. Customers can carry out the most frequently required transactions 24 hours a day, 365 days a year. The services were a response to pressure on banks generally to extend their hours of service availability, and National Westminster's aim was 'any phone, anywhere, any time'. For this reason, it chose to use voice recognition as well as tone, since the penetration of DTMF phones in the UK in 1988 was very low.

The bank's Actionline service, which was introduced nationally in December 1989, enables its customers to make payments, transfers and requests for items such as cheque books or for statements to be mailed. BusinessLine, a more comprehensive service launched in December 1992, provides balances on up to six accounts, aural statements, searches for transactions of specified amounts, and a review of past and scheduled transactions. These services were handling several million calls a year by 1992.

Since the main benefit to customers was having easy access to services outside of normal banking hours, it was a prime requirement that the services should be available 24 hours a day, 7 days a week, 365 days a year. The bank has therefore had to configure its systems (which encompass mainframe computers, data and telecommunications, and remotely sited IVR equipment) to permit routine maintenance without interruption to the services. As an example, the equipment for Actionline is located at six sites around the country to provide some degree of local telephone access for customers. This is exploited by having calls diverted automatically to alternative sites under preset conditions. If there is no answer from one site, perhaps due to a power failure or maintenance downtime, calls will be routed automatically to another site. Spreading call-handling facilities across more than one site therefore has improved reliability as well as customer access.

The accuracy of IVR equipment in recognizing customer responses is another issue of concern, particularly when using voice recognition. National Westminster estimates that its current equipment is about 95 per cent accurate on single-digit voice recognition. This is probably as accurate as live operators or bank counter staff recognizing similar data first time. However, the bank says that what really counts is how successful you are in taking the transaction, whatever it is, through to completion. Here, the design of the interaction with customers is crucially important.

National Westminster also stresses the importance of good 'error recovery', with help graded according to the problem being experienced by the caller. Imitating conversational style helps to win customer acceptance and to ensure that services can be used easily and accurately. The bank believes that the customers' perception of the service and the company is entirely influenced by what they hear.

Security is another vital requirement. Actionline and BusinessLine require callers to enter their account number and then their personal identification number (PIN). These, and all requested transactions, are voiced back to the caller for confirmation. Obvious hoax or fraudulent calls, detected at the account number or PIN stage, are ended quickly but courteously. Callers are referred to a service office for assistance and the system then says 'Goodbye' and disconnects.

After seven years' experience with automated account servicing, National Westminster Bank now has a large number of very active users. It has taken time to reach this stage because the technology was not widely known when these services were introduced. New services for customers and internal use are under development, but the bank believes that the full potential of IVR will not be realized until there is widespread public acceptance of the technology.

There are many other ways in which technology can help to improve the efficiency of telephone account servicing and to add value. One UK taxi firm, controlling 2200 black cabs in central London, has 32 agents handling an average of about 5500 calls a day from account customers. The company uses an Aspect CallCenter ACD which enables it to differentiate between calls from account customers and general enquiries, according to the number dialled. This has been used to offer a specialized service to disabled customers and lone female travellers (who are often concerned for their safety), whose calls are routed automatically to specific agent groups knowledgeable about their special needs. Other technologies that can enhance telephone-based customer service, and thereby help to nurture relationships and gain maximum value from each customer, are examined in Chapter 16.

While telephone account servicing is not applicable to all businesses (heavy engineering companies, for example), or for all customers (such as the most valuable or prestigious accounts), it does offer many companies the opportunity to maintain a higher level of contact with their customers, and deliver better service, while stabilizing costs.

11
Selling

Modern-day telephone selling bears no relationship to the telesales operations that emerged in the USA in the early 1960s and spread to Europe a decade later. Calling then was generally unstructured and inconsistent. There was little planning, control or measurement of activity that would allow companies to evaluate and improve their approach. Activity was dominated by the need to sell – to sell hard and to sell fast.

The pace in a professional telephone selling environment today is often no less frenetic, but everything – from lead sourcing through call structures to follow-up – is planned and controlled with precision. It is still dominated by the need to sell, but it is selling in a customer-oriented environment. Rather than dulling its edge, this controlled environment makes the telephone a much more incisive tool for selling to markets nationally and internationally. Most professional telephone selling is conducted in this manner.

Cultural differences are accommodated by differences in approach. In the USA, for example, people are accustomed to, and accept, a hard-sell approach, while European markets require more subtle tactics. The codes of practice for telemarketing in the UK, Germany and Italy, for example, state explicitly that high-pressure tactics should not be used, and these are codes designed for the benefit of telemarketing operators. The hard-sell approach is not productive in European markets, although cold calls (to people with whom the company has not previously had contact) are generally acceptable (except in Germany, where they are illegal) provided that they are made at the right time with the right offer and are handled courteously.

Resistance to telephone selling arises mostly when it is not used professionally. On the whole, people value the opportunity for personal contact with potential suppliers and often prefer it, particularly in business-to-business markets, because of the ease and speed of access. The increasingly widespread use of credit and debit cards means that people can order goods or services immediately by telephone, when the impulse or need arises, and sometimes take delivery the following day. For suppliers, telephone dialogue offers the opportunity to establish an immediate rapport with individuals, to identify their needs, tailor their approach to show how their offerings can meet those needs, and maximize the selling opportunity.

At the right time, in the right circumstances, it is a valued opportunity for both sides to develop a mutually beneficial relationship.

Almost anything can be sold by telephone, from a year's sponsorship of an African elephant to a forklift truck. The role of the telephone can range from simply taking the order and customer details through to a complete sale from pitch to close. Most telephone sales are not made with a single call but are generally the result of a cycle of communications that could have included direct response advertising, previous telephone contact, direct mail, perhaps with a brochure or catalogue, a sales visit or an exhibition. Many telephone sales are made within the context of an ongoing relationship which is nurtured with a rolling programme of timely personalized communications using appropriate media.

11.1 Planning and control

The success of telephone selling operations relies heavily upon the effective management of communications, across all media (inbound and outbound, print and broadcast, etc.) to ensure that people are contacted at the best time, with the right offer and in an appropriate manner. The planning and control measures that are fundamental to this process have a direct impact on results.

Case study 11.1

In November 1992, third party software supplier Wick Hill IMX introduced formal operational systems and procedures into its telesales operation, immediately after implementing a new training programme. The following month sales leapt by over 57 per cent. Even allowing for a seasonal variation in sales (60 per cent in the period September to January), this represents a substantial gain attributable largely to the new method of working.

Wick Hill IMX is UK market leader in its field, supplying a range of PC to mainframe connectivity software products. Over 60 per cent of the £7 million-plus sales (1992/93) are generated by the telesales operation, the remainder coming from corporate sales. The company supplies two markets: direct customers, including large corporate clients, and indirect customers, such as dealers and value added resellers (VARs).

Leads for the telesales team are generated through direct response advertising in computer magazines, using reader reply cards, direct mail and exhibiting at trade shows. Leads from these sources, as well as any callers requesting information, are put onto the prospect database and then mailed an appropriate information pack. Before reorganization, leads from the database were allocated according to who, in the team of four telesales staff, had the least number of leads at the time, and were prioritized as new leads.

The role of the telesales team was two-fold. Most of their time was spent taking inbound calls, put through by the switchboard operator to anyone who was not on the telephone at the time, from existing customers and responses to the information pack. They handled around 200–300 calls each month, taking orders, providing technical advice, answering general enquiries and trying to convert to sales. The team also made outbound calls to prospects who had been sent an information pack but had not responded. There was little time for this activity, however, and only a small proportion of leads were followed up. It was left to individual team members to decide who they called, and when. There was no system to measure the number of leads followed up, the outcome of calls, the proportion resulting in sales, and so on. By the time of the reorganization, a database of about 5000 prospects had built up.

At this stage, the telesales team were responsible for all direct and indirect customers except those dealt with by the corporate salesman. He generates nearly 40 per cent of sales and concentrates on building relationships with customers whose requirements could be large volume and who are also more likely to require support. He used a database of major companies for prospecting, as well as following up on relevant leads from exhibitions, and dealt with some of the larger dealers and VARs. However, the responsibilities of telesales and corporate sales for different types of prospect were blurred.

In July 1992, Wick Hill IMX decided to reskill the telesales team and called in consultant Brenda Spiller to discuss their needs. It quickly became apparent that there was a major opportunity to make the selling activity more productive and profitable. As a result, the consultant presented a proposal to review and restructure the telesales operation as well as deliver training.

The company directors agreed to the outlined changes, which had three main objectives: to generate maximum revenue by introducing structured working practices; to convert an essentially inbound, reactive telesales operation into a more proactive, outbound team to ensure that all relevant leads were followed up; and to clarify the telesales role and train the team in effective telephone selling techniques.

The first stage of the consultancy was to review all areas of the business which impacted on the sales operation. The consultant discussed a wide range of issues with the company's management, including territory planning, sales targets and forecasting, telesales management and motivation, call rates and record keeping, technical support, sales administration, the computerized lead-tracking system, timekeeping and career development.

As a result of this review, the consultant provided detailed proposals for changes in the operation, including recommendations to recruit a full-time telesales manager and increase the telesales staff from four to eight to ensure complete coverage of the UK.

The new systems and procedures were designed to ensure that all inbound and outbound telephone activity could be monitored and measured against preset standards and targets. All leads would be followed up within a specified time, the outcome of calls would be recorded systematically so that leads could be tracked effectively, call rates and sales incomes could be measured, and the results could be monitored continuously by management.

Prior to implementing the changes, the consultant conducted a training needs

Monthly sales (£s)

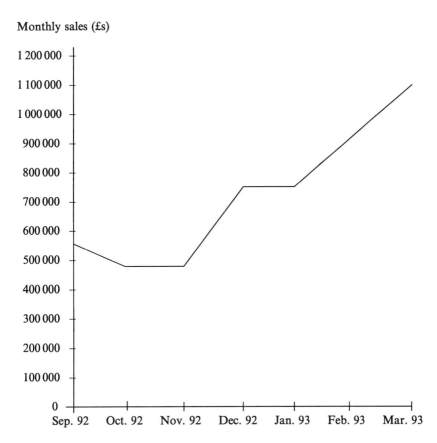

Figure 11.1 Impact of introducing formal telesales systems, procedures and training. (Courtesy of Wick Hill IMX)

analysis. Since there were no full job descriptions at this stage against which to measure competences, this was done by recording and listening to inbound calls to assess how individuals handled them. The consultant found that there was little structure to any of the calls and little or no 'technique' was being used to encourage sales. The training programme was designed to give telesales staff appropriate telephone selling skills, to encourage commitment to pure selling as their role, and to ensure that they understood the new systems and could follow procedures. Refresher product training was given prior to the initial three-day telesales training course delivered at the end of October 1992.

The reorganization began in October and went live in early November 1992, with a plan to monitor and refine it, as necessary, over a five-month period. The telesales manager, recruited during November, made any necessary operational adjustments as staff settled into the new style of working.

Additional telesales staff were recruited in January and February 1993 to form two teams: one dedicated to direct and one to indirect customers. Team members now have responsibility for their own leads, grouped alphabetically by prospect name. Inbound calls are put through by the operator to the relevant person according to the type and name of the prospect. All new leads have to be followed up within one week of an information pack being sent.

The corporate salesman's customer and prospect base has been identified as 35 of the UK's largest companies, which no member of the telesales teams is allowed to contact. However, the salesman has given up the large indirect customers (dealers and VARs) to the telesales team. Prior to reorganization, the company's managing director had guaranteed that no member of the sales staff would lose as a result of the changes.

Despite the disruption to the company and sales personnel caused by the reorganization, sales for December were up nearly 58 per cent, rising to £743 000 against £471 000 in November (see Figure 11.1). This was before the new telesales team had been recruited, and without any additional expenditure on lead generation.

Corporate sales revenues did fall, initially, as a result of the salesman handing over his large indirect clients to the telesales team. However, by making contact with the larger base of direct clients, some of which were previously direct telesales customers, his sales soon recovered (to £269 000 in January 1993, against a target of £186 000) and since then have been increasing steadily. Another corporate salesperson was hired in February 1993, and also a corporate sales administrative assistant.

Telesales staff motivation has increased dramatically, as a combined result of having their own customer and prospect base and achieving higher sales. The management information made available by the new operating systems enables better sales forecasting and marketing planning.

The early success of the unit is being consolidated with an ongoing programme of development, of which regular training forms a vital part. According to the consultant, Brenda Spiller, one of the most important contributing factors in this success was the commitment to the project of the Wick Hill IMX management.

11.2 Software support

The simple act of following up leads at the right time, with calls made by a skilled telephone salesperson, can overcome prospects' inertia to act, or encourage them to act now rather than later, and secure their business. Telemarketing software provides valuable support for telephone sales-people. In addition to contact details, including any personal information gathered through earlier contact, it can provide sophisticated scripts to guide the salesperson through the selling process. Counters to objections can be incorporated, along with product information, stock availability, service arrangements, special offers or free trials (and to whom they can be offered), and any other information required to promote sales. Linked to a database it provides access to customer records bearing information, such as usual lines stocked, which may be essential to service their needs efficiently (see CCSB, for example, on page 96).

Software can also support cross-selling and up-selling. Cross-selling is encouraging customers to buy goods or services related to what they are ordering but which they may not have realized the company supplies. An example is someone calling to arrange motor insurance and the telemarketer encouraging the customer to consider taking household insurance as well. Up-selling refers to encouraging customers to buy a more expensive option, or commit to longer-term business (e.g. a two-year subscription instead of one year), or to take more of the goods they are ordering. Increasing average order values by cross-selling and up-selling can increase profitability dramatically, since the major expenditure in building interest has already been made.

Case study 11.2

UK marketing services company Mailcom uses its computer system to help operators gain maximum order value on each call, by providing prompts for cross-selling and up-selling. The company won the the merchandise contract for British Sky Broadcasting (BSkyB) satellite television in August 1992. This includes handling subscribers' written and telephone requests for merchandise advertised on-screen. To fulfil these orders, Mailcom holds a wide range of goods, from holdalls and movie guides to T-shirts and jogging suits.

Mailcom's computer system prompts operators to ask for and capture the name, address, type of product, and payment method and details from callers. It also highlights items appropriate for cross-selling and up-selling, dependent upon the item a caller wants to order. The operator's screen will show instantly if the item requested is out of stock and will list alternatives. If the customer wants a green sweatshirt in a particular size, for example, and it is not available, the screen will show the other colours that are available in that size. The operator can suggest these alternatives and ask whether the customer would like one of those or wait until new stock is available at a date also shown on screen. When a customer orders a sweatshirt, the enquiry 'Did you realize that we also have matching jogging pants and baseball cap?' can trigger extra sales, as can information about discounts available on multiple purchases. All the relevant prompts are provided on operators' screens, to allow them to concentrate on selling.

When selling goods or services off the page, by direct mail, or via television or radio, there is no better way to capture impulse buyers than to offer them a telephone number through which to place their orders. The combination of a credit card, telephone and an express delivery option means that those customers who cannot wait any longer can have their goods within 24 hours of making the call.

Rapid response is also invaluable for marketers, as it gives immediate feedback on a campaign's success or failure. They can look at the response figures and calculate whether they need to order extra merchandise to cope with demand, or place extra advertising or change the creative concept to stimulate more sales. It takes a week or more before this can be done with postal responses, but it is in that first couple of days that companies are planning the next wave of advertising. Rapid feedback shows – in time to make the necessary adjustments – which products, advertisements and media are pulling response and which are failing.

11.3 Television selling

Off-the-page selling has been growing significantly in the UK since the mid-1980s, and rapidly in some sectors such as the computer and software industries. Television is the next boom area. Some advertisers have used UK terrestrial television since the 1980s to sell such goods as records and 'innovative' products, which are often not available through retail outlets. The biggest growth area in the early 1990s, however, has been direct selling on satellite television. This has been boosted by two new European dedicated satellite home shopping channels launched in 1993 – Sell-A-Vision, a joint initiative between Flextech and Quantum International, and a joint venture between BSkyB and Quality, Value, Convenience (QVC). QVC is the largest USA operator in this area, broadcasting 24 hours a day, seven days a week to nearly 50 million satellite and cable homes.

A TV advertising format which is likely to grow in Europe is infomercials – advertising, packaged as informative programming, of up to 25 minutes' duration. The concept was established in the USA in 1987 and has grown dramatically. An infomercial aims to involve the audience using a 'fun' format, which is both informative and interesting, often with a celebrity guest to endorse the product. Regular breaks invite the viewer to order the product and provide information on how to order. Quantum International is one of the world's major exponents. It buys air time directly from channel owners, to make productive use of their 'quiet time', and produces a complete programme package. In 1992 the company also began offering 2-minute advertising in the form of short infomercials.

Apart from air time costs, infomercials are very expensive to produce and their profitability relies heavily upon maximizing the value of responses. This is achieved partly by cross-selling and up-selling on the initial call, but also by subsequent outbound calling. Outbound calls are used to encourage repeat sales of consumables, for example, around the time when the initial order is likely to have been used. A database determines when people should be contacted. Repeat business can also be encouraged by the fulfilment pack containing the initial order. Business gained after the first sale can account for a large proportion of the business generated overall by an infomercial. Establishing a database is extremely important, so that the long-term potential of a customer can be exploited in the same way as any direct marketing operation. It delivers all the benefits of a marketing database, and identifies those products that can be promoted profitably by this method.

11.4 Financial services

The fastest growing areas of direct selling in the UK since the late 1980s have been insurance and banking, and they seem set to continue this growth throughout most of the 1990s. By early 1993 there were 15 UK banks and building societies offering telephone banking services, using three main ways for customers to transact business by telephone: direct with bank staff, using DTMF (tone) telephones and/or voice recognition, or using dedicated terminals (some with screens). Callers to First Direct, for example, are answered by operators (page 90), while National Westminster Bank offers an automated service (page 100).

Direct insurers controlled around 10 per cent of the £10 billion UK general (e.g. motor and household) insurance market by the end of 1992. Buying policies over the telephone rather than through a broker was becoming increasingly common, with keener prices often offered by operators by-passing the intermediary. One of the characteristics of these operations, however, is that they tend to cater for the mass market and not for customers with special needs. Even so, some predictions forecast that direct sellers will capture up to 30 per cent of the UK market by 1997, largely due to the convenience, the ability to shop around, and the cost savings.

Case study 11.3

Touchline Insurance Services, part of the French-owned European insurance and banking firm Groupe Gan, was launched in the UK in January 1993. The company initially offered motor insurance, with plans to move into household insurance later, and hopes to capture 2.5 per cent of the direct market overall. Launching into an already crowded market, where existing operators accounted for 15 per cent of the UK motor insurance market, meant that Touchline faced stiff competition from established, often well-known companies. Its strategy to win market share was based on delivering premium service, supported by the latest technology.

Effective call handling is paramount in service delivery and Touchline relies on its Aspect CallCenter ACD to help cope with peaks of calls. One of the features used is call-back messaging, which enables callers to leave a message, rather than waiting on hold, when all agents are busy. Messages are passed to agents during less busy times and the calls are returned. As well as enhancing service by reducing waiting times, it increases agent productivity (and thereby reduces costs to customers) by smoothing out the peaks and troughs in call volumes. Equally important, it minimizes the loss of sales calls and helps Touchline to obtain maximum value from its advertising spend.

11.5 Automated order capture

The convenience for customers of ordering by telephone varies directly with the quality of service delivered at the other end of the telephone line.

Case study 11.4

With a growing membership, ECI Book & Record Club looked to automation to help deal quickly and efficiently with members' calls. As Holland's largest mail order company for books and compact discs, in January 1993 it had 1.7 million members to service.

About 50 operators in ECI's Clubservice department handle members' queries on everything from deliveries to special offers. They are always busy, with peak call traffic occurring every three months at the end of each ordering period. ECI wanted to maximize automation to enable it to maintain levels of service to an increasing number of members. The installation of an Aspect CallCenter ACD with Application Bridge (Aspect's intelligent ACD/computer interface), in 1992, has enabled ECI customers to place their orders automatically.

ECI members can order by phone from the quarterly catalogue, at any time, without speaking to an operator. Voice prompts from the CallCenter guide them through the process of inputting their membership number and the catalogue numbers of the items they want to order, and this information is fed directly into ECI's computerized order-processing system. The system directly recognizes tones from DTMF telephones, while pulse signals from older telephones are converted first into digital signals. If customers experience any difficulties registering their orders, they can either speak to an operator or leave a voice message. Voice messages are passed to operators automatically, to return the call, when the Clubservice department is less busy. A rapidly increasing number of customers are now placing their orders automatically.

ECI members have benefited in two ways from the automation. They can place their orders quickly and at any convenient time and, if they do require personal assistance, operators can answer enquiries more speedily because less of their time is now spent taking orders.

Technology is providing increasingly convenient ways for people to place orders automatically from the home or office. For years the French have been able to order goods or services advertised via Télétel (page 99) using a special terminal. Limited versions of this type of service have been available in other countries, such as catalogue shopping via the Prestel service in the UK, but the arrival of the 'smart' telephone gives wider access for consumers and small businesses. In addition to normal telephone functions, smart telephones include a screen, smart card reader and computer technology for data communications over the telephone network. A smart card provides access to a specific service database, operated by a service provider, and business is transacted by following on-screen prompts and using the telephone keypad to input instructions. The potential applications are wide-ranging (ordering from catalogues, banking and insurance, booking travel, retail stock ordering, seeking credit approvals, etc.) and simply require the 'seller' to set up the appropriate service. Businesses are already using them in Japan and they have been trialled in Europe.

Combined with the ease and speed of access by telephone, offering customers a toll-free number can have a substantial impact on sales. One UK company, offering a nationwide round-the-clock emergency windscreen replacement service, experienced an increase of more than 30 per cent in enquiries and sales after it introduced a toll-free number.

11.6 International opportunities

No matter where a company is located, the telephone provides a direct two-way channel to its markets, and this is particularly relevant for companies operating internationally.

Case study 11.5

Anyone in Europe, Africa or the Middle East wanting to book a room at one of Holiday Inn's 1900-plus hotels world wide can call the company's pan-European reservations centre in Amsterdam. The company chose this location because it offered a higher proportion of multi-lingual speakers than elsewhere in Europe. Calls can be answered in any one of 12 languages.

Advertisements in travel magazines, newspapers and directories in Israel and 17 European countries offer travellers international toll-free numbers to call the centre direct. Calls from other countries can be made to the centre on a standard international number or to any Holiday Inn hotel.

The centre's 65 reservations agents handle approximately 70 000 calls each month from Israel and all over Europe. They can check availability and confirm bookings of 360 000 rooms world wide, instantly, through the company's Holidex reservations system run on a mainframe computer in Atlanta, USA.

An Aspect CallCenter ACD identifies the country of origin of each call, from the number dialled, and routes it to an agent with the appropriate language skills. Callers may also be given a choice of language. A call from Switzerland, for example, might typically require a German-, French- or Italian-speaking agent. In these situations, a voice menu from the ACD allows the caller to choose the preferred language before the call is routed to an agent. Calls from any country can be dealt with quickly and without customers having to struggle to make themselves understood. Average queuing time is only 10 seconds.

Another hotel chain has its European reservations centre in London. By centralizing operations it has been able to provide an efficient service to customers at a fraction of the cost of maintaining local booking facilities. Reservations costs were reduced by 50 per cent and, as a bonus, bookings increased by nearly 10 per cent.

The telephone is equally useful for selling goods in overseas markets. Outbound and inbound calling can be used to service intermediaries or to sell direct to end users. It offers a low-risk, minimal-cost method of entering new markets, either instead of or prior to establishing other sales channels. There is also the option of using local telemarketing expertise to service customers' needs, as in the case of Elégance.

Case study 11.6

When Elégance, a leading Germany-based fashion house, decided to launch into the UK catalogue shopping market in 1992, offering high-quality, high-value womenswear by mail order, it chose a telemarketing agency, Brann Contact 24, as its UK operations centre.

The company was starting with no market presence in the UK and Brann was selected to assist with the strategy and implementation of the launch. It was to handle all UK activity for Elégance, from media buying strategy through catalogue requests and fulfilment to order taking and processing. The core objectives in the first phase of activity were to create awareness of the Elégance brand and image among the target consumers with a major press advertising campaign, and to create a customer database to whom future seasons' collections could be targeted.

Brann handled all inbound response, including catalogue requests (fulfilled by Brann), product orders (from the catalogue and off-the-page advertisements, fulfilled by Elégance from Germany) and order queries. There was also a significant customer service element, dealing with product enquiries and returns, which was handled by a dedicated team at Brann.

Telephone was integral to the project because 'ease of access' was a key selling point. Lines were open 24 hours a day, 7 days a week. Potential customers responded to advertising, in national press and women's quality monthlies, which offered both telephone and coupon response mechanisms. Each respondent was logged on a database to enable them to be identified immediately in any future contact.

Clients ordering products from the catalogue were offered three ways of ordering: telephone, mail or fax. Again, the telephone was stressed as a simple means of responding and a quick way to obtain the desired goods. All telephone orders were captured on-line onto the database and order-processing system. This enabled the operator to view the customer's details and update them if necessary. Customers were advised, during the call, of the availability of the items they wished to order and, if the order was confirmed, the customer's credit card details were taken.

The telephone was used extensively in servicing individuals' needs. If a customer called asking the whereabouts of an order, for example, the Brann operator was able to query the system and immediately advise the customer of the despatch status. Where an enquiry could not be answered immediately, the customer would be telephoned the same day.

Personal contact was considered to be a key factor in both managing customer expectations and building a long-term relationship. This is why Elégance chose a telemarketing agency as its centre of operations. Brann Contact 24 offered personal answering, in the name of Elégance, together with computerized data capture, processing and analysis. Its dedicated customer service team was fully trained on both Elégance product information and telephone techniques to ensure a seamless operation.

Sophisticated monitoring and evaluation were especially important to Elégance because this was a major new venture. Information captured at the time of a call, including media source, coupled with the development of customer order histories, enabled Brann to conduct very sophisticated campaign analyses. It was possible to measure comparative conversion rates across the range of media used, to monitor and review customer behaviour, and to report regularly on campaign performance, received order values and cost per order by media. Brann also conducted outbound telephone research to evaluate customer perceptions of the products and the service provided.

Brann served as the sole UK market representative for Elégance for three months, before the company acquired a UK managing director and opened a retail outlet in London. Buying international couture from a catalogue was a new concept in UK home shopping and the telephone, used strategically, proved to be a powerful marketing tool in opening up the market. As anticipated, telephone orders far exceeded mail orders, validating the strategic decision to emphasize the telephone as a communications channel.

11.7 A numbers game

Despite modern telephone selling being very customer-oriented, it remains a numbers game. The more people the company speaks with, the more sales are likely to be made. As telemarketing with operators is labour intensive and good sales communicators are not inexpensive, it is important to optimize their productivity. On outbound calling, traditionally as little as half of a telemarketer's time has been spent productively talking to contacts. A large amount of their time is spent setting up calls (identifying who to call, dialling and waiting for an answer), recording information during the call, and 'wrapping up' (completing necessary administration work) after the call. Telemarketing software helps, for example, by delivering the next contact record to the screen automatically, offering an autodial facility, and allowing single keystroke entry of commonly captured responses. However, even this does not maximize the amount of selling time. Currently, the most effective option is predictive dialling.

Case study 11.7

One of the UK's leading mail order companies makes between six and eight million outbound calls a year for itself and other group companies, a significant proportion of which have a sales objective. To handle this volume of calls, the company uses three Davox predictive dialling systems supplied by Datapoint UK.

The diallers are used for three main applications – cash collection, customer recruitment and sales promotion – although work for other parts of the group includes market research and selling financial services products such as motor and household insurance.

Recruitment calls are made to new customers who have requested and been sent a catalogue but have not yet placed an order. The timing between receipt of a catalogue and the recruitment call varies according to marketing priorities. Once decided, prospects for calling are selected automatically from the company's powerful marketing database and the list is downloaded to a Davox dialler.

The sales approach varies, but may include the offer of a further discount or higher value free gift (with the first order) than was offered initially. The agent discusses the catalogue and the product areas that might interest the prospect, logging responses for future reference.

Obtaining an order is usually a two-call process. The agent arranges a time to call again when the prospect has viewed the catalogue and made a decision. Most of the calls made by the company, other than cash collections, involve calling to make an offer then calling again to collect the business. The database automatically produces call-back lists and numbers are dialled automatically at the times arranged with prospects.

A wide range of sales promotion calls are also made, prompted by the marketing database and as a follow-up to mailings by the marketing department. The highly sophisticated database enables a wide range of data-driven activities, such as targeting customers at different points in their cycle or those likely to be sensitive to specific promotions.

The supervisor's workstation is used to drive and manage the dialling and provides statistics on line and operator activity. Most diallers provide statistics of the type available from advanced ACDs, plus other information such as busy and unobtainable numbers, no answers, and even success in getting through on particular dialling codes. The mail order company, however, uses a Smart Management Centre (SMC) supplied by Datapoint.

The SMC provides real-time graphic monitoring and control of call activity through the dialler. The objective is to make information more readily accessible and to provide more flexible, dynamic control over dialling across multiple applications. In addition to the usual statistics, which can be displayed in various graphic forms, the system provides real-time monitoring of the success of individual campaigns or applications. On a sales promotion campaign, for example, the supervisor can look at the number of orders individual operators have taken and the number of call-backs they have booked. With the graphic presentation the supervisor can view progress at a glance and even make printouts to show operators.

An important feature of the SMC is the ability to flow different lists, dynamically, across all the workstations, without operators having to sign on and off different lists. The mail order company's system has been tailored so that workstation screens are colour-coded for different applications, alerting operators to a list change. The supervisor can also broadcast messages instantly, from the SMC, to all or selected workstation screens.

An alert facility on the SMC enables the supervisor to specify conditions, for each calling list, which will trigger an alert at the control workstation. The SMC then offers an option – either the supervisor can take action, or the system can be set to respond automatically to an alert by invoking a control script which reconfigures the dialling operation in a predetermined way. If an agent's performance falls below a predetermined level, for example, the alert function can invoke a control script which suspends the calling list on which the agent was working and reassigns that agent to a new list for the next call. The drop in performance could indicate that the agent requires a change of pace, or perhaps does not have adequate skill for the application and list. Whatever the cause, automatic reconfiguration minimizes the loss of operator talk time.

Compared with other systems trialled by the mail order company, the SMC gives an additional 20 per cent productivity gain, largely due to the ability to flow different lists. In a fast-moving sales environment like mail order, where multiple applications are running simultaneously, this dynamic control is important. Overall, the company has seen operator talk time increase from 25 minutes to 45 minutes per hour using the Davox diallers and SMC.

A large proportion of the company's outbound calling is closely linked to manipulating customer data on its marketing database, so calling lists are usually generated automatically from the database. However, the SMC's list filtering facility is used occasionally for further sorting.

Case study 11.8

Warrantech Corporation, in the USA, is one of the world's largest third-party administrators of extended service contracts. Originally, it gained warranty business when retailers sold service contracts at the point-of-sale. In 1990, the company established Warrantech Direct to expand its already successful business by soliciting maintenance contracts and renewals directly from consumers. This operation initially used a paper-based system with manual dialling.

Warrantech realized it required something that would help it to move quickly and manage lead information more comprehensively. Service contract extensions, for example, have to be sold while there is still time remaining on the original contract. The company chose a 20-station EIS Call Processing System, which combines sophisticated computerized call management, including scripting, with predictive dialling.

After installation, what used to take three manually dialling operators an hour to complete could be accomplished in the same amount of time by one operator. But speed was not the most important benefit for Warrantech Direct. The major advantage was the ability to increase capacity without increasing the labour force. The company could maintain higher levels of quality assurance because it no longer needed to train or manage a lot of new staff. It also stabilized operating costs because Warrantech was able to increase sales performance while holding down labour costs.

One sector that is likely to make increasing use of predictive dialling is insurance, to prompt renewal of policies. Renewal programmes commonly involve a series of communications, traditionally by mail, starting before the expiry date of the current policy and extending beyond expiry if it has not been renewed. A telephone call in this cycle would have more impact than mail alone and it would also enable the insurer to learn why certain people are not renewing their policies. Predictive dialling can also reduce the costs of occasional tactical campaigns, such as aiming to reactivate lapsed or inactive customers.

11.8 Customer focus

When orders, or any other significant commitments, are taken from customers by telephone, it is vital that instructions are confirmed by the operator so that customers are fully aware of the details, terms and conditions of the transaction. This is of such importance that operators' adherence to this rule is sometimes checked periodically, either by monitoring calls or having someone make verification calls to a sample of customers. Any verification calls should be carried out as a form of customer service. Some national codes of practice for telemarketing recommend a cooling-off period for sales calls, allowing customers time to change or cancel their instructions. One UK office supplies company, which delivers within 24 hours, offers all customers the option to return any unwanted goods, at the company's expense, simply by calling a toll-free number given on the delivery advice note. In Europe, good practice in telephone selling will be brought under legislative control with the European Commission's Directive on distance selling. However, this could also limit some applications, for example, by prohibiting cash-with-order advertisements.

Capturing orders is only a part of the selling process; they must be fulfilled efficiently. Coordination between telephone selling, production and/or distribution is therefore essential. Information management technology provides many options to ensure that a customer's instructions, once noted, are carried out efficiently. This is particularly important for companies which capture customers' orders centrally but fulfil them from remote sites. Mail order companies, for example, may have several warehouses and many distribution points to speed the delivery of goods.

Orders can be transmitted instantaneously, over public or private telephone lines, to the relevant warehouse, where a picking list, delivery note and billing advice are printed automatically. Tracking distribution of orders, so that customer enquiries about delivery can be answered quickly, is also a part of the process. Again technology can provide solutions (see page 185).

The telephone is not the ideal channel for all situations, even though it often has a role at some stage in the sales cycle. Complex technical information, for example, is best conveyed in print or face-to-face by a representative. Wherever it is used, however, it requires highly trained and well-motivated operators to make it successful. Telephone selling is a highly skilled activity which, above all, relies upon excellent communication skills. At the same time as offering effective solutions to prospects' needs and maximizing the selling opportunity, the operator has to establish or build upon relationships with callers to encourage their continued business. It is a challenging and rewarding job but it requires sustained high levels of effort. Some form of motivational package is commonly used to encourage continuous effort.

One of the questions arising frequently in telephone selling operations is whether the company should use performance-related commission or bonuses, or other incentives, to act as a motivator. Rewarding operators per sale, or for sales over a specified target, can improve results although it generally requires a particular type of selling environment (see page 142, for example) that does not encourage the use of high-pressure tactics. High-pressure selling is generally unproductive, often leading to cancelled orders and/or the loss of customers. Whether using commission, bonuses or incentives, it is important that all operators, or teams, have an equal opportunity to earn them (e.g. having contact lists or geographical areas of equal sales potential). Rewards beyond basic salary are best awarded on the basis of the quality of sales rather than just their value. For example, an operator who achieves a high level of cross-sales or up-sales, and is thus gaining good value from every customer, should be rewarded more than someone who is making twice as many sales but is 'using up' twice as many contacts.

The telephone is being adopted as a direct sales channel by an increasing number of businesses, either to complement other channels – as in some account servicing applications – or to replace them. But, however it is used, it cannot operate in isolation. The effectiveness of telephone salespeople depends partly upon factors beyond their control, such as the quality of leads available and the levels of service provided at all other stages of the sales cycle. These are equally as important to the long-term success of a telephone selling operation as the salespeople themselves.

12
Sales promotion

Sales promotion aims to bring end users into contact with a company's products or services, either directly or indirectly. It is the most diverse marketing discipline, employing techniques ranging from advertising and public relations, through exhibitions, demonstrations and merchandising, to sampling, price promotions and competitions. All are designed to promote sales, immediately or in the longer term, by reinforcing customers' buying habits and changing those of competitors' customers.

The focus in sales promotion, in common with other marketing disciplines, is predominantly on establishing a direct relationship. The telephone is ideally suited to this task and is an increasingly common element in promotional campaigns. As a response mechanism it allows prospects to react spontaneously to an offer and enables the promoter to capture their interest immediately. In outbound applications the telephone offers rapid access and precise targeting. Inbound and outbound calls both offer the opportunity to reinforce brand values, to capture data for subsequent marketing activities and to initiate a relationship.

Most of the telephone activities described throughout this book employ promotional tactics, but among the more traditional sales promotional activities the telephone is used most widely in the UK for competitions, sampling and editorial promotions.

12.1 Sampling

One international FMCG manufacturer ran a major sampling promotion in the UK in 1992 as part of an ongoing programme to grow a relatively new market.

Case study 12.1

The FMCG company's aim was to encourage trial of a fledgling product launched under the company's market-leading personal hygiene brand. The promotion was supported by a £250 000 spend on advertising in general interest and women's magazines, as well as on packs of the market-leading product.

Consumers were invited to call a toll-free number to obtain a free introductory pack and money-off voucher. Because of the scale of the promotion, and the potentially large response, an automated response-handling facility was chosen to capture consumers' details. Callers were asked to give their name, address, postcode and where they heard of the offer, which was recorded digitally for subsequent transcription.

Advertising ran between July and November 1992, with the on-pack offer still in circulation a little beyond that date. A total of around 370 000 calls were received, of which approximately 295 000 (80 per cent) were completed. The average call duration was about 80 seconds.

The fulfilment pack contained the product sample and a personalized letter with a tear-off coupon for 15p off the product purchase price, valid until 31 March 1993. The coupon was barcoded (for easy database entry) and bore the name and postcode of the recipient.

The data gathered from consumers was put onto a database for fulfilment and subsequently analysed to identify multiple applications across media and within media. It also provided the first good opportunity for the manufacturer to conduct geodemographic profiling, which revealed some polarization in age groupings and showed users to be more 'upmarket' than expected.

Redemption of the money-off coupons was tracked and showed that over 30 per cent had been redeemed by the expiry date. The database then provided the basis for ongoing direct promotions. Consumers who had not redeemed their coupon, for example, were mailed a personalized offer – buy one and get the next pack free by returning the pack barcode, the till receipt and the personalized application form. Further sampling offers and feedback from the direct promotions are being used to expand and enrich the database, providing ever-more detailed knowledge of the market for ongoing development of the promotional programme.

Automated call handling, rather than live operators, is a popular choice for major consumer promotions because the cost savings, usually around 50–60 per cent in the UK, can be substantial on large call volumes. However, there are other considerations, such as consumer perceptions of automated systems and their willingness to use them (see page 164). Low exposure of the general public to these systems can result in a significant proportion of potential customers abandoning their call. The impact on brand image must also be considered.

Case study 12.2

Disposable nappy manufacturer, Peaudouce, conducted its first major sampling promotion in 1990. The primary objective was to build a database of customers and prospects for research. Advertising in consumer magazines and on radio invited parents to call a premium rate number, giving details of their baby and the nappy brand they use, to obtain a free sample pack. About 100 000 calls were received over a 10-month period, all of which were handled by an automated service.

Peaudouce then ran another promotion in April/ May 1992. The main objective this time was to encourage trial of its new nappy range. Advertising in a mix of consumer and women's magazines and national press offered readers a toll-free number and freepost coupon to apply for their free sample plus a 75p money-off coupon. The campaign generated over 250 000 responses during its seven-week run, with a further 50 000 responses accepted after the closing date. Coupon and telephone responses were split 60/40.

Free response mechanisms were offered this time because Peaudouce felt it was more in line with brand positioning. In addition, all calls were answered by operators – to reflect a caring brand and the intimacy associated with parenthood. A secondary consideration was to ensure that data was captured accurately. Some calls had been lost in the earlier promotion, due to poor data capture by the automated system, and even more information was being gathered this time. Peaudouce also felt that calls would have been unreasonably long if answering was automated; the average call duration with operators was around 60 seconds.

The data gathered in these two promotions has been merged and is being used for campaign planning and direct promotions (tracking the growth of the baby and the changing size and type of nappy required). Peaudouce subsequently launched another promotion, in December 1992, to expand the database. A direct response TV commercial, with a toll-free number, offered a sample pack plus a £1-off coupon.

Automated call handling does have advantages other than lower cost and high volume capacity, however. Tambrands, for example, use it for sampling promotions of Tampax, the UK's leading sanitary brand. The promotions, often using direct response radio advertising, provide on-line educational information as well as the opportunity to obtain a sample. The target audience is typically young girls beginning their menstruation periods, who generally are unwilling to discuss this topic with a live operator.

Capturing competition entries is a very popular application for automated call handling in the UK. The majority of competitions use premium rate numbers, capable of generating large revenues in major promotions to help offset the promoters' costs. The cost is not unreasonable for the entrant, even with relatively low value prizes, provided the duration of the call is short. It can compare well with the cost of a first-class stamp and envelope, not to mention the time it takes to complete and post a coupon.

Offering a telephone response mechanism for off-the-page and on-pack promotions has the advantage that, unlike a coupon, there is no need to cut the page (before the reverse has been read) or the pack (before the product is used). For the promoter, call handling, especially if automated, is certainly more convenient, and can be less expensive (or a money-spinner on premium rate), than handling sacks full of mail.

12.2 Media promotions

One of the biggest areas of growth in telephone promotions in the UK since the late 1980s has been their use by the media to enhance editorial content. It began as part of the general boom in audiotex (recorded information) services. Readers, listeners and programme watchers could dial to access further information on horoscopes, weather forecasts, traffic conditions and any other information they would pay to obtain on a premium rate line. Although this provided an extension to the editorial, its value as a promotional device was probably marginal.

Radio programmes had already used the telephone with incredible success. Inviting listeners to telephone and speak live on air not only provides them with the opportunity to comment, but can also provide highly entertaining programming. Live 'phone-in' competitions became increasingly popular with the growth in commercial radio.

An increasing number of television programmes gradually adopted the telephone as a means of enabling viewer participation, with applications falling into three main areas: televoting, competition entry and information lines. Live 'phone-ins' have also become a regular element in some magazine-style TV programmes. However, inviting live calls should be treated with caution, as time only permits a small number of people to talk on air and those that call but cannot take part are potentially dissatisfied viewers. The majority of TV promotions use automated call handling to cope with the potential surge of calls, and premium rate. Using premium rate instead of a standard Public Switched Telephone Network (PSTN) number actually benefits callers overall, because everyone pays the same rate irrespective of their location.

Televoting – using the telephone to register votes – is growing on TV and radio and in newspapers and magazines. Capitalizing on consumers' desire to comment on issues about which they feel strongly, the results provide valuable editorial copy on 'what you, the public, think about this important issue'. Dedicated numbers are usually used to register different responses, either YES/NO or agreement with one of several statements. The immediacy of the telephone is crucial in live situations. On TV and radio, much can be made of the ongoing polling results that are available in real-time with automated call handling.

Live televised talent contests can generate 100 000 or more votes within minutes, although the time constraints on voting within the programme's duration can produce frustrated viewers who were unable to get through to register their vote. The largest response to a premium rate promotion in the UK in 1992 was when BBC Television's Health Show offered viewers a free Government health pack. Over 1.6 million calls were received.

Although premium rate lines can generate considerable revenues, particularly with mass media, the promotional objective has become increasingly important. Involving viewers, listeners and readers helps to build and retain their interest and encourage loyalty to a programme or press title.

Case study 12.3

Involving viewers is the philosophy behind the competitions used in the UK's Channel 4 Television weekend Italian football programmes, produced by Chrysalis TV Productions.

Chrysalis produces an hour-long Saturday morning magazine-style show, presented by Paul Gascoigne, and a live game, plus other match highlights, on Sunday which attracts around three million viewers. Two weekly competitions are held in conjunction with the programmes. The first, run on the Saturday morning show, features a question relating to the next day's match, while the Sunday show features 'Gazza's Golden Goals', where viewers are asked to select their 1–2–3 from the previous week's games.

The choice of questions encourages viewers to watch both programmes on succesive weeks. The use of Paul Gascoigne's voice on the competition lines, designed and run by service provider Greenland Interactive (formerly Legion), creates continuity between the programmes and the competitions. The scripting also incorporates Channel 4 and Italian football branding. To encourage participation, the competition line numbers are displayed constantly on screen while the competitions are being detailed, and both offer attractive prizes such as trips to Italy, football merchandise and kits.

Case study 12.4

Associated Newspapers is another UK convert to the editorial value of telephone-based promotions, for which it uses various service providers, including Greenland Interactive. Following the lead of a number of USA newspaper groups, Associated Newspapers now offers a range of premium rate services, from competition and information lines to horoscopes and dating services.

It was the first national UK newspaper group to introduce the idea of selling property off the page using automated telephone services, with its Talking Ads (*Daily Mail*) and Talk Volumes (*Evening Standard*) services. The theatre booking service, Theatrecall (*Evening Standard*), offered in conjunction with leading booking group Ticketmaster, was also innovative. As London's leading newspaper, the *Evening Standard* regularly contributes a large amount of space to entertainment reviews and listings. Theatrecall enables readers to dial a premium rate number, listen to details of shows and events and then, if they wish, divert to an operator at the Ticketmaster agency to make bookings.

The newspaper group measures the success of these services not only in terms of the volume of calls and the revenues they generate, but also in terms of their editorial contribution. Even if revenues do not cover the cost of space used to promote them, the editorial contribution in terms of added value for readers can make it worth while.

With competitions, the company also looks at whether it increases response rates and makes administration easier. In most cases, where telephone response is offered in addition to a traditional coupon, the number of entries is almost doubled.

A recent development in newspaper publishing has been the use of the telephone to provide direct access to a computerized system to capture classified advertisement details automatically and to give readers access to a database of recent adverts which they can 'interrogate' and search for a product or service they require. No operators are required.

Consumer magazines have also adopted premium rate lines as a way of extending editorial content, by providing information on products and services featured in their pages. This has the added benefit of creating closer ties with potential advertisers.

Recorded information services have potentially wide-ranging applications in sales promotion. They can be used to provide additional product or service information when people call to leave their name and address for fulfilment, or as stand-alone services. Advertising can be supplemented by more detailed information, with the ability to change messages frequently to give details of current special offers. Our Price Music has used premium rate lines to generate traffic through its UK chain of music stores, offering television viewers a number to call to hear excerpts from newly released albums.

12.3 Supporting product usage

Helplines, carelines and information services have obvious promotional value if they enhance product usage or product satisfaction and thereby encourage purchases directly or through recommendation. Carelines, offering consumers advice on product usage, can improve perceived product performance and directly stimulate sales of consumables by suggesting new uses.

Computer applications software and video games are examples where the level of satisfaction can be largely dependent upon the customer's skill in using the product. On the basis that a happy customer is likely to remain a customer, Nintendo of America aims to ensure that video game enthusiasts get as much as possible out of their products.

Case study 12.5

In 1992, Nintendo had 80 per cent of the multi-billion dollar USA video games market and provided players with their own magazine and something special in the way of telephone support.

Nintendo Power, an $18 subscription magazine with a circulation of one million, provides players with monthly news on products and tips on game play. If that doesn't satisfy their cravings, they can call a Game Play Counsellor.

For general advice, such as help with questions about installing games and subscriptions to the magazine, customers can call Nintendo's Consumer Service on a toll-free number. Calls come in to an Aspect CallCenter ACD which voices a menu of services available for the caller to select. Consumer service agents handle about 300 000 to 350 000 enquiries each month, but the Game Play section is even busier.

There can come a point in playing a video game when the challenge turns to frustration. The counsellors are there to ensure that this is not terminal as far as the customers' business is concerned.

Counselling was introduced as a response to customer demand. When Nintendo's call centre opened in 1985, game play counsellors did not exist, but the number of callers with questions about playing the games increased to a point where it was practical to introduce full-time counsellors. Their sole job is to teach others how to play the games. Nintendo employs about 200 counsellors who answer an average of 300 000 to 400 000 calls every month.

Originally this service was provided on the toll-free number, but the call centre was overwhelmed. Many regular callers began friendships with counsellors and were often calling for a chat. Switching to a standard number helped to reinforce the message that this was a serious helpline rather than a chatline.

Although the counsellors are experts, they have access to a vast database of information on every Nintendo game and the games sold by its 60 licensees. If they do not have the answer, they can implement a key word search of the database to find possible solutions. This search may also point to other situations the caller has not yet encountered, but the counsellors aim to provide only clues to ensure that the challenge and excitement of game play is not ruined.

Other Nintendo subsidiaries, like Nintendo of Europe based in Germany, offer similar services, although they are not available in Japan, the company's home territory.

12.4   An innovative sales approach

The above idea has also been extended to offering proactive telephone support before the product is purchased.

Case study 12.6

In an innovative use of the telephone, software giant Microsoft tested a new method of sales promotion for the 1991 UK launch of the word-processing package Microsoft Word 2.0 for Windows. The idea was to offer a free trial and provide proactive telephone support throughout the trial period.

A launch event was organized at Wembley Conference Centre, London, on 6 November 1991. Attendees were sourced through trade magazine advertising and among registered Microsoft product users. The event was designed to inform delegates about the key features of Word 2.0 for Windows and generate enthusiasm to try it. Each of the 5120 delegates was given the product on a 60-day free trial and briefed on the type of telephone support available. The program was being offered at a special launch price of £99.

Telemarketing agency The Decisions Group had been contracted to provide an innovative mix of telephone support and promotion. It selected telephone staff specially for the campaign, a key selection criterion being computer literacy. Selected operators then underwent two days' intensive product training, conducted by Microsoft's direct marketing manager and the Word for Windows product manager. After additional telemarketing training by Decisions, there was a half-day briefing on the campaign.

Decisions set up a dedicated helpline for users with queries, and would also make outbound calls. As most of the people involved in the trial were business users, these calls were made during office hours.

Decisions phoned users initially about 10 days after the launch and offered to help them, if necessary, through the installation of Word 2.0 for Windows and guide them through a demonstration and explanation of the program's major features and benefits.

Not all users wanted a full demonstration. Some had already installed and were using the program, while others had not yet installed it or wanted a demonstration only of features of particular interest to them. Those who wanted more time to evaluate the program were called a second time about 40 days into the trial period. (Christmas fell in between). All were given the opportunity to be called again at a convenient time and most (99 per cent) were pleased to receive a call.

Calls which involved a demonstration lasted about 20–25 minutes because many users were enthusiastic about the product and wanted to discuss it. As a result, the average call rate was initially only 1.7 per hour against a target of four per hour. Eventually, as fewer demonstrations were required, the call rate rose and finally averaged 4.2 per hour.

Throughout the trial period, users also had access to a technical helpline provided by Microsoft. However, only about 20 calls were received as most difficulties that might have arisen had been pre-empted by the demonstration calls.

The campaign was even more successful than expected (Table 12.1), with 74 per cent of the 5120 launch delegates purchasing Microsoft Word 2.0 for Windows, against an expected conversion of 45 per cent. Of those purchasing, 88 per cent switched from using competitors' products. Equally as gratifying was the high proportion (60 per cent) of purchases by users of the earlier release of Word for Windows. An additional benefit of the campaign strategy was a reduction in the amount of technical support required post-sales.

The success of the campaign, which won The Decisions Group a Direct Marketing Association (UK) Gold Award in 1992, has encouraged Microsoft to use this as a method of encouraging adoption, with only minor changes to accommodate what was learnt during the campaign.

Table 12.1 Results of computer software trialling promotion with proactive telephone support. (Courtesy of Microsoft)

Launch delegates	Number trialling	Number purchasing	Conversion rate (%)
Users of competitors' products (49.2%)	2519	2217	88
Users of earlier Word for Windows release	2601	1572	60
Total	5120	3789	74

Growing emphasis on establishing a direct relationship with customers and prospects means that the telephone will play an increasingly important role in many forms of sales promotion. However, there is an acute danger, particularly in promotions generating large volume responses, that not enough attention is paid to fulfilling the promises that have been made, or to meeting callers' expectations. There is widespread evidence among past UK promotions that the fulfilment element (both telephone service and subsequent follow-up) is not given the consideration or resources it requires. In effect, a proportion of people responding to such promotions are disappointed. The execution of a promotion should meet the same stringent service standards set for the rest of the organization.

13
Traffic generation

Traffic generation aims to bring people into contact with the company or its products or services by encouraging them to visit either a sales outlet or an event. In some instances, such as paid-for seminars, the visit constitutes the sale, while in others, such as retail traffic generation, it aims to encourage sales.

Generating retail or event traffic involves: (a) reaching the right sort of prospects and generating interest; (b) checking that they need or want what is on offer; and (c) encouraging firm commitment to the visit. The telephone can play a role at each stage – as a response mechanism for advertising and direct mail, for screening and qualifying prospects, for 'selling' the idea of a visit, and for gaining commitment.

13.1 Event traffic

The costs of staging events such as exhibitions, roadshows, open days, product launches and demonstrations have escalated dramatically in the past decade. However, they remain a cost-effective medium provided that the organizer can entice the optimum number of highly interested people to attend. The economics are clear from the example of paid-for seminars. If the organizer does not target the right people and get a sufficient number of them to give their commitment to attend (a cheque), then the event will lose money. Organizers of any event are in the same situation, even though the return may be less tangible.

Assuming the viability of the event has been researched, perhaps by telephone, the profile of the target audience will be known and an appropriate contact strategy can be formulated. Initial interest may be generated by advertising (press, TV, radio, direct mail) and PR, using coupon and/or telephone response mechanisms, or directly by telephone. The two most commonly used contact strategies for business-to-business events are illustrated in Figure 13.1.

The call–mail–call strategy is typically used where the accuracy of contact details (for mailing) is uncertain, or where the organizer wants to identify all relevant decision makers within a company, or where contacts need to be

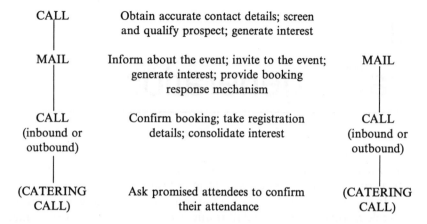

Figure 13.1 Two contact strategies commonly used for event traffic generation

screened to determine if they qualify to attend the event. Screening is vital if little is known about the prospect. The organizer must ensure that the best value prospects attend – especially to avoid 'freeloaders' who can be a problem with free events. The initial contact, whether by telephone or mail, should be made at least three weeks before the event. More time may be required if, for example, the prospects' work commitments mean they have to plan their diaries far in advance, or if international travel is required. Some other operational aspects are summarized in Table 13.1.

Both contact strategies may end with a catering call, which is made just a few days before the event. The objective is to have people confirm their

Table 13.1 Some operational aspects of event traffic generation by telephone

The timing of successive contacts is important; initial contact should be at least three weeks before the event.

Requests to attend should be confirmed by mail within 24 hours.

When more than one call is being made to prospects, it is preferable to have them made by the same person.

If event capacity is limited, close monitoring of conversion rates is required to avoid over-booking.

The more stringent the qualification criteria, or the higher the cost (event fee, travel, accommodation, etc.) generally the lower the conversion and the more leads required.

The number of leads required to achieve capacity is best calculated by working backwards from maximum capacity.

attendance. It serves as a final check on the prospect's commitment, under the guise of having to 'cater' for the correct number at the event. The theory is that people are more likely to be honest than cause unnecessary wastage. If appropriate, either the catering call or the previous telephone contact can be used to arrange appointments for prospects with company personnel during or immediately after the event. With the call–mail–call strategy, the number confirming at the catering call will normally be approximately 90 per cent accurate.

The call–mail–call combination is generally the more successful of the two strategies in generating traffic because the mailing is more accurately targeted. However, the mail–call strategy can be very successful provided that accurate prospect data is available.

Prior knowledge of delegates, obtainable from telephone screening or when taking bookings, can be invaluable for events where company representatives will have the opportunity to talk on an individual basis with delegates. Representatives can be briefed on delegates' businesses and their particular needs to show the company's interest in meeting those needs.

The primary objective of the majority of free events is to prime prospects for a sale. Existing customers form an often neglected audience who can help to achieve that aim. A handful of selected customers mingling with prospects can do more for the company's credibility than any salesperson. It is also a way of showing the customers that they are still valued.

Integral promotion

Events, and the process of encouraging attendances, should not be viewed in isolation. In many cases the contact strategy can be exploited to further the sales objective even among those who do not wish to attend the event.

Case study 13.1

As part of the launch strategy for its EDIpost service (see page 68), Royal Mail organized two seminars for prospects during the EDI '92 exhibition being staged in October 1992. The exhibition and seminars were being used as an opportunity for initial face-to-face contact with prospects and the objective was to build on the interest already generated by earlier communications.

A conventional mail–telephone–telephone strategy (Figure 13.2) was being used to generate attendances at the seminars. An invitation and information pack would be sent to prospects, a proportion of non-responders would be followed up by telephone and, finally, a catering call would be made to companies intending to send delegates. However, as this was an integral part of the launch strategy, all contact opportunities would also be fully exploited to promote the new service and build interest beyond EDI '92.

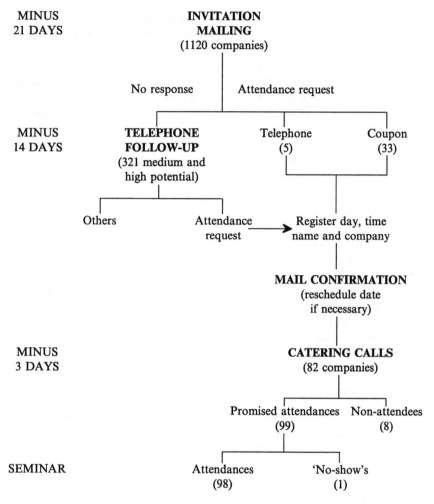

Figure 13.2 Contact strategy for generating attendance at seminars during the launch of Royal Mail's EDIpost service. (Courtesy of Ogilvy & Mather Teleservices)

The launch campaign, planned by telemarketing consultancy Ogilvy & Mather Teleservices, had begun with a market evaluation exercise in August, thus making accurate data available for targeting.

A total of 1120 prospects were mailed a seminar invitation together with an information pack. Coupon and telephone response mechanisms were offered for prospects to book a place at a seminar, and were also promoted as a means to obtain further information or to raise queries. A total of 92 companies responded (8.2 per cent conversion), including 38 companies wanting to send delegates to a seminar (Table 13.2). The majority (88 per cent) of responses were by coupon.

Table 13.2 Results of mail–telephone–telephone combination in encouraging seminar attendance during the launch of Royal Mail's EDIpost service. (Courtesy of Ogilvy & Mather Teleservices)

	Companies	Attendees	Conversion rate
Invitations mailed	1120		
Requesting attendance	38	55	3.4%
Other requests	54		4.8%
Calls to non-responders	321		
Requesting attendance	54	72	16.8%
Other requests	122		38.0%
Catering calls	82	107	
Attendees confirming		99	92.5%
Other requests	8		9.8%
Actual attendances		98	99.0%

All companies requesting places at the seminars were sent postal confirmation within 24 hours, and given the option to reschedule the date they attended if necessary. Details of those wanting to attend were registered for the appropriate seminar.

The agency providing telemarketing services made follow-up calls to a proportion of non-responders about one week after the mailing. Contacts were selected using data from the earlier evaluation exercise. A total of 321 high and medium potential prospects, with EDI implemented for more than 12 months, were contacted. The rationale for a follow-up call was that it overcomes prospects' inertia to respond, it provides an opportunity to answer questions and overcome objections, and it represents (and is perceived as) good customer service.

The calls were used not only to generate seminar attendances but also to build and convert interest in the EDIpost service. As a result, in addition to a further 54 companies requesting a seminar place (nearly 17 per cent conversion), 34 per cent of prospects asked to be mailed further information, over 20 per cent were given additional information during the call, and three companies requested an appointment.

Around three days before the seminars, the telemarketing agency made catering calls to 82 companies to confirm attendance. At this stage, only 8 out of 107 delegates withdrew (i.e. 7.5 per cent). Subsequently, of the 99 attendances confirmed during these calls, only one failed to show at the seminars. The exceptionally high accuracy of the catering calls in predicting attendances (almost 99 per cent compared with a more usual figure around 90 per cent) is probably the result of earlier elements of the contact strategy which, at each stage, had sought to qualify, build and convert prospect interest.

The strategy used to encourage seminar attendance had, at the same time, generated four sales appointments, answered 15 queries and provided additional information on EDIpost to 224 prospects (20 per cent of the target audience).

If encouraging event attendance is not part of a wider contact strategy then attendees and 'no show's should be followed up, within seven days, either by mail or telephone depending on their value and the stage in the sales cycle. Among people who do not show it is important to determine the reasons and, if they really did want to attend, to make alternative arrangements to fill the gap.

The inclusion of outbound calling in a traffic generation contact strategy serves to obtain early commitment to attend, rather than leaving it to chance that an event will be well attended or fully booked. It is not a last-minute contingency measure.

Organizers of large-scale events, such as trade and consumer exhibitions, increasingly offer telephone and fax numbers to encourage visitors to pre-register. For some major international events the promotion and pre-registration campaign may begin more than six months before the event. A major benefit in selling tickets to consumer events early, apart from generating bankable income, is that people are more likely to attend once they have bought their tickets. For trade exhibitions, pre-registration provides valuable data for the organizers to show committed exhibitors and to attract new ones.

13.2 Retail traffic

A very common application of the telephone for retail traffic generation is nearest store, stockist or dealer location. Advertising a number to call to get the name and location of an appropriate outlet has several benefits. First, the advertisement does not need to carry the names and addresses of all the outlets, which is impractical for TV and radio and creatively inhibiting for press. Second, response levels can be used to test different advertising media and creative treatments. Third, and most significant, leads can be generated at the same time, simply by capturing appropriate details from callers (see Fiat, for example, on page 139).

There are many possible permutations of the basic outlet location service. When there was uncertainty in the UK about whether retailers trading on a Sunday would be prosecuted, one national retail chain, tentatively opening some stores, advertised a telephone number in the press for consumers to find out which stores would be open the following Sunday.

Location services can be automated using the caller's telephone number or postcode, captured with tone or voice recognition, to identify the nearest outlets from a database. Automation also provides an effective way to disseminate additional information, such as current special offers available in stores. If the retailer has a national, high-profile presence, then the location element of the service is not necessary. A leading UK travel company has offered a variety of services on premium rate numbers advertised via the holiday section of a TV teletext service. As well as obtaining information on weather conditions in popular overseas resorts, callers could obtain details of the latest holiday bargains available at the company's high street branches. In a similar vein, Our Price Records in the UK has advertised a number for music fans to call to hear excerpts from the album being promoted – those who wanted to buy were encouraged to 'get down to Our Price'. In business-to-business markets, especially, a fax-back system can be used for callers to obtain immediate hard copy product information and a list of local dealers.

An integrated approach

One reason for using the telephone is that information is provided immediately, striking while interest is high when people respond spontaneously to advertising. Of course, there is no guarantee that people will visit an outlet once they have the information. Capturing callers' details for follow-up is one way of encouraging them to make that visit. Another is to offer an inducement, such as a prize draw.

Case study 13.2

A Belgian company, Bijttebier, has used an innovative mix of techniques, combining traffic generation with retailer support, sales promotion and lead generation, with remarkable results.

Bijttebier is one of Belgium's biggest tableware importers and wholesalers, supplying a range of porcelain, glassware, cutlery, ornaments and other gifts to mostly independent retailers throughout Belgium. Since 1990, the company has undertaken a highly successful annual St Valentine promotion designed to increase traffic and sales at the shops it supplies. The 1991 campaign resulted in sales of US$18.9 million against costs to Bijttebier of only US$242 500 (Table 13.3).

Direct marketing agency De Visscher & Van Nevel (DVN) developed a strategy, including national direct response advertising and local outbound telemarketing, to encourage store traffic and stimulate sales only in shops supplied by Bijttebier. The target audience was people planning to marry within a year, estimated at around 60 000 couples (1991), and the objective was to encourage them to deposit their wedding gift list with one of the shops. Secondary targets were parents and grandparents, who have an influence on wedding gift purchases.

There were a number of challenges in designing the campaign. First, it would have to involve the shopkeepers and give them tangible results. Previous initiatives by other suppliers had not proved very successful, so shopkeepers were sceptical and were not prepared to make a high investment. They also view potential customers as *their* property, and would not want their supplier 'poaching' their business by following up contacts made through the campaign.

As a further problem, no suitable prospect lists were available. DVN knew, from

Table 13.3 Results of a retail traffic generation campaign developed by De Visscher & Van Nevel. (Courtesy of Bijttebier)

St Valentine–Eschenbach campaign	1991	1992
Target audience (couples, estimated)	60 000	55 000
Number of responses (couples)	21 000	18 000
Response rate	35%	33%
Wedding lists deposited	15 750	13 500
Conversion rate	75%	75%
Sales value per response (US$)	1 200	1 000
Total sales value (US$)	18 900 000	13 500 000
Campaign costs (US$)	242 500*	242 500*
Cost per response (US$)	11.55	17.96
Number of shops participating	302	250
Sales increase at participating shops	10–25%	10–25%
General market decline in sales	7%	7%
Real increase in sales	17–32%	17–32%

*8 000 000 Belgian francs

experience, that by the time the names of people about to be married appeared on lists they would have already decided upon their wedding gifts.

St Valentine's Day was chosen as the platform for the campaign, capitalizing on the positive emotion, associated with marriage, of 'being in love'. Shops were to stage a special open-door afternoon, from 2 to 6 p.m., on the Sunday before St Valentine's Day. This would be a festive occasion, where couples would have the opportunity to view products supplied by Bijttebier, receive help in choosing gifts for their wedding list and take part in prize competitions.

Bijttebier distributes various brands, many of which are supplied by other wholesalers. To make the promotion exclusive to Bijttebier, the Eschenbach range, for which it is the sole importer, was chosen to be featured.

A media campaign, in Dutch and French, was planned to promote the event, offering various incentives for people to visit a participating shop. Each shop would have a display of 10 festive set tables, which all visitors on the Sunday would be invited to judge with the opportunity to win an Eschenbach coffee service (one winner per store). Couples about to be married who deposited their name, address, telephone number and wedding date, and who took part in this contest, would be given two free champagne glasses and could enter a competition to win a Volkswagen Golf. All visitors would be offered a free drink.

In January, Bijttebier supplied shopkeepers with the table displays and various point of sale materials, in Dutch and French, including posters, competition vouchers and a special 50-page product catalogue. Shopkeepers were encouraged to buy advertising space in local newspapers, for which the company supplied sample advertisements, and were also supplied with leaflets that they could distribute locally.

Direct response television advertising, offering a toll-free number, was used in

1990 and 1991, demonstrating to shopkeepers that Bijttebier was willing to make a substantial investment. Since the budget was limited, advertising was restricted to one station, VTM, which reaches only the northern, Flemish part of Belgium. However, this is where the majority of participating shopkeepers are situated. Fifteen 30-second spots were used in 1991, concentrated in the two weekends and off-peak during the week.

In 1990, Bijttebier had used full-page direct response advertising in six women's magazines. Subsequent market research and analysis of results revealed that newspapers were the most effective medium, in terms of recall, awareness and response. For 1991, therefore, media spend was concentrated on newspapers and television.

Bijttebier had reserved space, at a special rate, for full-page advertisements to be published the day before the event in the major national newspapers. The adverts included a coupon, a list of the participating shops by region, and an invitation to call the toll-free number for further information. Couples intending to marry were invited to complete the coupon and take it to a participating shop, on the Sunday, to collect their free champagne glasses.

In succeeding years DVN has searched for ways to enhance the campaign (see Table 13.4). In 1992, for example, radio was used in preference to television. Three versions of a direct response advertisement, each of 30 seconds duration, were produced in Dutch and French. One version was broadcast, mainly at weekends, during the 10 days before the event, one version on the day before the event, and one on the morning of the event. A total of 104 spots were used, concentrated in the mornings and around 7–8 pm.

Table 13.4 Development of a retail traffic generation campaign by De Visscher & Van Nevel. (Courtesy of Bijttebier)

Campaign elements	1990	1991	1992
Media used for direct response advertising	Women's magazines		
	Television	Television	Radio
	Newspapers	Newspapers	Newspapers
Creative execution	Progressively more dynamic and aggressive		
Shopkeepers participating	262	302	250
Shopkeepers placing ads (estimated)	50%	50%	75%
Calls received on toll-free number	1816	2651	2420
Media source of calls	80% TV and radio		30% radio
	10% magazines		30% press
	8% press		40% word
	2% word of mouth		of mouth

Callers to the toll-free number were given information about the promotion, asked for their personal details and told the name and address of the participating shop(s) according to their postal code. Bijttebier had developed a special computer program that allowed operators to give details of participating shops not only in the caller's town but also in the surrounding areas. The reasons for this were primarily that Bijttebier wanted to remain neutral towards individual retailers. The company also recognized that individuals may prefer not to visit their local shop, perhaps because of a previous bad experience, or because they had previously used another shop, or because they lived on the borders of a town and a shop in another district was more convenient. Leads from these calls were sent to the appropriate shopkeepers before the event.

People visiting a participating shop on the Sunday were given the competition voucher, which asked for their personal details, where they learnt of the promotion and whether they wanted to receive a catalogue. The campaign proved extremely successful, both in encouraging visitors to the shops and gaining sales. A total of 21 000 couples visited a participating shop on the day of the event in 1991. Of these, 15 750 subsequently deposited wedding lists worth a total of US$18.9 million in sales.

Shopkeepers played a major role in achieving these results. They were responsible for follow-up, by personal contact, mailing catalogues and phoning those who had left their details, to encourage couples to deposit their wedding list. Follow-up activity continued throughout the year, depending on when a couple's wedding was scheduled, but was concentrated in February and March. An estimated 80 per cent of the participating shopkeepers used telemarketing as a means of follow-up in the 1991 campaign.

The telephone can play a diverse role in retail traffic generation, by delivering pertinent promotional messages and by providing some elements of the retail service (such as what is available and at what cost) direct to prospects over the telephone. However, it is important to remember that, for both event and retail traffic, the quality of the telephone activity reflects on the company and its products or services.

14
Dealer, distributor and retailer relations

Many businesses use intermediaries of some type – wholesalers, retailers, dealers, local branches, franchisees – to supply their goods or services. In doing so they distance themselves from direct contact with end users and all but the first level of intermediaries. The longer the distribution chain the more the supplier relinquishes control over the sales process to the intermediaries. Since the buying experience impacts on customers' perceptions of the product and the manufacturer, intermediaries have varying degrees of control over how the manufacturer is perceived in the marketplace. And this control is increasing, particularly in the retail environment. At the same time, the lack of contact with end users (and with some intermediaries) means that manufacturers are more reliant on the intermediaries to get essential feedback for marketing planning and product development.

The challenge for manufacturers and service providers is to ensure that their intermediaries deliver the required levels of service to *their* customers (whether other intermediaries or end users) and that they gather appropriate marketing intelligence. Some of the key issues in addressing this challenge are summarized in Table 14.1 and the telephone can play a varied role in managing these issues.

The quality of intermediaries, and therefore the recruitment process, is obviously crucial. When a company needs to maintain a large number of intermediaries, such as a dealer network, prospects can be screened and qualified quickly and effectively by telephone to determine whether they are likely to meet the company's requirements (see page 86, for example). Thereafter the telephone is an ideal channel for providing both systematic and *ad hoc* support.

Table 14.1 Some considerations in maintaining a customer-oriented supply chain

Casting the net widely to attract prospects will yield a better choice of quality intermediaries.

Prospects should be screened carefully to identify those who can best represent the company.

Ongoing support should be tailored to meet the varying needs of different types of intermediary and individual businesses.

Intermediaries will require product service training, perhaps ongoing, and regular promotional support.

Information relevant to serving the market's needs should be exchanged freely between supplier and intermediaries.

A routine of regular dialogue is required to service intermediaries' needs and to prompt feedback on business results and other market activities.

There should be an open direct channel of communication by which intermediaries can obtain immediate advice or support for themselves or their customers.

Performance of the supply chain, its individual elements and overall, should be monitored continuously.

14.1 Dealer support

Many companies supply through intermediaries that also act for their competitors.

Case study 14.1

One computer manufacturer addressed this problem by establishing a dialogue with its registered dealers, designed to encourage them to think of its products, rather than a competitor's, when discussing end users' needs. Most of the dealerships were small businesses whose priority was to sell rather than to market the brands they stocked. One of the devices the manufacturer used was a manual to help dealers market the company's products. In return for supplying qualified leads to the dealers, the company expected them to run local promotional campaigns. Direct dialogue was essential to encourage dealers to use this manual and to position themselves as the local centre for the manufacturer's products.

The company established a careline which was staffed by a specialist in marketing information technology products. The specialist called each dealer every four weeks to discuss any promotions they were undertaking, to provide advice and generally to keep the marketing manual at the forefront of their minds. For the dealers, the prospect of a regular telephone call was a gentle persuader to carry out some form of promotion. They could use the careline at any time to obtain advice or to discuss any difficulties that arose. It was a very personal service, where the manufacturer's marketing expert was on first name terms with the dealer principals.

The monthly calls were also used to establish the results that dealers were achieving with their leads and to identify any problems they might be experiencing with end users. The manufacturer's salesforce concentrated on supporting distributors, who supply the dealers, and originally made only *ad hoc* visits to dealers. With the regular telephone contact, the salesforce could target visits to those dealers who needed them and therefore manage their time more efficiently.

The same principal, of support through telephone dialogue, can be applied across many sectors where competitive products vye for customers' attention at the point of sale. It helps to ensure understanding of the products, to engender commitment to serving customers' needs and, crucially, to get feedback on the intermediaries' needs and help resolve any problems they experience. Without this dialogue minor issues may never be discussed, feedback may be arbitrary and the supplier can easily lose touch with both the intermediary and the marketplace.

Intermediaries in some sectors are notable for their lack of zeal in finding and converting prospects. To compensate, suppliers have developed increasingly sophisticated support programmes. Historically, car dealerships in general have had a poor reputation for generating and exploiting leads. A 1992 survey of telephone enquiry handling by dealers for the UK's Top 10 car manufacturers produced fairly damning results. Only 23 per cent of salespeople offered to send prospects car details and just 31 per cent mentioned the possibility of a test drive. Only one-third (34 per cent) asked for an address or telephone number, over two-thirds (69 per cent) did not ask prospects any questions and 20 per cent failed even to invite the prospect to the showroom.

Not surprisingly, car manufacturers invest heavily in dealer support. In the UK, all the major motor manufacturers use direct response advertising, mainly press, as part of their support programmes.

Case study 14.2

Fiat Auto UK ran a combined lead generation and traffic-building promotion in June and July 1992. A three-page advertisement appeared in *Radio Times* and *You* magazines, under the banner 'Fiat's Green Paper', publicising free catalytic converters on the new Fiat range, special price deals, free test drives and a competition to win one of 25 Fiat Unos.

The first page promoted trade-ins and other 'unbeatable deals' and invited readers to call a toll-free number for further information. On the second page they were encouraged to call the same number to obtain a free test drive by leaving their details for a local dealer to contact them. Everyone taking a test drive would receive a free house plant worth up to £25.

The last page of the advertisement carried a detachable card bearing the image of a leaf. Readers were invited to take the card to any one of the 250 Fiat showrooms before 31 August 1992 and check if the leaf matched (in shape, colour and type) the one on display. A match meant that that person had won a Fiat Uno. Instructions, and the toll-free number to locate the nearest dealer, were printed on the front of the card. On the reverse was a form requesting details of the car owner, the make and model of car currently driven, its age, and the month and year in which the owner expects to change it. Each card carried a media code and unique number.

Fiat had five operators taking calls during the day and an automated call-handling service between 6 p.m. and 9 a.m. Operators recorded details of the driver, current car and expected renewal date, and provided details of the nearest Fiat dealers. Callers to the automated service, provided by agency Greenland Interactive (formerly Legion), were asked to speak their telephone number or enter it using a DTMF phone. The system recognized the number, searched its database for the nearest three dealerships associated with that number, and voiced the details back to the caller. Callers were also invited to leave their name and address to receive a Fiat information pack.

This promotion created four opportunities to obtain lead details for dealers (and to get an information pack into the hands of prospects): callers wanting to obtain further information on special deals; those requesting a test drive; those wanting to know their nearest dealer; and completed competition cards. All lead details were entered onto a database for subsequent tracking.

The value of such campaigns is heavily dependent upon how effectively the leads and traffic generated are exploited. Lead management systems are commonly used to help plan subsequent contact strategies (implemented by the manufacturer) based on the data gathered, which is updated at each contact, and to track leads long term.

14.2   The value of regular dialogue

Gaining feedback on lead outcome from dealers, in all markets, is a potentially weak link in the lead-tracking cycle. Manufacturers in regular telephone contact with their dealers can pursue this information routinely, if necessary, in the course of normal business, such as checking on their need for replacement stock.

Case study 14.3

Canon (UK) distributes its wide range of business equipment mainly through national dealer networks. Dealers for the Office Trade Products (OTP) division are variously supported by a national field salesforce, Dealer Support Officers, and telemarketing through agency BPS Téléperformance and an in-house telesales team.

Canon's aggressive marketing policy is underpinned by delivering high-performance products at competitive prices. The company spends 12 per cent of total sales revenue on research and development. New product launches and product enhancements are featured in national brand and direct response advertising, designed to interest existing and potential dealers and to attract end users to support the growth and development of dealers' businesses. Increased demand for products, in turn, interests more dealers in becoming part of the dealer network, with the added attraction of comprehensive dealer support.

Owing to ongoing expansion of Canon's product range and changes in UK distribution channels, the company adopted a policy of selling direct to its UK dealer network in the late 1980s. It began working with BPS Téléperformance in 1989 as these changes were implemented.

One of the first major projects to be undertaken was a dealer recruitment drive in 1990 (see pages 86-88), with the launch of Canon's FC1 and FC2 personal photocopiers. As dealer recruitment is continuous, BPS continues to screen and qualify prospective dealers, booking appointments for Canon's field salesforce when appropriate. BPS maintains the central database of existing, prospective and lapsed Canon OTP dealers, who are targeted regularly by mail and telephone.

The OTP division supplies all Canon equipment aimed at consumers and small businesses and for personal use by senior executives, including desktop copiers, personal typewriters, small fax machines and calculators.

Prospective and lapsed dealers are mailed information on new products and the benefits of being a Canon dealer, which include 24-hour delivery and easy ordering by fax, telephone or mail. Incentives are offered to encourage immediate response, by phone or using a Dealer Trading Agreement. Level of interest is logged on the database for appropriate follow-up action. BPS coordinates all dealer mailings and telephone follow-up.

Product launches are also used to attract existing and potential dealers to high profile events such as road shows. BPS mails invitations and follows up by telephone. After the event a mailing, with a toll-free response number, encourages positive action.

Dealers requiring support literature, such as brochures and mailers, call BPS where their request is logged and fulfilled. The agency reports to Canon regularly on current live dealer accounts and dealer literature requests by sales area. Newly recruited dealers are tracked as to what, and how often, they order, with the objective of turning them into range dealers through subsequent communications.

End users are targeted frequently with special offers, such as free copier or fax paper, and sometimes prize draw incentives to encourage immediate response. All end-user toll-free telephone and coupon responses to advertising are channelled directly into BPS for processing.

Information gathered from callers includes media source, product interest, buying timescale and reason for interest. BPS also validates coupon responses for some products, such as copiers; end users are called and taken through the same questionnaire as telephone respondents. Leads are entered directly onto a database and a lead sheet is despatched within 24 hours to either Canon telesales or field sales, depending on who is best able to support a sale. BPS provides Canon with a regular breakdown of enquiries received, by media source, product type, lead quality, destination of leads, and so on.

Since early 1993, responsibility for servicing OTP dealers' ordering needs has been split between 12 in-house telesales staff and 14 national field salespeople. The telesales team services approximately 1800 dealers. Each team member looks after between 120 and 190 dealers, spread across the UK so that the sales potential is equitable; they work on a part-commission basis for sales exceeding individual monthly and half-yearly targets. Field salespeople look after about 200 dealers, generally the larger, high value accounts.

Leads from BPS are allocated by telesales and field sales to their dealers according to which is best able to fulfil a particular end user's needs, dependent upon equipment stocked, their location and the support required.

Telesales staff make regular calls to their dealers, although there is no fixed call cycling. Timing of calls is partly influenced by special promotions run by Canon's marketing department, which can be every two weeks and sometimes targeting specific sectors of the dealer base. On average, telesales will speak to 25 per cent of their dealers at least weekly, 25 per cent bi-weekly and the remainder at least every month.

Although telesales staff work on a part-commission basis, it is unproductive for them to use a 'hard sell' technique. They come to know their dealers and their buying patterns and, unless a promotion has been targeted at the dealers or relevant end users, they do not generally push for sales outside these patterns.

Regular calls are oriented towards relationship building, based around such topics as asking if leads have been successful, how good trade is, if dealers are thinking of stocking new products, and generally discussing their plans for the next three months. Staff tailor their approach according to the dealer's known preferences, ranging from quick business-like exchanges to calls with a preamble about family, holidays and other personal matters. In effect, this mirrors the type of relationship field salespeople maintain with their dealers.

There are six Dealer Support Officers (DSOs) serving Canon's OTP dealers. Their primary role is to give product demonstrations in the field and to provide on-site training. Because they cover large territories, their time needs to be planned carefully in advance. The smaller dealers, serviced by telesales, are less likely to plan their requirements and the DSOs are not always available when required. On these occasions, two or three of the more experienced telesales staff are available to make site visits. This has the advantage of helping to build a closer relationship with the dealers. Telesales staff are not under great pressure from inbound enquiries, most of which are channelled through BPS, and can therefore afford this time in the field.

All sales and other feedback from dealers is logged onto a database. This completes the lead tracking cycle and enables Canon's marketing department to analyse the effectiveness of end-user marketing initiatives, such as the value of different media channels. This results in more effective end-user promotions. At the same time, by maintaining regular contact, Canon builds up a profile of each dealer's business, buying history and support needs. The company is then better able to help each dealer to service the growing demand from end users.

Maintaining direct contact with intermediaries means that their performance can be monitored continuously. A company does not have to wait for an end user, or an intermediary in the middle of the supply chain, to complain before action can be taken. Telephone research can be conducted among end users to provide information on how they view the level of service being provided, and the 'mystery shopper' technique provides a way of measuring how well intermediaries handle customer telephone enquiries.

14.3 Retail branch support

The investment a company makes in promoting its products or services must be protected throughout all stages in the supply chain. However attractive the offering, a prospect disappointed by lack of supply or poor service will, more often than not, turn to another supplier. A UK survey of the retail market in 1991 revealed that customers' desire for better service ranked second only to wanting lower prices.

Supporting local branches is perhaps even more important than supporting independent intermediaries, since branches carry the company name. Although a company has a great deal more control over its branch operations, staff skilling, marketing support and the selling environment, there are occasions when local expertise or resources are insufficient to deal with a situation. The telephone is the most direct and flexible means of support available for these occasions.

Case study 14.4

National Westminster Bank, one of the UK's leading high street banks, places a high priority on the use of information technology (IT) both to improve its operational efficiency and to provide a premium service to its customers. In such a fast moving service-oriented environment, it is vital that any problems staff experience with IT equipment are resolved quickly. The bank therefore provides its branches and other IT users with a central help desk, dealing with all machine, application, procedural and reconciliation problems within the retail banking operation, as well as some departments and some subsidiaries.

The Information Technology ServiceLine (ITSL) was established in 1988, at the bank's Data Centre in the Midlands, to deal with reports of operational problems on all IT equipment, including automatic teller machines (ATMs). It serves approximately 2300 branches, plus approximately 700 sub-branches and 2000 Personal Financial Advisers, 2 subsidiaries and approximately 12 departments. The objectives in setting up the ServiceLine were:

– to provide a single telephone number staff could call for help;
– to transfer problem ownership from individual sites to a centralized department,

and resolve problems within agreed service levels and budget; and
– to 'de-skill' the help role.

The de-skilling of help is achieved by providing ITSL operators with a computerized knowledge-based system called COLA (Contextual On-Line Assistance). This is installed on their PCs, which are connected to file servers on a Local Area Network (LAN).

The IT ServiceLine uses an Aspect CallCenter automatic call distributor together with Aspect's Application Bridge (an intelligent ACD/computer interface). Each site using ITSL has a unique direct dialling in (DDI) telephone number, which is used to identify the source of calls to the ServiceLine.

As a call arrives, the CallCenter interfaces with the file servers, via Application Bridge, and uses the DDI number to identify the site calling. The file servers hold details of each site, including the IT equipment used and the last five incidents about which the site has had occasion to call ITSL. Information on the site calling is then passed to the operator's screen at the same time as the call is connected.

The operator uses COLA to help define the problem being reported and to identify a route to the solution. The COLA knowledge base holds a vast amount of information relating to the bank's IT equipment, including operating procedures, potential operational difficulties, equipment faults and their probable causes.

In conversation with the caller, the operator systematically works through a succession of screens, presented by COLA, each with a list of options. At each stage, the operator selects the option most appropriate to the problem being reported. COLA then searches its knowledge base to find the next relevant set of options or questions. Each successive option selected by the operator takes COLA nearer to isolating the cause of the problem, through a process of elimination and deduction, and suggesting a route to its solution. COLA keeps track of the selections made, which describe the problem, and automatically creates an incident record in the background. At the end of this process, one of three things will happen.

1. COLA may have identified the problem, and suggested how it can be resolved. The incident is then closed.
2. COLA may have identified the problem as hardware-related and an engineer is required. At this point the caller terminates the call, but another section of ITSL calls an engineer and monitors progress through to solution.
3. The extent of the knowledge within COLA is reached without solving the problem. In this case it is necessary to pass the call to a human expert.

When a human expert is required – and there are some 50 specializing in different subjects at the bank's offices around the country – the operator will call the appropriate person. On making contact, the operator gives the expert the incident number and sends the incident record to the file server. This enables the expert to key the incident number on a local terminal and bring the record up on screen. At the same time, the caller reporting the problem is connected with the expert, who can immediately assess the situation with the full problem history on screen. Progress from here on is still monitored at the ITSL.

Around 50 per cent of all incidents are resolved by the ITSL, without referral to an expert, although this figure is probably nearer 75 per cent for hardware problems. The average is brought down by application, procedural and reconciliation problems. Having immediate access to previous problems experienced at a site, together with details of the existing equipment base, enables a quicker and more effective response to reported problems.

If a 'global' problem occurs, affecting many sites, the CallCenter's voice response unit can be used to play a recorded message as calls are received by the ACD. If this solves the problem, callers are asked to terminate the call; if not, they are asked to hold to be connected to an operator. In this way, ITSL operators are free to deal with problems where the cause is not known.

The ITSL is staffed by 56.5 full-time operator equivalents, including 15 part-time staff. Agency staff are called in to assist with peaks in call traffic. The ITSL aims to answer 85 per cent of calls requiring an operator within 30 seconds and, except in times of extreme pressure, this is achieved. The average time to answer is approximately 8 seconds, and call duration averages approximately 3 minutes.

Since the ITSL was established, the COLA knowledge base has been expanded with the addition of many more topics, machines and procedures. Incident records, produced automatically by COLA, help in development of the system. Two of the bank's subsidiaries also now use the ServiceLine, while a third has introduced its own help desk.

By being able to respond immediately to any IT problems experienced by its staff, wherever they are situated in the UK, National Westminster Bank is able to maintain premium levels of service to its customers.

Providing direct telephone access to central support resources can be exploited in many ways (see Table 14.2), not only to help intermediaries but also their customers. An in-store hotline, for example, could be offered to customers should they fail to get a satisfactory solution to a problem from branch staff. A hotline could be used by staff to check stock availability, centrally or at other branches, or delivery status. When a local dealer is closed, customers might value the opportunity to speak to the supplier direct to find out if the dealer has an item in stock, or to check delivery status on an order. With today's information management systems there are few areas of enquiry that could not be dealt with immediately (see Chapter 16 for examples), and many types of service can be automated, dispensing with the need for large investment in additional personnel or 24-hour staffing.

Ease of contact makes the telephone the ideal medium for supporting overseas agents. When a company is competing with local suppliers it must deliver a service to agents that is at least equivalent to that available from local firms. Offering an international toll-free number for enquiries, orders and general support goes some way towards providing this, while regular outbound calls to the agents provides support, keeps them up to date with

Table 14.2   Central telephone support for intermediaries

Stock availability enquiries, order hotlines and delivery tracking

Traffic generation

Direct response lead generation, supply and tracking

Local marketing support (information, advice, representative appointments)

In-store hotline (for customers and staff)

Local branch/dealer locator

Out-of-hours customer service

Branch service line

the business and makes them feel a significant part of the company's international operations.

Developing, managing and supporting a supply chain is a complex business. It is a dynamic system that must respond flexibly to the demands of the marketplace. Regular dialogue between supplier and intermediaries is required to stimulate business, monitor performance and identify when and where action and change are required. The telephone meets these requirements. It provides suppliers with a direct view of the needs and activities of both intermediaries and end users. Overall, by helping carefully selected intermediaries to deliver a better service to their customers, suppliers support their own image in the marketplace and contribute to the success of the sales channels that are essential to reach their markets.

15
Direct response

All inbound telephone calls start with a number being dialled. The aim of direct response 'campaigns' is to make a target audience aware of the telephone number appropriate to their needs and encourage them to use it. This is a looser definition than is usually applied to direct response. It encompasses any situation in which a telephone number is promoted as a method of contacting an organization for brochure requests, placing orders, requesting service, making complaints, questioning bills, etc. The reason for the broad definition is that the concept of 'accessibility' is at last being realized. Businesses are beginning to fulfil the promise of the telephone as a means of direct access. They are encouraging people to telephone them, *en masse*, whatever their needs, sometimes using a single telephone number. This has important implications for the more 'traditional' direct response applications, such as lead generation, because now they must be viewed as part of a broader plan and definitely not as isolated activities.

In the caring, welcoming spirit of the 1990s, a company's openness to, and encouragement of, dialogue with the marketplace is becoming an integral part of brand and corporate image. In this context, using the telephone as a channel of direct inward communication needs to be planned strategically, across all applications, and managed effectively. This ensures not only that brand and company image are promoted positively, and consistently, but also that the company gains maximum benefit from such dialogue.

The reasons for the growth in the use of the telephone as a response mechanism are many. Technology has been a major facilitator through more sophisticated network services, automatic call distributors and computerized information management. Growth in the use of credit and debit cards has facilitated direct selling. Rising media costs mean that companies want their advertising pound to work harder, while increasing media segmentation is improving opportunities for more accurate targeting. With the need for greater accountability in the marketing spend, companies have welcomed the ability to use the volume and quality of response as a comparative measure of the effectiveness of different strategies. Increasing competition has forced companies to respond more quickly, and more personally, to market needs in order to maintain competitive advantage.

Instant access and dialogue are the two key benefits of the telephone in today's markets (see Table 15.1). The telephone enables people to receive an immediate response, and the company has a 'captive' audience which it can influence positively whatever the nature of the call. Offering telephone access to all-comers has certain disadvantages, however. The promise of instant access heightens callers' expectations of an immediate response and one which satisfies their needs. So a company must respond quickly and appropriately to each call.

Uses for direct telephone response include lead generation, database building, sales hotlines, technical support, service, sales promotion, traffic generation, carelines, crisis management, market research, database building, recruitment and *ad hoc* enquiries. Many of these applications use traditional direct response advertising, while others, such as technical support and carelines, generally target users in more specialized ways. The principles are the same, however, with four main areas to consider when undertaking direct response activity: the objectives, the media, the message, and response handling and fulfilment. Across these four areas there are many factors to take into consideration, both individually and their interactions. This chapter does not examine these factors in detail, but it identifies the key issues which impact upon the success of direct response activity.

15.1 Objectives

It is quite easy to recognize some of the direct response advertising that has been executed without clear objectives. It is most obvious in the response mechanism itself. A coupon too cramped to complete easily and clearly, or a telephone number lost in a sea of body copy, or included at the end of a television commercial but shown fleetingly without a voiceover. While encouraging response may not be the primary objective of a particular piece of advertising, it is a serious error of judgement to include a response mechanism that does not make response easy. The advertiser is simultaneously being welcoming and rejecting. Mistakes of this type are not uncommon, and they highlight the importance of thinking through the reasons why a response mechanism is being used and planning how to use it effectively.

Response solicitation can be combined successfully with other objectives, provided that the reasons for doing so are clear. A direct response mechanism may be incorporated in brand advertising to get maximum value from advertising expenditure. The brand element aims to build awareness and build or change brand perceptions, which is the primary objective, while the response mechanism helps to capture interest to convert those in the market or to extend the weight and content of the advertising through fulfilment.

Table 15.1 Advantages and disadvantages of using the telephone as a response channel

Advantages	Disadvantages
A dialogue is initiated	Requires real-time response handling
Callers gain immediate access to information, advice or help	Requires skilled operators if answering live
It capitalizes on impulsive responses (quicker and easier than a coupon)	Introduces risk of lost opportunities, or poor service, if call-handling capacity is inadequate
Respondents can be screened and qualified, live, with follow-up action agreed and actioned immediately	Requires accurate prediction of response rates to optimize cost-efficiency of call handling by operators
Rapid response can increase conversion rates	Introduces variability in response if using operators
Additional data, for profiling and planning subsequent contact strategies, can be captured quickly and easily, including ad hoc comments	Operators need immediate access to any information required to handle enquiries
Data is accurate and more complete (no illegible coupons, fewer unanswered questions)	Handling open-ended calls, e.g. complaints, can be time-consuming
Dialogue helps to improve conversion rates, and to increase order value by cross-selling and up-selling	Offering response by telephone heightens expectations of rapid fulfilment, follow-up or answering of enquiries
Used with a coupon it can more than double response levels	Some people would rather not respond by telephone
Rapid feedback enables early analysis of campaign effectiveness	
Cost to the respondent is flexible	
Call handling can be cheaper than handling written enquiries	
Some people prefer to respond by telephone	
It is quicker to note down a telephone number than an address	

An integrated approach, giving roughly equal prominence to brand objectives and response solicitation, seeks to generate response *and* build awareness and influence brand perceptions at the same time. Some campaigns aim to achieve both objectives with the same advertisement. Others use two, or sometimes more, advertisements placed in the same medium. For example, a TV brand commercial may be shown early in the break and followed later with a direct response commercial. This concept is even extended across different media. Satellite TV company BSkyB, for example, has used brand commercials, including news of a special subscription offer, to forewarn subscribers that they will be receiving a letter through the post. The letter contains more information on the offer and the response mechanism. Integrated campaigns cater for long-term strategic objectives at the same time as providing immediate feedback and tangible results in the short term.

The primary objective of pure direct response campaigns is to generate the maximum possible number of good-quality responses from the target audience although, in so doing, they may also seek to build awareness and influence brand perceptions. Direct selling campaigns also aim to generate maximum response, but from people who want to make an immediate purchase.

All these uses of response solicitation are equally valid in appropriate applications, but it is vital to understand why a response number is being offered and the type of calls or callers the company wants to attract. A lead generation campaign, for example, might exploit brand values to pull response, while a product recall advertisement might avoid associating the brand with a product fault. The availability of a free 24-hour technical support line might be featured in brand advertising, as evidence of added value, but it may be unwise to give the support line number. The purpose, after all, is to provide after-sales support and not to encourage technical enquiries from prospects. An FMCG company, on the other hand, might include the number of a careline in its brand advertising. While the existence of the careline shows added value, the provision of the number as well can help to achieve sales promotion objectives. The company can resolve callers' queries about the brand, inform them of its varied uses, perhaps in a fulfilment pack with money-off vouchers, and give them information about where it is available locally.

The objectives of soliciting response have to be considered carefully because they can affect the whole campaign, including media selection and buying, advertising design, and the fulfilment resources required. An appropriate balance must be struck between brand and response objectives so that the correct mix of brand builders and response motivators is selected. This, in turn, will influence media selection and buying (conditional upon the need to reach the target audience), creative execution and the planning of response handling and fulfilment. These factors are not considered in isolation, however; for example, it is both a waste of resources and damaging to the brand image if a massive response is generated and the response handling and fulfilment resources are incapable of coping effectively. The call handling has as much, if not more, influence on brand image as the values promoted in advertising. Inviting a response, or welcoming people to make contact, carries a risk. It opens the company to scrutiny. The planning, implementation and management of direct response should ensure that the company is up to that inspection.

15.2 The medium

There are many considerations in deciding which medium is most appropriate for soliciting response in particular circumstances, but they cover areas such as the target audience, reasons for inviting response, the nature of the message, and cost-efficiency. Sometimes the medium is determined largely by the application (e.g. an on-pack careline number), while in others (e.g. lead generation) there is a wide choice of media. Some of the individual issues that bear on media selection are summarized in Table 15.2.

Direct response advertising is becoming more flexible and the cost is decreasing with increasing segmentation of media, new media and new applications of established media.

Table 15.2 Some factors bearing on media selection for soliciting telephone response

Does the application limit choice of, or dictate the medium?

How quickly must the campaign be implemented? (Production and lead times vary widely.)

What precision is required in targeting?

Is a personalized message required?

What volume of response is required, and within what timescale?

Does the message require longevity, i.e. will it be required for reference at a later date?

How long is the message and how much detail does it contain?

Can the message be conveyed more effectively using the qualities of two or more different media?

Are visuals, still or moving, essential to communicate the message effectively?

What cost per response is acceptable (bearing in mind the probable volumes and quality of response)?

What is the competition in the available media?

What call-handling and fulfilment capacity is available? Could it cope, for example, with response from prime-time television?

- Targeting is becoming more precise, which not only decreases costs but also enables a more pertinent (and therefore more effective) message to be delivered.
- Database technology is enhancing targeting not only of customers but also of prospects identified through geodemographic and lifestyle comparisons.
- The increasing diversity of programming in commercial television and radio is creating new opportunities to target niche markets.
- The growth of satellite television is doing the same, as well as giving access to developing markets in such areas as the Middle and Far East.
- The use of interactive television will give precise details of viewers' preferences, and so enable precise targeting.
- Data services delivered by television, e.g. teletext, are becoming more sophisticated, with greater capacity and faster searching.
- The number and variety of supplements delivered with newspapers is increasing as a result of circulation battles, while magazines are being personalized for individual subscribers or subscriber segments.
- Electronic newspapers will enable individuals to select the type of news and features they want to read.

All these developments are increasing the opportunities for ensuring that a telephone number is seen by the right people at the right time.

Direct response television

The growing range of options means that testing has become all the more important to find the best medium and treatment, as illustrated by Weight Watchers' testing of direct response television.

Case study 15.1

Weight Watchers is the best-known brand and largest company in the slimming industry. Each week it delivers its service through over 5500 weekly weight loss meetings throughout Europe. Direct marketing is vital to the company's business. Firstly, the Weight Watchers weight loss service has very little retail presence. The bulk of its meetings take place in premises rented from other organizations for only a few hours on each occasion. Walk-in traffic is therefore negligible and every member has to be actively recruited. The business is also highly seasonal. The majority of enrolments are recruited during the three key promotional periods: just after Christmas, just after Easter and after the summer holidays. These relatively short periods are the only times when consumers are really motivated to take action about their weight, which means Weight Watchers has only one attempt at getting the campaign right each season. Finally, weight control is a crowded market and so it is vital to communicate a powerful reason why consumers should make Weight Watchers their choice.

The telephone plays a key role in the recruitment process, providing immediate access for consumers to act impulsively when motivated by powerful advertising. There is an inevitable reduction in enquiries to sales, like any two-step sales process, so it is essential to generate high volumes of enquiries cost-effectively. Weight Watchers has found that direct response television (DRTV) delivers these high volumes at an acceptable cost.

In France, for many years, the television strategy used was traditional. Advertisements carried a response number and, for this to work, the company felt maximum frequency and exposure were required. Since Weight Watchers' primary audience is women aged 25–54 with a full- or part-time job, this inevitably led to a buying strategy based on prime viewing periods. Within these periods, the media buy was targeted on programme quality, net coverage and frequency. However, the company gradually became disappointed with the cost-efficiency of television compared to print media being used, particularly direct mail. Cost per enquiry eventually reached a level that the company was no longer prepared to pay and it moved to other media, such as radio. However, even though this produced cost-effective results, volumes were reduced.

Weight Watchers decided to return to French television in January 1992, but with a radically revised buying strategy which followed a pure DRTV route. This entailed a revision of most of the TV advertising principles previously adhered to. The new rules were that:

- rating points bear no relationship to results (i.e. the number of enquiries and their cost);
- air time would be bought purely on the basis of the time of day that produces the best response results; and
- selection of quality (i.e. 'watchable') programmes could, in fact, be a disadvantage.

Essentially, the rules add to a philosophy that commercials should only be aired at a time when the potential respondent is able, and willing, to use the telephone; that is, when less than absorbing programmes are showing and when there are few other distractions. Inevitably, this meant using a day-time mix, which seemed to conflict with the rationale behind the company's previous tactics. If the target audience works, how would they see commercials aired during the day? Weight Watchers' new buying strategy also meant losing the large audience for prime-time TV. However, prime-time does not meet the 'able and willing to use the telephone' criterion. Another variable considered was the effect of the length of the commercial block in which an advertisement appears. Too many commercials in the block produces 'clutter' and seems to diminish impact. Buying, therefore, needed to be targeted on blocks that contained fewer commercials.

After three complete enrolment seasons using this strategy, Weight Watchers had isolated the most effective time slots for producing healthy volumes of enquiries at cost-effective rates. Repeated usage had proved that the only times producing cost-effective results were during the morning (9.00 a.m. to midday) and after lunch (1.30 p.m. to 5.00 p.m.). Breakfast and lunch times, despite the relatively cheap air time, are seemingly too distracting a period for response; while prime-time is expensive and, despite the large audience size, response is poor.

One rule that has remained valid, whichever air-time buying strategy is used, is the synergistic effect of combining media. Under both strategies used by Weight Watchers, stronger results are achieved from both TV and the other media when they are run concurrently.

The company found French media owners particularly amenable to the idea of DRTV, and adopting the purist DRTV strategy not only improved cost-efficiency but also lifted volume. In the first season, Weight Watchers spent 40 per cent less on TV than in previous campaigns but volume increased by 66 per cent; and cost per enquiry fell by 65 per cent. Slightly lower results, but still significantly improved, were achieved in the two subsequent seasons using this strategy.

Creatively, the four key ingredients of successful Weight Watchers' DRTV commercials are the portrayal of simple emotional triggers, the problem solution, a powerful promotional offer and the all-important telephone number.

The situation in the UK has been different. Weight Watchers has used TV consistently for many years, based on a media buy of 60 per cent prime-time and 40 per cent off-peak. During the 1980s, a succession of commercials, while not specifically DRTV spots, were aimed primarily at getting prospective members to call and attend a meeting. However, TV became more inefficient each year and the company decided to reach out to a new audience. It was time to go back to creative basics. The company had found that combining image advertising with a telephone number was not effective direct response television. DRTV results from a single-minded focus on generating response.

The company undertook new consumer research which reinforced existing knowledge and confirmed that the four key rules on creative execution were still valid. The formula was to find an emotional trigger, present the problem solution, communicate a powerful offer and get across the telephone number. After adopting DRTV principles in the UK, as it had done in France, Weight Watchers experienced unprecedented success.

Testing and retesting
The company was determined to obtain maximum return on its TV spend and chose three main measurement criteria with which it could evaluate precisely the impact of changing different campaign variables. First, it looks at top-line results (number of calls and members through the door) versus TVRs (TV ratings) used, and calculates a ratio for each result. Second, telephone calls are monitored carefully, particularly those in the first 20 minutes following a commercial. This provides a comparison of prime-time performance versus off-peak, how 10-second spots perform compared to 30-second, and so on. Third, it looks at telephone calls per million impacts and, most importantly, enrolled members per million impacts – which Weight Watchers regards as the acid-test of efficiency.

The company has a strategy of testing and retesting variables in each campaign, in addition to the main promotional thrust. One of these is different types of telephone number, comparing operated-connected toll-free, toll-free, local call charge and standard 'responder pays' numbers. The most cost-efficient has been found to be responder pays. Another variable tested is money-off offers. Not surprisingly, price promotions do increase response volumes and the company has found TV to be an excellent testing medium with a high degree of sensitivity. (In 1992, UK healthcare company BUPA discovered that £9 per month was the 'magic' figure for pricing its healthcare insurance in DRTV commercials.) A third area of testing is campaign duration and switching campaigns on/off/on. The company has found that its campaigns have an effective life of 3–4 weeks before efficiency falls dramatically (a reflection of the short 'season'), while campaigns that are continuously 'on' perform better, in terms of cost-efficiency, than if they are switched on/off/on.

Weight Watchers' decision to depart radically from its advertising tradition has paid dividends and has proved that DRTV is not only cost-effective for lead generation but also allows quantifiable measurement of the return on investment.

The proportion of European television advertising carrying a response mechanism is only a fraction of that in the USA, but is growing rapidly. The value of the mass media in creating opportunities for dialogue, either directly or indirectly, is now well proven. In 1992 a number of leading USA advertisers launched campaigns costing tens of millions of dollars to establish and improve dialogue with their markets. General Motors, for example, used television to alert consumers to an imminent special offer mailing, while magazine advertising encouraged them to call direct on a toll-free number. The response far exceeded the company's expectations. Not that the volume of calls generated by advertising is any measure of success; it is the quality of response that counts, as demonstrated by one of BT's promotions.

Lead value – a key criterion

As the UK's principal telecommunications supplier, BT feels it has a responsibility to other companies to set an example in how to use the telephone effectively as a marketing tool.

Case study 15.2

BT is constantly looking for creative applications which not only assist in its communications but also show other companies just how effective a marketing tool the telephone can be. As an example, BT launched a promotional campaign in October 1992 for its toll-free (0800), local call charge (0345) and 0891 premium rate services.

A series of direct response press advertisements invited readers wanting more information to call a toll-free number for a brochure. This described the services and their possible application areas, with short case studies explaining how businesses in different sectors are using them to gain competitive advantage. The brochure was unusual: apart from its very lively graphic design, it offered, throughout, a further 17 toll-free numbers. Prospects could dial and listen to different users of the 0800, 0345 and 0891 services talking first hand about their experiences, via an audiotex service provided by the agency Greenland Interactive (formerly Legion). At the end of each recorded case study, prospects could divert to an operator to arrange an appointment with a BT specialist. Alternatively, they could use another toll-free number given in the brochure.

The objective of this 'talking brochure' promotion was not to attract a high volume of calls. Its purpose was, first, to educate businesses on the spectrum of free/ variable charge BT calling services, second, to brand the product as delivering competitive advantage and, third, to generate leads. Even allowing for the tremendous growth in the use of toll-free numbers in the UK, the promotion was hugely successful. Approximately 25 per cent of people requesting a brochure subsequently asked to speak to a BT sales representative, compared with 0.3–6.0 per cent in previous promotions, and over a third said they planned to invest in one of the BT services within six months. In independent research, commissioned by BT, 90 per cent of leads said the literature brochure made them think that the 0800/0345 services help companies to attract new business (Table 15.3).

Although this was a fairly straightforward use of direct response and audiotex, the way in which the promotion was structured proved very powerful.

Table 15.3 Results of independent research into lead perceptions of a BT services brochure. (Courtesy of BT)

25% claimed to have been influenced by the brochure
79% filed it
93% read or glanced through it
90% said it made them think that BT's 0800/0345 services help companies to attract new business
78% said they learnt something new
90% claimed it was informative
60% found it thought provoking.

In some situations, such as competition entries, the quality of response is relatively unimportant (unless entrants' details will be used for targeted marketing). In most campaigns, however, it is the most important criterion of success. Lead generation campaigns, for example, should aim to generate response from good-quality prospects. In a sampling promotion, the company wants response from people who are likely to use the product long term. A campaign resulting in a relatively small number of high-quality responses is much more effective than one generating a large number of low-value leads. Careful selection of the advertising medium helps to target the potential high-quality respondents and minimize those of low value.

Capacity to handle the volume of response expected should also be considered. In generating leads to book appointments, for example, how many appointments can the salesforce cope with so that leads do not have to wait an unreasonable time for a meeting? It is best to select media and place advertising in a way that generates a steady, manageable flow of leads.

The combined use of different media in encouraging response is becoming more widespread. Sometimes this is done to capitalize on the particular qualities of the different media, such as using television for powerful promotion of brand values and direct mail to communicate more quietly in a personal and informative way. In some instances the second medium might not even be stated explicitly. A business-to-business television commercial, for example, might end by encouraging executives to 'call your local dealer for a demonstration' without any reference about how to make contact. This would be done in the knowledge that those who are interested in the product will find the number from the most convenient source on return to the office. The commercial serves simply as a reminder of the brand values and the availability of a local demonstration. Using two or more media for the same direct response application can often also introduce a synergistic effect, one medium lifting response generated by the other. This is most noticeable in combined television and press or television and direct mail campaigns, where TV raises awareness and increases response from mail or press advertising.

Obviously it is important to identify how each medium is contributing to results in terms of both response volume and quality – for example, by asking where callers saw the number advertised – so that maximum cost-efficiency can be achieved.

15.3 Design for response

The manner in which a response mechanism is to be offered must be planned carefully, irrespective of the balance between brand and response objectives. Response must be made easy; people should be made aware of what will happen when they call and what they will receive in return. Obviously this becomes more important when the primary objective is to generate response, but it must be thought through in every situation where response is invited.

The scope for advertising design will have been determined partly by the medium selected and the mix of objectives, but in terms of a telephone response mechanism there are many ways in which response can be facilitated and promoted. An interesting situation arose in the UK when direct response television first gained momentum in the late 1980s. As advertisers were beginning to recognize the potential of including a response mechanism, many advertising agency creative people opposed the idea on the grounds that it would interfere with the creative execution of their ideas. The UK is renowned world wide for its advertising creativity and its executors understandably did not want to put their reputation at risk. It is true that, in such a highly evocative and provocative visual medium as television, the image properties of a brand should not be put at risk for direct response. They play a vital role not only in building brands but also in encouraging response when required. The mixing of the two objectives in the same advertising, even when direct response is the primary aim, presents a challenge. One of the most successful UK direct response TV campaigns was that designed by agency Hoare Wilkins for Direct Line Insurance. The first campaign was launched in January 1990 and requests for insurance quotations rose by 14 per cent in the first three months. The commercials introduced consumers to a red telephone, on wheels, which came hurtling to the rescue of people who needed insurance, to the accompaniment of a battle-cry musical jingle. As well as a significant increase in brand awareness, the campaign helped Direct Line to make a profit of over £10 million (1990/91) at a time when 'lookalike' competition was becoming fierce. It has also helped the company to double motor insurance telephone quotations year on year since April 1991. Furthermore, the advertising has won a string of awards.

The overall design of advertising can have a major impact on the effectiveness of the invitation to respond. Most of us are bombarded by many hundreds of advertisements each day and we actually notice only a small proportion. So the design can serve to get attention. It can then be used to focus attention on the reasons for calling and on the number to call. Within this area there are three significant factors: the type of number offered, the call to action and the display of the number.

Choice of number

Direct response advertising became more popular in the UK and other world markets after the introduction of toll-free calling. While it is not applicable to every situation, the concept of a free call fits well with the ethos of accessibility. It signals an open invitation, saying we will pay for the call, no strings attached. Cost to the advertiser is obviously an issue, and this has to be weighed against the value of the response. However, in the USA, where it is commonplace for companies to offer toll-free calls, access at no cost is generally now seen by consumers as a right and not a privilege. The rapid growth in toll-free calling in other countries (over 30 per cent annual increase in volume in the UK) is likely to engender the same view.

There are alternatives to toll-free calls which have benefits in different circumstances. Local call charge, for example, can reduce the number of hoax calls and other time-wasters, if this is likely to be an issue, while still benefiting people who have to call long distance. Premium rate, on the other hand, enables the advertiser to charge for a service or to generate revenues towards the cost of a promotion. Premium rate has many applications, but its use by some advertisers is questionable. One UK company offers a premium rate number for consumers to obtain brochures on its leading brand, maintaining that it reflects the 'premium' nature of the brand, and if people are genuinely interested in the product they will have no objection to paying a premium. Furthermore, the calls are answered by an automated system, not an operator. The wisdom of this type of application is questionable. The type of number used must be thought through carefully; some of the many issues to consider are summarized in Table 15.4.

Table 15.4   Some factors influencing the choice of direct response numbers

General issues
- Availability of easy-to-remember numbers is limited.
- Memorable numbers can reduce unmanageable peaks in response from TV advertising because people can call at their leisure.
- Consider the cost to the company of providing the service and how much customers and prospects will be willing to pay to use it.
- Consider the cost of the call in relation to the value offered, the existing relationship with callers, and the purpose, e.g. is charging for a call compatible with the objectives of a careline?
- The cost to the company of providing free or subsidized calls should be clearly justified, e.g.: How many more calls, will it encourage?, What will be the cost of servicing these? and What benefit will be derived from the extra callers?
- Take account of levels of awareness of the call cost with special codes, e.g. local call charge and premium rate, when advertising numbers.
- Variations in numbering systems in different countries make international advertising difficult, e.g. having to give a different toll-free number for each country.

Standard numbers
- The variety of national dialling codes make these more difficult to remember.
- Call costs are not obvious unless the relative location of the advertiser is known.
- Numbers can always be found in telephone directories.

Toll-free
- Can encourage a high volume response.
- Misuse is higher than with other numbers; non-legitimate calls can reportedly amount to 25–40% with long-running campaigns.
- The full cost of calls is borne by the advertiser and quickly mounts up on large-scale or long-running campaigns.

Local call charge
- Can reduce time-wasters
- Less cost to the advertiser than toll-free, but it makes a big difference to long-distance callers.

- Requires more commitment from callers than toll-free.

International toll-free
- Some misuse can be expected.
- High cost, but may be much less than the cost of setting up overseas agencies or offices.
- Offers a quick way to evaluate and tap into overseas markets; enables overseas companies to compete with local suppliers.

Premium rate
- The growing number of premium rate codes can lead to confusion among users.
- Callers' interest is qualified since they have to pay a premium for the call; virtually cuts out non-legitimate calls.
- Revenue from call charges helps to finance services or campaigns.
- The value obtained by callers must match or exceed the cost of the call; callers must know what they will get and be confident that it offers value for money.
- Flexible tariffing, available in the USA, enables a wider range of services to be financed and offered.
- Premium rate numbers can have dubious associations due to their use for providing 'adult' services.

Alphabetical translations (e.g. 727 2357 = PARCELS)
- No need to remember number, only the dialling code
- Can be used in combination with any telephone dialling code.
- There is a finite number of 'specials'.
- Serves a branding function, but generic branding, e.g. AIRWAYS, FLOWERS, could lead to confusion between suppliers.

Other specials supporting branding
- Offer many of the benefits of alphabetical translations.
- Virgin Atlantic Airways in the UK, for example, uses:

toll-free	747 747
local call charge	747 747
standard	747 747

Easily remembered numbers are the most sought-after. Again this is in line with the concept of accessibility. If consumers can remember a number associated with a particular company, then they will use it when they want to contact that company. A memorable number is easier to note from transient advertising such as television and radio. It can also reduce the burden on call-handling capacity, since some people will call at their leisure rather than respond immediately. The ultimate goal is to ensure that people know the company's number and it is thus available to them at any time. Currently the best types of number for this purpose are alphabetical translations and others which offer some form of branding. Letters on telephone 'dials' were withdrawn in the UK during the modernization of the telephone network, while they remained on phones in the USA. The USA market has made great use of this feature to create memorable branded 'numbers'. Someone wanting to buy a floral gift, for example, can dial toll-free FLOWERS. This is equivalent, numerically, to dialling toll-free 356 9377 – which is hardly memorable. BT began reintroducing letters on telephones in the UK in the early 1990s, but it will be some time before they are sufficiently widespread for advertising alphabetical number translations to be viable. Some UK advertisers have found another solution; for example, the Forte hotel chain uses an access code followed by 40 40 40, and Virgin Atlantic Airways uses 747 747 (see Table 15.4).

Toll-free calling is likely to become and to remain the standard for most applications, with an increasing trend towards branded numbers which are both more easily remembered and recalled and are recognizable as 'belonging' to a particular advertiser or brand.

Call to action

The call to action in an advertisement explains why people should call (i.e. the benefit they will gain), and sometimes when, and how to make contact. It is the most crucial part of a direct response advertisement and must be clear and unambiguous. The aim is to attract and encourage the right type of people to call (those who want what is on offer, e.g. information, help, a product sample or a service visit) and make it easy for them to respond. If the call to action is not specific, or is ambiguous in any way, it is likely that some people in the market for the offer simply will not respond while other people, perhaps not in the market, will respond for the wrong reasons. As a result the campaign could lose valuable prospects and attract calls of little value but which add to the cost of response handling.

The incentive used to encourage people to call will depend on the offer being made. An advertiser wanting a quick response, for example, might say 'Call us free now for an instant quotation', or 'Call us before 4.00 p.m. Monday to Friday and we guarantee free delivery the following day'. A time limit could be put on a special offer, or a free gift offered for orders placed before a certain date. Anything which clearly reinforces the benefits of calling will help to lift response levels. Even a sticker giving a service line number can use a call to action which supports proper usage (e.g. 'If you experience a problem with ...') and offers an incentive (e.g. 'If you call before 1.00 p.m. we guarantee to put it right before the end of the day').

A call to action serves to manage the expectations of callers, by telling them what they can expect in return for their call. Some direct response advertising goes even further in managing expectations. One UK insurance company, for example, has used a TV commercial which, first, talks about the product, the offer, and to whom it appeals (i.e. who should call), then it invites people to call and explains the entire process, visually and verbally.

With the number on screen, it shows the number being keyed into a telephone, an operator answering the call and asking questions, and the brochures that will be sent to the caller as a result of the conversation. This process prepares callers and makes the process of responding much easier and less daunting for those who, perhaps, dislike using the telephone for personal business.

A call to action should never raise expectations above what the company can deliver. Obviously there is no point in advertising an instant response if some prospects repeatedly get an engaged tone; but sometimes the situation is not as clear-cut. An advertisement might give the impression of a welcoming company and some prospects might call, looking forward to a friendly chat about their personal needs. When the call is answered with a recorded message they are inevitably disappointed and abandon the call. A call to action should be designed in such a way that callers know exactly what they can expect. If the company can then deliver something more when people call, all the better.

Research in the UK by BT and Channel 4 Television in 1993, summarized in Appendix 3 (page 286), identified certain values that all TV commmmercials carry for viewers. Three of these 'action values' – relevance, quality, expense – were found to be the most powerful in stimulating viewers to respond to DRTV commercials. Overall, the two key factors affecting response rates were the timing of the broadcast (both the day and the time of day) and the creative elements (including the duration of the commercial, the display of the number, and the use of a voiceover).

Number display

Ensuring that people notice the response telephone number and, if necessary, have time to make a note of it, is most difficult where advertising is transient, as on TV and radio. One method is to forewarn people that a number will be given shortly, so that they can watch or listen for it and, if they wish, have time to get the telephone or pen and paper. The clarity of a number on the TV screen, its size, the length of time for which it is shown, and having it spoken, are all important. Obviously the number must be very visible, with a clear typeface and contrast against the background. Around 15 to 20 seconds on screen, depending on the length of the commercial, is generally the minimum acceptable duration, together with voiceover repetition two or three times. Simply adding a voiceover can double and even treble response rates (see page 291, for example). It should also be borne in mind that portable televisions are used widely and the size of display should make appropriate allowance. A flashing number can attract attention, but it should not become difficult to read at any time. The use of a shot of a number being dialled, while the number is on screen, is a

Table 15.5 Conveying telephone numbers to aid assimilation

0800 770 800		0800 77 0800
0500 445 566	REPLACED BY	0500 44 55 66
0345 122 333		0345 1 22 333

great device to draw attention to the number. However, this is not appropriate for the majority of commercials.

Radio advertising is obviously totally reliant upon voicing the telephone number. Clarity and a 'writing speed' are important, as well as repetition. For both radio and television, the way in which a number is spoken/displayed can help the audience to assimilate it more easily and more quickly. It depends on the number being used, but if the digits can be grouped to provide a pattern, as shown in Table 15.5, the audience will find it easier to remember and to dial. Print advertising can also make use of this device.

While print advertising does not present the same problems as TV or radio, the design of the advertisement must still give appropriate priority to the response mechanism. The key to success is to direct attention to the telephone number, both through design and the call to action with its incentives, while retaining the creative integrity of the advertisement. Various devices are used, such as repetition and bold highlighting of the number in the body copy, or making a feature of the number through its dominant display.

The effort made to attract attention to a response number and to encourage people to respond depends on the objectives of the advertising. The advertiser may only want to attract people who have specific questions they want answered, such as through a careline. Whatever the circumstances, giving a telephone number is the first step in establishing a dialogue. Those who want to call should already feel 'good' about responding as a result of the way they were invited to call. The capital that is made of that 'feelgood' sensation then depends on the call handling.

15.4 Fulfilment planning

Fulfilment in the context of this chapter refers to everything that happens from the time prospects dial the number, through the handling of their calls, to any appropriate follow-up. Making the most of every call requires sophisticated planning, including, for example, ensuring that there are sufficient lines and operators so that callers do not have to wait an unreasonable time for an answer, having operators appropriately trained, and setting up systems and procedures to ensure that promised follow-up action (such as sending a brochure or keeping an appointment) is carried out efficiently.

Automated call handling

If a company is expecting a large response it may consider using automated call handling rather than live operators. A majority of people responding to a TV commercial, for example, will generally call within 7–8 minutes of broadcast. If it is a popular offer on prime-time TV, the volume of calls can be enormous and swamp even the largest call centres. Automated call handling has many benefits, not least the lower cost and the ability to handle many hundreds of calls simultaneously if necessary. It relies upon interactive voice response technology (see page 36) to service the callers' requirements. The level of interaction varies from recording callers' details to completing complex transactions over the telephone. Several examples are given in other chapters (see, for example, pages 100, 110 and 140).

Automated call handling can provide a very effective solution in many circumstances, but it does have disadvantages (shown in Table 15.6). Consumers in Europe have received little exposure to automated call-handling systems and there is some resistance to their use. One study found that almost 50 per cent of consumers replace the telephone on their first call to an automated system, falling to around 24 per cent on the second to fourth calls to the same or a similar service. Many companies have used them more successfully but there is still a high risk that a significant number of calls will be lost. In the USA, where these systems are more commonplace, the abandoned call rates are comparatively low.

Research in the UK, conducted by telemarketing consultancy Ogilvy & Mather Teleservices with network provider BT, suggests that consumer acceptance can be encouraged by careful planning. The research examined consumer perceptions of automated call handling and identified the major influencing factors (see Table 15.7). Using this information it is possible to construct guidelines for planning an automated service (Table 15.8) to try to improve consumer acceptance and minimize the number of abandoned calls. Although these measures have not been tested, many of them are based on general good practice in direct response advertising and therefore have relevance even to situations where automated systems are more widely accepted.

There are alternatives to fully automated call handling when operator resources are limited. The introduction of digital technology has enabled network providers to offer a range of sophisticated services for automatic call routeing. When call volumes to a particular site reach a certain level, or when all lines are busy, subsequent calls on a particular number can be diverted automatically to an automated answering facility.

Table 15.6 Two sides of interactive voice response services

Advantages	*Disadvantages*
Can handle high volume call traffic	Not as flexible as live operators; cannot as easily accommodate callers' differing needs
No lost calls as a result of engaged tone	High capital investment
Low unit cost of call handling	Not 100% reliable in data capture
Enables services/campaigns which otherwise would not be cost-effective	Can only capture information it is programmed to capture; cannot easily exploit *ad hoc* responses
24-hour service delivery	In some applications a high proportion of callers may ring off if they are not expecting an automated service
Service levels preset and guaranteed	
Consistent delivery of accurate information	Only suitable, by itself, for a minority of applications
Can reduce levels of hoax calls	Requires careful planning to be acceptable to many consumers, i.e. user/target audience profile, application, call to action, scripting, deliverables
Positive consumer perceptions:	*Negative consumer perceptions:*
– 24-hour convenience	– inflexible; loss of control over interaction
– no engaged lines; quick, guaranteed answering	– tedious and less enjoyable than a live conversation
– consistent presentation of information	– difficult to absorb and understand information
– no direct sales pressure	– impersonal
– can access/provide information that would be embarrassing to ask of/give to a live operator	– a money-maker for the advertiser

Table 15.7 Factors influencing consumer acceptance of interactive voice response services. (Based on research by Ogilvy & Mather Teleservices and BT)

Technophobia. Familiarity and comfort with using technology varies. Even willingness to use the telephone may be lower among some audiences, e.g. elderly consumers.

Convenience. Consumers recognize that it enables companies to offer services for their convenience, e.g. 24 hours, no engaged lines and speedy, guaranteed answering.

The experience. Automated call handling is felt to be tedious and less enjoyable than talking with an operator.

Callers' stage in the purchase cycle. Acceptance is higher at the beginning of the decision-making process and declines steadily the nearer the caller is to purchase. However, consumers are often deterred from responding to advertisements because they feel the person who answers their call might pressurize them into buying. Regular customers often react favourably to the convenience of automated services.

Complexity of the dialogue. Consumers feel it will be difficult to understand and absorb information.

Nature of the product or service. Some consumers are reluctant to divulge certain personal information, such as financial details, on an automated service. On the other hand, some personal matters, e.g. the onset of menstruation in young women, are regarded as too embarrassing to discuss with an operator.

Severity of decision required. In general, the more important the decision to be made, the more likely consumers are to prefer talking with an operator.

Relationship with the service provider. Customers find an automated service more acceptable than prospects.The more established the relationship the more acceptable an automated service, provided users have been informed and educated about it.

Perceived value. Toll-free calling increases acceptance. Premium rate is acceptable when merited by the value of the service. Consumers feel it is the 'cheap' option and could lead to active money-making by the advertiser. TV advertising lends greater credibility, but consumers expect to have trouble getting through.

Concerns about their 'performance'. Consumers are concerned they will not be able to provide the information requested, or will not do correctly what is asked of them.

Length of call. Automated services make callers more aware of time passing and they dislike long, annoying, time-wasting gaps.

Flexibility of the service. Consumers tend to feel that automated services are inflexible and they have no control over what happens.

Table 15.8 Encouraging consumer acceptance of interactive voice response services. (Based on UK research by Ogilvy & Mather Teleservices and BT)

Generally
- When planning interactive voice response services, use the combined skills of telemarketing and systems programming. Marry best practice in both disciplines to exploit the technology while remaining true to accepted wisdom in telemarketing.
- When deciding what number to use (i.e. what it will cost to call) consider what value callers are getting in return, e.g. a brochure, free sample or quotation. Also remember that automated services are generally perceived as a 'cheap' option, so the value of whatever is being provided may be perceived as being lower than it would be otherwise.
- Conduct market research among the target audience, or a test campaign, if there is a risk of alienating a large proportion of customers or prospects.

Targeting/application
- A divert to live operator option is a good idea in all but the simplest of automated services. It can be especially important when:
  - some of the target audience may be reluctant, or find it difficult, to use an automated service, e.g. technophobes, or the hard of hearing;
  - you are targeting people early in the purchase cycle;
  - users will be asked to make an important decision;
  - the interaction between system and user is complex;
  - the information being requested is of a type which some people may not want to divulge to 'a machine';
  - the application is of a type where people may need the 'warmth of human kindness and understanding', e.g. emergency repairs and other crisis situations.

Call to action
- The call to action is critical and must be very clear.
- The primary objective is to manage the expectations of users to ensure ease of use and to avoid disappointment. So, forewarn them of what to expect, including the length of the call, how to use the service, what information they will be asked to provide, and what they will receive in return.
- Always make it known when a divert to operator option is provided.
- Always emphasize the benefits of making the call, e.g. 24-hour service, guaranteed answering, and the 'offer'. This is even more important when users are paying for the call.
- When using TV advertising it is especially important to emphasize that all calls will be answered, and quickly.

Scripting
- Keep the script as straightforward as possible, e.g. not too many options to choose from, and the call as short as possible.
- Lead users by the hand and build flexibility into the script. Ensure that callers know when to listen and when to speak. Maximize their control over the

interaction, e.g. by providing a help option, similar to on-line help on computers, so that they can have information or questions repeated. Repeat any important information they give and request confirmation. Let them know at an early stage if there is a divert to live operator option.

• Have a short, fast introduction, then give callers something 'up front', e.g. ask 'Which brochure would you like?' before asking for their name, address and telephone number.

Deliverables

• Be careful in the selection of the 'voice' of the service. Unlike talking to an operator, where spontaneous reaction to the caller gives warmth and colour to what they say, an automated service has a disembodied voice which can seem totally disinterested in callers' needs.

• Deliver all that has been promised, and more if possible. This extends from ensuring that the system has sufficient capacity to answer all calls through to delivering brochures, samples, etc., on time.

Case study 15.3

The National Society for the Prevention of Cruelty to Children (NSPCC), a UK charity, has used an automated facility since December 1992. It has developed a very successful formula for direct response TV advertising since first testing the medium in 1991 and was one of the first UK charities to find television viable for fund raising. For Christmas 1992, the charity was planning a major campaign using television, radio, posters and national press. Until this time, all donation calls on its toll-free number had been handled by operators at telemarketing agency Merit Direct. With the prospect of a massive response to the new campaign, the NSPCC added an automated call-handling facility, provided by agency Greenland Interactive (formerly Legion), which would handle all calls on Christmas Day and the overflow of calls from Merit Direct during the normal working week. As well as recording details of credit card donations, the automated service enables callers to access information about the NSPCC during the same call. Over the Christmas 1992 period, the service handled tens of thousands of calls which contributed over £200 000 to the funds raised. (Incidentally, the NSPCC feels that a number of factors contribute to the success of its television campaigns, including the use of discounted air-time rates, commercials that are long enough to allow the message to be absorbed, keeping the response number on screen long enough to allow people to respond, requesting a specific sum of money (£15) and the creative treatment, which includes a hard-hitting emotional appeal centring on the loving care and safety of children.)

Overflow calls can just as easily be diverted to another site with operators. Using more sophisticated network services, calls to a particular number can be shared across multiple sites (see page 33) at different times of the day and week. The routeing of calls to ensure that they are answered quickly and appropriately is examined in more detail in Chapter 16, together with methods of helping operators to service calls of different types.

Creating the right impression

With increasing emphasis on accessibility, no advertiser can afford to lose calls or keep callers waiting. One of the problems with direct response advertising is the unpredictability of response levels. Testing a campaign can give some indication of probable call volumes, as can records from similar previous campaigns showing call traffic over time. Even if arrangements have been made for calls to be routed to a second site, it is important to have some idea of call volumes. An optimum number of trained staff will be required – sufficient to avoid keeping callers waiting but not so many that some skilled personnel have nothing to do. Provisions will have to be made for sending out any fulfilment literature, or keeping appointments within a reasonable time, or undertaking any other follow-up action. The better the forecasting of response levels, the better the service that can be delivered to callers.

Close liaison between the telemarketing facility and those responsible for creating and implementing the advertising is essential. The advertising people will need to know what can be achieved during a telephone conversation, such as the extent of information that can be gathered or given. The promises made in advertising will be fulfilled as a result of the telephone conversation, so advertising must not make promises that telephone resources cannot fulfil. Telemarketers require knowledge of the content of advertisements and when and where they are being placed, because it determines the type of calls that will be received, and when and how they will need to be handled.

In addition to the creative treatment, the type of information required for planning call handling when using the press includes the number of advertisements, size (or prominence), insertion dates, whether a coupon is also being offered, circulation and the readership profile. For radio and television it would include catchment area, profile and number of listeners or viewers, transmission times/frequency and campaign duration. For mailings it would include volume, when they are likely to be received, the profile of the target audiences and, if they are existing customers, their names and addresses so that, if necessary, customer records can be made available to operators when they answer calls. Media schedules have a tendency to be changed and liaison is essential to ensure that telephone resources are available when required. Telemarketers need to know when the first and last calls are expected to be received. For example, is a limited period special offer being made?

The information necessary to calculate the number of operators required to handle calls efficiently includes the probable volume of calls, how call volumes will fluctuate throughout the day and on different days of the week, the types of call, the average length of conversations, and the time required between calls to complete associated tasks and prepare for the next call. Records of similar previous campaigns and testing can be used to gain a fairly accurate picture of the resources required. Voice-messaging facilities, enabling callers to leave their details when all operators are busy, can help to cope with the busiest call periods and provide work (the call-backs) for the operators during quieter times (see page 97, for example).

However well targeted the advertising, and however clear and precise the call to action, some callers almost inevitably will make enquiries other than those the advertisement has been designed to generate. Inviting people to call for a brochure, for example, might result in some people calling to ask for the name and address of their local dealer. In some applications, like a careline, the range of enquiries and requests can be enormous. Adequate operator training, and access to relevant information resources to cover all eventualities, is vital. The call is a relationship building opportunity and the handling of each and every call must reflect company and brand values in a positive way.

Computerized systems can help operators, in many ways, to make the most of this opportunity. The case studies in Chapter 16 on customer service illustrate the range of support available.

Support technologies

Data entry directly into a computer is invaluable for completing the fulfilment process speedily and efficiently, as well as for analysing the response. In some applications, such as dealer location, callers' needs may be met fully by only the telephone conversation; in others, e.g. lead generation, further action is required, such as sending literature or keeping an appointment. With data already in the computer, many types of fulfilment activity (such as printing a label and personalized letter, notifying product despatch, generating lead sheets for dealers or salespeople, faxing product literature, notifying service personnel) can be fully automated. Apart from speeding fulfilment, this also reduces the likelihood of introducing errors by re-entering data.

Speed in completing fulfilment is important. Apart from reflecting the efficiency of the business and its care for customers, rapid fulfilment can affect results directly. The quicker prospects are put in a position to buy, the better the chance of winning their business.

Monitoring the outcome of fulfilling the callers' immediate needs is essential. Thus, for example, service visits might be followed up with telephone calls to ask customers if they are happy with the outcome. At the very least feedback should be obtained from the relevant service personnel. Despatch of a brochure might be followed up with a call to prospects to check that it arrived and to try to influence the buying decision and perhaps obtain orders.

Rapid feedback on campaign success, through the volume and quality of response, enables decisions to be made quickly about changes in strategy or tactics. Response can be analysed within hours to show, for example, which time slots in which television regions are performing best in terms of volumes and how well callers match the profile of the target audience. Testing can be undertaken quickly and relatively inexpensively to identify the most effective campaign strategy within and across media. Rapid feedback in testing also helps to identify the resources required to fulfil the expected response when a campaign is rolled out.

Unlike coupons, which are dealt with away from the scrutiny of respondents, the manner in which telephone calls are handled directly influences callers' perceptions of the company and its products or services. The quality of call handling, as well as the execution of any follow-up, should create a positive image. The aim is to build a rapport which adds value to the relationship. Response handling is not an isolated incident but part of an ongoing process of communication designed to increase the value to the company of each caller. The company's reputation depends on it.

16
Customer service

With less and less to distinguish between different suppliers' products and services, the battle for competitive advantage is being fought on the service front. Service relates to how a company meets the needs and expectations of the people with whom it deals in the process of carrying on its business. There is a service element in almost everything that a company does, whether it is dealing with customers and prospects, intermediaries in the supply chain, suppliers, shareholders, the press, its own staff, or anyone else whose impressions of the company are significant. The ultimate aim of service delivery is to improve 'satisfaction' with the company and its products or services. It does that by meeting individuals' needs and expectations quickly and efficiently at every viable opportunity. This chapter looks at service from the perspective of the supply of goods or services, but the same principles apply, and the same techniques can be used, in servicing any significant audience.

16.1 What does service mean?

Basically, service encompasses offering products and services designed to meet the market's needs, the process of promoting and selling them, and ensuring that they perform as required. This covers all the activities described elsewhere in this book, including such things as market research and crisis management. In order to distinguish themselves from the competition, companies now look for ways of adding value by delivering a better service than an individual could reasonably expect from the nature of the relationship. The majority of value-added service is delivered by improving the way in which the basic service is provided – i.e. meeting needs more quickly and efficiently – although this may include new initiatives. Providing pricing information and details of special offers, for example, are routine activities, but the information may be made more accessible by setting up a toll-free recorded information line.

Helplines and carelines can play an important role in delivering service, particularly for certain products. Nicotinell TTS patches, marketed in the UK by Zyma Healthcare, are designed to help people give up smoking. The patches are supplied with printed support materials giving practical guidelines on how to 'kick the habit'. A pocket-sized emergency help card lists five things the smoker can do, in times of desperation, instead of reaching for a cigarette. The fifth and final option suggested is to phone the 'smokefree helpline' which offers practical advice, in the form of recorded information, together with the telephone number of a professional counsellor who can offer one-to-one support. Marion Merrell Dow, in the UK, offers a branded pollen line for its Seldane hayfever treatment. The country is divided into eight regions and each is assigned a different premium rate number which hayfever sufferers can dial to listen to the daily pollen count in their region. Innovative products are obvious candidates for user support. The Boots Company, the UK high street pharmaceutical retailer, offers a helpline to users of its blood cholesterol measurement kit. The use of helplines in the UK in association with pharmaceutical products is tightly controlled by Medicines Act legislation and the Medicines Control Agency (MCA). The MCA guidelines, for example, state that 'Any proposed "helplines" should be educational and must **not** be promotional'. Approval is now required for any recorded messages.

Service can be enhanced in many ways, whether it is through the products offered, or in the way that they are promoted, or in the conduct of the sale, or through after-sales support. Some of the opportunities for delivering service by telephone are listed in Table 16.1.

The boundaries between basic and value-added service are continually shifting. The expectations of the market are continually rising and what once represented added value becomes the basic service expected of any company. Toll-free order hotlines, for example, once represented added value and are now commonplace. The same is true of the boundary between value-added service and customer care activity. Welcome calls to new customers, for example, while still not common, will probably become almost routine in some markets and therefore expected. Many customer care activities are part of the same gradient. So it is important to remember that there are no finite goals in service delivery; it is a continuous process of trying to meet new needs and exceed current market expectations.

The measurement of service delivery by telephone has become increasingly important for the monitoring and improvement of call centre performance. Sophisticated methods have been developed which go far beyond the use of simple statistics such as time to answer and abandoned call rates. One example is BT's Telephone-Based Customer Satisfaction Measurement tool examined in Appendix 1 (page 269). Such methods, although currently used by only a tiny proportion of companies, are all the more important because a recent study in the UK by the Henley Centre (Appendix 2, page 272) suggests that the poor quality of telephone service

Table 16.1 Opportunities for service delivery by telephone

Service delivery points

Providing product/service information (e.g. product specifications, pricing, stock availability, outlets, booking information)

Appointment making/arranging demonstrations

Sales/sales promotion

Credit approvals/cash collection

Order hotlines

Customer account servicing

Transaction queries, e.g. delivery, invoice

Complaint handling

Helplines and service requests

Crisis management

Impacting on service image

Carelines

Welcome calls and courtesy calls

Ancillary information services

Post-crisis comfort calls

Invitations to events

Customer satisfaction surveys

Product/service improvement surveys

New product/service testing

---

offered by many businesses is inhibiting growth in the use of the telephone for 'telebusiness'.

Delivering good service goes beyond showing respect and courtesy. It requires a prompt, accurate and helpful response. It requires a company to make itself easily accessible and welcoming to people who want to make contact. Above all, it requires skilful matching of individuals' needs and expectations with the company's resources available to meet them.

16.2 Bottom line impact

The concept of service is difficult to conceive in its entirety, particularly on a company-wide level. It means different things to different people and to different types of business. However, its importance to the success of a business is far less intangible. Service levels affect the bottom line. Research has shown that a reduction in service levels reduces customer spend. One study found that customers would reduce their buying by over 20 per cent if there was a fall of only 5 per cent in service standards. The converse, that delivering better service improves business results, is also true.

Case study 16.1

Adopting a customer service philosophy, implemented mainly through telemarketing, enabled Dental Linkline to expand profitably into a new market and possibly saved the company from oblivion. In 1984/85 turnover was static, at less than £1m, and the family-owned business was losing money. It is now a leading supplier to dental practices throughout the UK and continues to expand.

Based at Leigh, in the northwest of England, Dental Linkline originally specialized in supplying precious metals and amalgam alloys for dental fillings and bridges. This small, highly competitive market accounted for 90 per cent of sales, with general surgery supplies contributing only 10 per cent. The company had built a good reputation and a strong customer base of around 1500 dental practices, but there was obvious room for expansion. The UK dental market comprises some 10 400 surgeries. Market analysis had confirmed the opportunities to expand this side of the business, but it would mean educating the market in a different style of trading. The market for dental sundries had been serviced mostly by salespeople working from local depots. Customers were accustomed to personal visits from local suppliers. To win market share, Dental Linkline had to become a national supplier offering the full range of surgery requirements. Escalating costs meant that a national salesforce was not viable. So the company would have to persuade dentists that there was another, better way of buying. At the same time, the large investment required to expand their product range meant that a fast return was essential. Only one marketing approach met both objectives.

In late 1985 Dental Linkline launched a telephone sales department, offering dentists a toll-free number to call for advice on products, check delivery times and place orders. Marketing consultants were commissioned to completely overhaul the company image and presentation. The toll-free number was placed prominently on all trading materials, including a new full supply catalogue. With the aid of a government grant, a programme of telephone marketing and sales training was implemented. Direct mail informed dentists of the new service, the full range of supplies, and the company's philosophy – to provide an unmatched level of service only a (free) phone call away. Surgery sales almost doubled in the first full year, with a further 128 per cent growth the following year.

Since then, the service has been developed continuously. Specialist management and telesales appointments have been made through a combination of head hunting and advertising to dental surgeries. Between 1985 and 1992, staff numbers were increased from 6 to 26, including three telephone account managers and eight staff handling calls.

Customers use a single toll-free number for product and price enquiries, stock availability, orders, account queries, technical support, and to discuss problems or complaints. The number also provides access to a general dental information service (see page 198). Goods supplied cover a range of 5000 leading and own-brand stock items, plus any of 20 000 items to special order. Telephone staff are trained to establish precisely what customers require, even if they do not have the exact technical name. Catalogue numbers, used for order processing, are not requested.

The company aims to function as the dentists' stock cupboard, delivering within

24 hours. Immediate access and the opportunity for regular contact outweighs the disadvantages of customers not meeting their supplier face-to-face. To establish relationships on a personal level, telephone staff send out business cards bearing their photograph.

While the telephone forms the backbone of the sales operation, the overall service strategy includes:

- A comprehensive catalogue with competitive prices.
- Immediate free telephone advice on prices, promotions, bulk orders and special requirements.
- No minimum order charges; no delivery charges.
- Same day despatch of stock orders received by 3.00 p.m.; 24-hour delivery by carrier.
- Urgent requirements given priority; special delivery arrangements can be made.
- Invoices sent with goods; prepaid envelopes supplied for account payments.
- All account queries by toll-free number.
- Regular account payment terms; credit card payment accepted with order.
- Goods may be returned for credit within three months; faulty products are replaced immediately, with no time limit.
- A customer loyalty scheme, offering an annual rebate at specified spending limits.
- Access to information of general and professional interest.

Regular direct mail campaigns, planned with the help of the customer database, are used for prospecting and promotions. Several thousand catalogues are printed and distributed every six months. Sales of advertising space, introduced in 1988, now recoup the major part of catalogue production and distribution costs.

Almost 1000 calls a week are received on the toll-free number, and 90 per cent of them are orders. These calls account for 99.6 per cent of all orders, with values varying from £1 to over £1000, yet the line and inbound call charges for 1992 amounted to little more than one-third the cost of keeping a salesperson on the road. An additional toll-free number, for faxed orders, was introduced in February 1993.

Business growth proves the effectiveness of the strategy. Turnover in the target market grew by an average of over 49 per cent per annum between 1986 and 1993. Profitability has risen steadily over the same period. Turnover remained steady even during the depths of the recession, when some competitors ceased trading and others reported a significant reduction in business. Dental Linkline's value added service has enabled it to ward off competition even from companies offering cut-price product ranges.

Over a two-year period the company expects to deal with over 4500 of the 10 400 UK dental practices, compared with less than 2000 in 1986. The number of active customers is growing steadily, as is their average annual spend. Market penetration has been achieved at a time when dentists have become increasingly price conscious, with margins being eroded under the National Health Service.

As a business solution, telemarketing offered Dental Linkline relatively low investment, flexibility and ease of expansion. In the circumstances, no other marketing approach could cost-effectively have created this added-value market positioning and such rapid market penetration.

16.3 Priority – meeting customer needs and expectations

While delivering good service improves business performance, it is not an end in itself. It is a by-product of normal business communications or 'transactions'. The closer a company can get to its markets the easier it will be to identify needs and match them with the appropriate company resources. The telephone is becoming a central feature in service strategies because it facilitates this process. All of the positive qualities of telephone communication come into play.

- It is personal and interactive, enabling the needs of individuals to be addressed directly.
- It is fast, with no geographical or time barriers, enabling the company to respond much more quickly.
- It enables centralization, facilitating the control of the 'matching' process and delivering cost savings.
- It is flexible and can be used in a wide variety of situations.
- It enables a company to make itself accessible.

There are two components to consider in the matching of needs and resources: the infrastructure supporting the business transactions, such as the communications media and strategies used, and the actual exchanges that occur during transactions. The infrastructure includes everything that helps to bring together, for the transaction, information about individuals' needs and knowledge of the company's resources that can meet them. The telephone, backed by appropriate information resources, is a highly significant part of this infrastructure in modern businesses. The transaction relies upon the skilled matching of needs and resources, and in the case of the telephone this depends upon human skills in most cases.

The human element is generally the weakest link in service delivery by telephone. Since it is a personal medium, the quality of telephone staff is the single most important factor in delivering good service. (This applies to all people who use the telephone within an organization, but especially to those who use it routinely to talk with 'influential' audiences.) Even being civil, when under pressure, does not come easily to some people. The importance of rigorous selection criteria and thorough, as well as ongoing, training cannot be underestimated. Delivering first-rate service throughout each and every call is extremely demanding. In addition, specialist skills will be required for different applications and to use information resources and other operational systems. Some evaluation criteria for the handling of inbound calls, summarized in Table 16.2, highlight the demands made on telephone staff. Fortunately, there are many ways in which a company can support telephone staff, mainly through the use of technology. Computerization of telemarketing operations can deliver huge benefits in productivity and service. Some of the main benefits have been described in Chapter 4.

Table 16.2 General evaluation criteria for the servicing of inbound calls

- *Ease of contact.* Is the appropriate telephone number easily available to all who want to call? Is the cost of the call reasonable? What proportion of callers receive an engaged tone?
- *Time to answer.* On average, how long do callers have to wait for an answer? Are they paying for this privilege? While waiting, is the time used constructively, e.g. providing useful recorded information? Are they told how many people are ahead of them in the queue?
- *Welcoming statement.* How is the greeting perceived, in terms of appropriateness of tone and message, by the full range of callers? How often do operators fail to recognize callers well known to them?
- *Listening.* Do operators actively listen to callers and accurately perceive their needs? Do operators allow sufficient time for callers to explain?
- *Needs evaluation.* How efficiently do operators identify precisely what callers require?
- *Interest shown.* Do operators reflect genuine interest in callers, their situation and meeting their needs?
- *Helpfulness.* How willingly do operators respond to callers' requests? And to their unspoken needs, e.g. offering information not requested but possibly of relevance or use?
- *Accuracy.* How accurate is the information or advice provided? How accurately are details of the transaction recorded? Can all promises made by operators be met realistically?
- *Ownership.* Do operators take responsibility for ensuring that callers' needs are met, either directly or by someone else more appropriate? If there is a delay in meeting their needs, are callers kept informed of progress with their enquiry?
- *Closing statement.* Do operators close calls in a positive way, such that the relationship and chances of further business are enhanced?
- *Professionalism.* Does operators' call handling reflect the best values of the company? Overall, is it professional and positive?
- *Caller satisfaction.* What is the perceived and actual level of caller satisfaction, e.g. do callers feel more positive about the company as a direct result of their calls?

Evidence from the Henley Centre study (Appendix 2, page 272) shows that UK companies generally have much room for improvement in delivering telephone-based service. Their report, *Teleculture 2000*, suggests that companies are failing to meet consumers' needs and expectations for a variety of reasons, including a lack of understanding of those needs and a failure to invest in the organization and technology required to meet them. More disturbing is the finding that a majority of people experiencing a badly handled call would prefer not to do business with that company again (page 276).

16.4 A role for technology

Knowledge of individuals' needs is a basic requirement in delivering good service. Where no prior knowledge exists, such as a prospect calling the company to request product or price information, it is the operator's job to identify precisely what those needs are. In many situations, however, there will be at least some information available. With outbound calling to prospects, for example, various profiling techniques can be used to segment the prospects so that telemarketers can deliver different messages appropriate to each group. Operators who speak to customers or known prospects on outbound or inbound calls, should be provided with direct access to their database records, or relevant information from them, to ensure that they can talk at a 'personal' level to tailor the call appropriately. Because new data can be entered instantly during a conversation, everyone with access to the database immediately has available the most up-to-date information on every known individual – which also helps them to deliver better service. Coca-Cola & Schweppes Beverages (page 96) provides a good example of how a database helps to deliver excellent service at the same time as achieving the main business objectives of the calling activity. The full significance of computerization will become apparent later in this chapter.

Data communications over public or private networks can link all of a company's sites and departments so that information resources, wherever located, are accessible instantly when required. The ability to link geographically remote sites for voice and data communications is especially important for some companies. Mail order firms, for example, may have several warehouses and many distribution points to help deliver goods quickly across a large area. Dial-up or dedicated data links enable orders to be transmitted instantaneously to the relevant warehouse where a picking list, delivery note and billing advice are printed. Where a company has different service functions located at different sites, or has a central service operation which sometimes has to call on expertise located elsewhere, the ability to transfer calls 'seamlessly' can improve service significantly. Any relevant computer files can also be transferred with the call. However, an area of more fundamental importance is the routeing of inbound calls to people in a company able to meet callers' needs.

Call routeing and distribution

People are beginning to expect easy access and rapid response. Some aspects of accessibility, and issues in managing inbound calls, were examined in

Chapter 15. Telecommunications network operators offer increasingly sophisticated services to help route calls so that differing needs can be met quickly and efficiently (see page 31).

Call diversion (page 33) provides the facility for 'overflow' calls to be diverted to another answering site, automatically, when all operators are busy at one site, or all calls can be diverted at predetermined times. The Calling Line Identity service (page 32) can be used to identify the caller's number. This allows a database to be searched to retrieve the customer's record, which can then be delivered to the operator's screen as the call is connected. The charitable organization World Vision U.S. uses this facility (see page 256).

When a call reaches a particular company site, automatic call distribution is essential for handling large volumes of inbound traffic. Automatic call distributors (ACDs) offer a variety of features to improve efficiency and therefore service. If a company has different operators dealing with different types of call, then DDI is a very useful feature (see page 32). This enables a telephone system to recognize the number dialled and route the call accordingly. Examples of the use of DDI can be found on page 101 (a London cab firm) and page 111 (Holiday Inn). Additional technology helps to coordinate the delivery of appropriate information to the operators' screens as calls are connected. National Westminster Bank uses this in combination with DDI to help deal with calls to its information technology helpdesk (page 143).

The installation of an ACD can have a remarkable effect on service levels. When the UK electricity company NORWEB installed Aspect CallCenters, for example, the average time to answer was reduced to 7 seconds, call abandon rates dropped to less than 3 per cent, and the number of calls handled per agent rose by at least 25 per cent. These figures reflect a much more efficient handling of calls and corresponding improvement in service delivered to customers.

Statistical data available from ACDs about call traffic and call-handling efficiency (see page 35) is invaluable for supervision and management of inbound telemarketing activity. A supervisor can see instantly how efficiently calls are being handled across different applications, and by different operators, and dynamically alter the number of workstations assigned to a particular application. The data also helps to identify individual and group training needs, or the requirement for additional briefing. Historic reporting provides management information such as average call length, average wait time, and call traffic over time showing any peaks and troughs. This data helps to plan staffing levels, schedule work and identify trends and influences on call volumes. For companies without the necessary technology, some network operators can now provide comprehensive inbound call statistics, even in real-time (see page 34).

Statistical data is also available on outbound calling when it is computerized. Even more advanced information is available when predictive dialling systems are used, and additional control technology, such as a Smart Management Centre (see page 114), can provide a remarkable insight into calling activity.

Historic data on call traffic helps to predict probable fluctuations in call volumes, thus enabling the appropriate number of staff to be put in place to help maintain service levels. However, unexpected influences on call volumes cannot be accommodated by staff scheduling. Unexpectedly hot weather, for example, can cause a surge in orders for such products as soft drinks and ice cream. Different types of automated call handling can help, e.g. the voice messaging and automated ordering described earlier. For businesses that require extra call-handling capacity only during seasonal increases in call traffic, technology provides another solution.

Case study 16.2

In March 1992, Aspect Telecommunications Corporation of San José, California, launched an enhancement of its CallCenter ACD, the Remote StaffCenter ACD. One of the first users was La Quinta Motor Inns Inc., a national USA hotel chain based in San Antonio. La Quinta has used the Remote StaffCenter to transform a classroom on the campus of the local Incarnate Word High School into a remote hotel reservations centre. Established in spring 1992, the centre has enabled the company to increase its capacity for handling reservations traffic without expanding its headquarters facility. The remote centre is equipped with 25 PCs and workstations, air conditioning, a power supply and security system, the Remote StaffCenter and a dedicated high-capacity telephone link with the Aspect CallCenter and Remote StaffCenter Controller at La Quinta's corporate headquarters. Students on the campus use the PCs to learn word processing during school hours and become part-time reservations staff after school and at weekends.

Incoming calls are automatically delivered to the first available agent at either location. Students at Incarnate Word handle calls and book hotel room reservations as if they were based in the main reservations centre, with voice and reservation data being transmitted between the two sites over the high-capacity telephone link. The classroom is equipped with the PCs to handle the data and Aspect Telesets to handle the telephone call. The PCs offer no hard disk. The School uses its Local Area Network (LAN) when using them for instruction. When the classroom operates as a reservations centre, La Quinta installs its disk to connect to the LAN at its corporate headquarters.

La Quinta handles over 3 million reservation calls a year and 30 per cent of calls received during the summer are handled at the remote centre. About 45 students are employed during the school year, the majority from Incarnate College and the remainder from the High School, rising to around 75 in the busy summer months. Students handle calls from 3.00 p.m. to midnight during the academic year, and from 6.00 a.m. to 2.00 a.m. during the summer.

The remote facility cost about $150 000 to install, but it has saved La Quinta having to enlarge its headquarters facility and given the company access to a flexible work force, which is particularly important in dealing cost-effectively with the peak summer call traffic. Training time is reduced because students are already computer literate. At the same time, the reservations centre has provided welcome employment opportunities for the students and Incarnate Word has gained a facility for word-processing instruction.

Interactive voice response

Interactive voice response facilities are invaluable for very busy call centres, helping to improve the speed and even the quality of response to calls. A basic function is the ability to play a digitally recorded message as calls are received. This can be played to all callers, selected callers (only on specified DDI numbers), or only those calls which cannot be answered immediately. The message can be used to advise callers of the number of people already waiting in the queue, as well as to give information, such as new product lines or special offers, to give callers some value while they are waiting for an answer, or to invite them to leave a voice message after they have been waiting a predetermined time.

Voice messaging has several uses. Callers can be invited to leave their names and numbers so that an operator can return their calls later; these messages are passed automatically to operators when they are less busy. Callers can also be given the option to request brochures, leaving their names and address details, or to place orders.

The interactive element of voice response facilities is perhaps the most useful. Some ACDs can recognize and respond to tones from DTMF phones, enabling callers to select different services or give instructions. Holland's leading book and record club, ECI, uses this facility to enable members to place their orders automatically without speaking to an operator (see page 110).

Many service functions involve routine (though not necessarily standard) activities that employ expensive human resources whose expertise could be used more efficiently servicing customers who merit personal attention, or performing more complex tasks. An increasing number of private and public organizations are using IVR technology to stabilize costs while providing enhanced levels of service.

A wide range of service functions can be fully automated, and not only those which involve completely standard responses. The ability to link IVR systems to databases allows the automation of quite complex functions such as transaction processing (see National Westminster Bank on page 100, for example). The combination of the database and caller response recognition has enormous potential for providing services tailored to individuals' needs.

The USA leads in the application of IVR technology. Voice messaging is commonplace and sophisticated applications are widespread. The Internal Revenue Service, for example, uses IVR equipment to provide the nationwide TeleTax service, designed to answer tax filing questions and give taxpayers information on their refund status. Social security claimants can call the Social Security Administration's IVR service to listen to prerecorded help messages about their benefit status.

Implementation in Europe has been slow, although it has gained momentum since the early 1990s.

Case study 16.3

In the UK, the Royal Navy Supply and Transport Services (RNSTS) uses a Periphonics system for handling stock enquiries and orders. The service, known as OSWALD (On-line System for Worldwide Access to Logistics Data), can be accessed by the entire Fleet (ships and submarines) and all Naval Bases via the Ministry of Defence telephone network or the public network.

OSWALD gives entitled personnel 24-hour direct access to the central computer of RNSTS stores by simply dialling a telephone number and PIN, using a DTMF phone. Up-to-date information can be retrieved from all the RNSTS store depots located throughout the UK and abroad. Callers are prompted to enter their ID number and to select the service they require. When checking stock availability, the caller enters the NATO stock number and quantity required and the system responds with the precise location of the items sought. If orders are required they can then be placed automatically with the appropriate depot.

As the Royal Navy operates worldwide, with store depots located internationally, easy access to information held centrally is vital. OSWALD answers stock availability enquiries immediately, around-the-clock, and enables orders to be placed automatically from anywhere in the world. Ships' supply staff can thus react more quickly to maintain a high level of operational readiness. Overall, RNSTS customers have been given a better service, over extended hours, without increasing staffing resources.

Case study 16.4

Wisconsin Electric Power Company (WEPCO) in Milwaukee, USA, makes wide use of technology to ensure that customers' calls are handled in the most efficient way. The Milwaukee call centre handles calls between 7.30 a.m. and 9.00 p.m. Monday to Friday and from 8.00 a.m. until midday on Saturday. Outside of these hours calls are routed automatically to one of three control centres using AT&T time-of-day routeing for WATS calls (over lines charged at a flat fee irrespective of volume and call distance) and a switching system from Ameritech for local calls. Callers to the

Milwaukee centre are offered a number of services. WEPCO uses an Aspect Application Bridge intelligently to link its Aspect CallCenter ACD to a CCS voice response unit (VRU) that accesses the company's customer database held on an Amdahl host computer. Customers can use their DTMF phone to select, from a menu, the operator group or service they require, or can leave a voice message, or can access their account on the computer. When WEPCO's representatives are unable to read meters, they leave cards asking customers to read their own meter and call a toll-free number to report the information. Guided by the VRU, the customers can enter their meter readings directly into their accounts using a DTMF phone. WEPCO also uses the VRU for message broadcasting. During a power outage in 1992, for example, there was a huge surge of calls, many of which could be answered quickly and efficiently by appropriate information relayed to callers by the VRU.

Expert assistance

Some of the ways in which computer software can support operators in meeting individuals' needs were described in Chapter 4 (page 37). Computerized scripts, for example, can hold a vast amount of information which can be structured so that it is easy to navigate and find the information relevant to answering a particular enquiry. In some situations, however, the amount of information that may be required to answer any one enquiry is so vast, or so complex, that computerized scripting is not enough. It requires expert knowledge. Computerized knowledge-based (or 'expert') systems can provide a solution, enabling non-specialist telephone staff to deliver accurate information and advice. National Westminster Bank uses one to help resolve problems reported to its information technology helpdesk (page 143). Telephone sales staff at a UK engineering company use an expert system to identify which products, from among the many thousands it supplies, match the technical specifications given by customers. Another user is ICL.

Case study 16.5

European computer company ICL, owned by the Japanese firm Fujitsu, has a large UK customer base built up over many years. The Customer Service (CS) division, which provides on-site repair services for the installed base of over 270 000 systems, comprising many different types of computers and peripherals, bases its maintenance strategy on teleservice. A key element in this strategy is LOCATOR, a computerized knowledge-based system which aids telephone fault diagnosis.

A team of fault diagnosticians take in excess of 900 calls a day from customers reporting hardware 'faults'. Using LOCATOR, they aim to elicit from customers the answers to key questions in order to identify the true nature of the fault. This results in a very high probability (over 98 per cent) of either clearing the problem without making a site visit, or sending an appropriate service engineer with the correct part to clear the fault first time.

LOCATOR is designed to help diagnosticians navigate quickly and easily through the vast amount of information on products, faults and their probable causes, and produce an accurate fault diagnosis. LOCATOR presents a series of screens, each with a question to ask the customer and a list of possible replies. The diagnostician works through successive screens of options until LOCATOR identifies the most probable fault and suggests a recovery action. This may be action the customer can take to resolve the problem, or the need for a site visit by an ICL Service Representative. Faults which require a service visit are automatically transferred into another system for action.

The system includes various features which provide added value. LOCATOR can 'park' partially completed diagnoses and resume them at any time. If a customer needs to check or find information, for example, or perhaps try a certain recovery action, the transaction can be resumed in a subsequent call without having to repeat all the questions and answers. The diagnostician can also navigate backwards through questions, so customers who change their minds about earlier answers do not have to go back to the beginning. LOCATOR also records the trail of questions and answers, which can be analysed later. This means, for example, that the Customer Service division can identify common problems, perhaps arising from lack of user understanding or product misuse, and take appropriate preventive measures.

Prior to the installation of LOCATOR, diagnosticians relied upon shelves of manuals, plus their own expertise, and were correctly diagnosing around 68 per cent of faults. After installation, correct diagnoses rose steadily, as diagnosticians became more practised in using LOCATOR, to around 98 per cent. Customers benefit through reduced response times for fault repair. Nearly all problems can now be resolved either during the telephone call or on the first site visit. At the same time, ICL has made savings in engineers' time, spares utilization is improved, and skill levels required for first-line service have been reduced. Overall, it is helping ICL to achieve one of its key business objectives – maintaining a high-quality but cost-efficient fault repair service.

Answering enquiries about deliveries of goods is an important service function for many businesses. Tracking goods *en route*, when they are not delivered direct, requires special arrangements. If goods pass through multiple distribution points, changing vehicles and sometimes modes of transport, each parcel has to be tracked through each node in its distribution path.

Barcoding of parcels is a common solution. The barcodes, corresponding to parcel numbers, are read at each stage in the journey. This data is fed into a central computer which registers the parcel, via its barcode, at a specific location at a particular time. Customer service agents can access this information, using the parcel number, to identify the location of any parcel in the distribution network. Some freight carriers in the USA use interactive voice response systems to answer delivery status enquiries. The customer dials the service and inputs the parcel number using a DTMF phone. The system then interrogates the host computer and voices the status of the parcel back to the caller.

Proof of delivery (POD) requests are not uncommon for business freight, where any one of many people could have received and signed for a parcel.

Case study 16.6

Securicor receives as many as 10 000 POD and delivery status enquiries a week. Second only to the Post Office in the UK for parcel deliveries, the company handles up to 300 000 parcels a day through its 120 branch offices.

In 1992, Securicor consulted Datapoint UK, specialists in call centre design and networking information technology, to advise on streamlining POD and other telephone-based service enquiries. The result was two dedicated Customer Service Centres, where a Pyramid computer and an advanced optical storage system from Standard Platforms form part of the delivery tracking system. The Pyramid computer runs Datapoint's Edge telebusiness software, which provides service agents with instant access to Securicor's main parcels database held on an ICL mainframe computer.

At the end of each day, drivers hand in their barcoded manifests. Each of these holds barcodes torn from the parcels delivered, together with the signatures of the recipients. The manifests are scanned into an imaging computer each night and the data transmitted to the central optical storage system.

When customers enquire about delivery status, agents enter the parcel numbers and the Pyramid computer interrogates the mainframe to identify the manifests on which the parcels reside and their current delivery status. This information is displayed immediately on the agent's screen. If a customer asks for proof of delivery, the agent can retrieve a copy of the signed manifest, on screen, to identify the signatory. Some customers request a copy of the manifest, which Securicor service agents can now fax instantly from the workstation. Previously, answering POD enquiries could take days as it involved locating the original manifest and making a copy for the customer. Securicor now handles these enquiries in an average of only 200 seconds, during which time the agent has verbally confirmed the name of the parcel recipient and faxed a copy of the signed manifest to the customer.

Facsimile can be used in many ways to improve service. Written or graphical information can be sent quickly, either to help illustrate something under discussion or as part of the fulfilment process. It can provide hardcopy confirmation of what has been discussed, or in-depth information on something covered only in outline, as well as visual images that cannot be described easily. The whole process can be automated with dial-and-receive fax information services (see page 42).

16.5 Delivering internal service

Servicing internal 'customers' is an important focus for management, since it has an inevitable knock-on effect. Whether, as a result, staff are better informed, more confident, better satisfied with their job, better equipped, etc., improving internal services supports staff in serving external customers' needs. National Westminster Bank's IT ServiceLine (page 143) is a clear example.

Here again, IVR technology can help to improve service levels without escalating costs. In the area of employee communications, for example, there is a continuous need to disseminate information, ranging from company policies through recent developments and job opportunities to the latest productivity levels and business results. More than ever, employees need to be kept informed and involved.

As well as providing access to information at any time, from anywhere, and relieving staff from answering routine enquiries, an IVR system provides consistency of message. This addresses problems commonly experienced in employee communications. Information conveyed indirectly through a succession of mediators, for example, is liable to personal interpretation and possible distortion at each stage. Enquiries may be answered slightly differently by different people. Lack of information can also cause problems, giving rise to rumour which is often inaccurate.

IVR services are very flexible and can offer call diversion at any time to a relevant staff member, dependent on the service being accessed. Fax-back facilities can be offered for callers to order an immediate hard copy of information on their local fax machine. Voice messaging allows callers to request printed materials or specific additional information, or to request a meeting, or give feedback on specific issues. Local information could be provided using departmental numbers as the identifier. Individual callers can be identified, from their works numbers and reference to an employee database, and referred to by name. Any information can be made available to all employees or to select groups. An example application is illustrated in Figure 16.1. Management reporting on system usage provides an insight into the information needs of employees and may help to identify specific areas where communications could be improved. Identifying the source of calls gives an insight into local information requirements.

Even simple initiatives using the telephone can enhance internal service levels. One UK-based international haulage company, for example, which delivers goods throughout Europe, provides its drivers with international toll-free numbers to contact base easily from wherever they are located at the time. Drivers can call direct to the UK free or, at most, for the cost of a local call (depending on the country's international 'toll-free' arrangements). Drivers are asked to call base periodically to obtain details of their next job

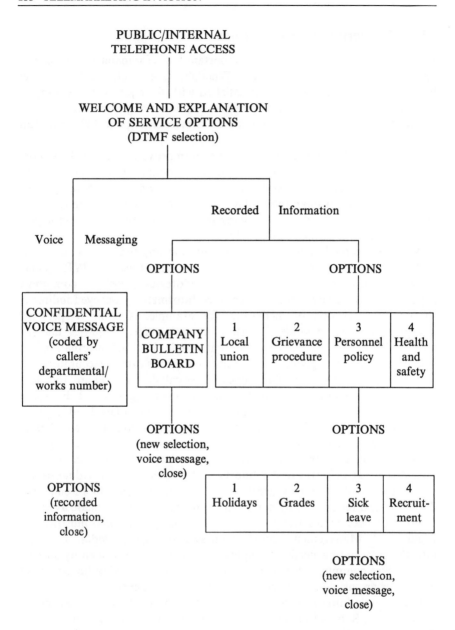

Figure 16.1 Example IVR application in employee communications. (Courtesy of *Cal*com Associates)

or to receive instructions for collecting return loads. When urgent jobs are received the relevant drivers can be alerted quickly to the necessary changes in their schedules. All this improves service to customers and is more convenient for drivers, who can call the UK direct at any time, from any convenient telephone, without the need for large amounts of change in local currency.

The telephone has been poorly used generally as a channel for delivering service inside organizations, perhaps because it is such a routine method of communication that the need for planning and formal systems and procedures are overlooked. In major applications it should be treated like any other customer service activity, with defined service targets and management controls. Seen from this perspective, the opportunities to improve service levels to internal customers are wide-ranging.

16.6 Central operations, local service

In striving to deliver better levels of service, many companies have set up central service operations either to replace the service function at local sites or to support them by handling the bulk of enquiries or enquiries of specific types. Centralization offers many benefits. It provides a clear access point for customers and, because the operation is dedicated to service, with no operational distractions, the company can ensure that their needs are met quickly and efficiently. It avoids the problems associated with providing service locally, such as staff being busy dealing with clients, or at lunch, or the single phone line being permanently engaged. Response is faster and more consistent. There are also cost savings because of efficiencies of scale. Staffing requirements are reduced and better information management resources can be provided to help meet customers' needs efficiently. Staff can also be more highly trained, with different operator groups dedicated to specific functions. The service function can be managed more efficiently, both in terms of meeting changing needs (because they can be monitored more closely) and ensuring that resources are deployed in the most cost-efficient way.

Centralization has also been given impetus by companies seeking to streamline through organizational re-engineering or process innovation, i.e. reorganizing the work effort to add value and to speed processes. One aspect of this is the replacement of dedicated work groups with multi-disciplinary teams that can react quickly with responses tailored to differing market needs. This ties in well with the idea of centralizing service functions, where multi-skilled personnel can deal with a wide variety of enquiries. Establishing voice and data links to create a national or international communications network is essential to support this type of operation. It enables a single centre to become the hub of customer-led operations, with direct links to all company resources that may be required to service customer needs.

Case study 16.7

Thames Water went live with its new Customer Centre in July 1993. The £30 million development, originally planned for completion in 1996, provides a single entry point to the company for all enquiries. As one of the world's largest utilities, Thames Water serves approximately 11 million people who previously were confronted by a bewildering array of telephone numbers, depending on the district they lived in, the subject of their enquiry, and the time of day. Customers often spent a long time tracking down the right person to deal with their enquiry and the response they received could vary according to who answered.

The company made a strategic decision, in the late 1980s, to establish a 'one-stop shop'. Customers would be able to call a single telephone number and talk to Customer Agents who would either resolve their enquiry there and then, or assume total responsibility for following the enquiry through with complete confidence on both sides that the necessary action would be taken. A major consideration in this decision was the increased visibility of the water companies, and higher expectations of their customers, as a result of their privatization in 1989. Thames Water predicted that this would result in more people wanting to contact the company. In fact, this proved correct. The company's call traffic in the early 1990s was increasing by approximately 25–35 per cent a year. Dealing effectively with this rapid growth was a key reason for the early completion of the project, achieved by buying-in systems rather than the slower process of in-house development.

Major new computer and telecommunications systems would be required to handle the growing volume of call traffic and, in particular, to ensure that 'local' service, relying upon local knowledge, could be delivered from a central point. The Customer Centre would require powerful information systems to replace local knowledge and instantaneous communications links with over 60 different sites around the Thames area. Thames Water conducted a worldwide search for the best system. Andersen Consulting had developed an advanced Customer Information System (CIS) for Baltimore Gas & Electric, in the USA, and Thames Water chose this as the basis for its new operation. The £30 million investment covered the cost of a new IBM mainframe computer, a GPT automatic call distributor, new software and telecommunications systems, training for up to 1000 staff, the project team and three years of operating costs (due to early completion).

Centralization of call handling was staged. Until the new Customer Centre building was completed, calls were channelled progressively into two other sites in Swindon. The first step was to bring together over 20 local revenue offices, which was completed in 1989. Next came calls on operational matters, which were brought together gradually, by region and by operational area (supply, sewerage and water quality), between November 1990 and May 1992. Thames Water's 24-hour emergency service was transferred in September 1991.

In parallel with these changes, the CIS was being developed. This would replace the existing billing system and link into Thames Water's work management system. Call handling was brought together in the new building early in 1993, ready for the launch of the Customer Centre with its new systems in July 1993.

From March 1993, Thames Water offered customers in any area just two contact numbers, both local call charge: one for billing or account enquiries and one for all other enquiries. Two sets of numbers were used at first, one for customers in London and one for those outside London, because most of Thames Water's customers are located in London while the Customer Centre is located in Swindon, well outside the local call charge area. Since the company has an extensive private telephone network, it made sense to route calls made in London over this system rather than pay the telephone service provider an additional levy for calls on a special local call charge number. So customers in London used two standard (local) numbers, thus saving the company hundreds of thousands of pounds a year in additional call costs. In June 1994, however, Thames Water started using the same two numbers for all customers. By switching to a competing telephone service provider, the company found it could save money by offering all customers the same two special local call charge numbers.

A key reason for not offering a single telephone number, as originally planned, was to improve call-handling efficiency. Using two numbers means that the basic type of call – billing or other enquiry – can be distinguished automatically by the ACD and routed to an appropriately skilled Customer Agent (CA). The alternative was either to transfer calls once answered, which was unacceptable from a service standpoint, or to have multi-skilled agents answering all calls. The latter option would require more investment in training and higher salaries and could present problems with recruitment.

Thames Water actually employs three types of CA: billing specialists, operational specialists and multi-skilled agents who can deal with calls on any topic and are therefore more highly paid. This arrangement provides operational flexibility. The company can predict basic trends in the types of calls it can expect in any one day, such as billing enquiries after bills have been sent out, or mains fractures after severely cold weather, and have appropriate CAs in place. If either the billing or operational CAs are over-stretched, calls can be routed automatically to multi-skilled agents.

The CIS combines bulk billing with advanced facilities for handling individual customer enquiries. It gives CAs access to a wide range of information. At its heart is a database, covering the company's 3.5 million customer accounts, which has three separate elements – details of the customer, the account, and the property. This separation is important. When customers move, for example, they retain their billing history but acquire a different property history, which may be relevant in responding to an enquiry.

When a customer contacts the centre, by phone or letter, any necessary action – which may range from adjusting a bill to repairing a mains burst – is entered onto the system. The need for action is then transferred automatically to the appropriate person. On receiving a billing enquiry call, CAs can access details of the customer's latest bill, past payment records, brief details of previous contact and any payment arrangements in force. If the enquiry cannot be resolved during the call, the CA enters a general action and it is delivered, via electronic mail, to back-office personnel. Within the CIS there is an electronic bulletin board on which is posted any information, from anywhere in the company, that may impact on enquiry handling. This can range from operational issues, such as work in progress, to new public awareness initiatives. Thames Water is working to ensure that all staff understand that something happening in their area of activity can generate, or impact on, customer enquiries and it is vital that this information is available to CAs.

For operational enquiries, such as reporting loss of water supply, CAs access the customer property record. Working from the property postcode, the bulletin board will display any known incident that might be affecting customers in that area and give an expected time for it to be resolved. If reported problems do not relate to known incidents, the CAs are specially trained to identify their exact nature. This is partly to ensure that they are the responsibility of Thames Water and are not, for example, a household plumbing problem. When it is the company's responsibility, the CA enters the details onto the system and the incident is logged automatically onto the work management system. This system automatically transmits the details to a computer screen at the relevant local depot to alert a local inspector or work gang. CAs can access the work management system at any time to check the current status of a job if a customer enquires. Each call is added to an incident record, automatically, so that management can obtain reports on the number and type of calls each incident has generated. To speed the notification of operational field personnel about newly reported incidents, Thames Water is supplying them with hand-held terminals which will instantly display new jobs. Field personnel will also use the terminals to notify the completion of work, thus updating the work management system immediately.

Thames Water is also adding a Geographic Information System (GIS) which will show CAs the location of a caller, and local incidents, on a map on screen during the call. One of the disadvantages of a centralized operation is that telephone agents lack detailed local knowledge and cannot relate directly to the caller's situation. With the GIS, the agents will appear to know the customer's street, the local shopping mall and all the other local details that help to inspire confidence, as well as helping to clarify the incident situation. The GIS was first used in Spring 1994 to help identify the location of water meters.

The CIS links into various other corporate systems such as metering, corporate ledger, debt recovery and word processing. When CAs are not on the telephone their time is utilized for simple items of correspondence that can be completed in less than 5 minutes, which is near the average call cycle of just over 4 minutes.

Thames Water has a policy of a maximum of one call transfer, when necessary. The majority of calls can be handled by the CAs, although there are certain areas in which the company is particularly cautious. One of these is water quality which, for obvious reasons, is given high priority. A higher proportion of these calls are therefore being passed to experts in the Operational Science Unit, at least until the company can evaluate the nature of the enquiries. During 1993, the company was examining ways of segmenting its customer base to enable CAs to develop specialist knowledge to help deliver better service. Commercial customers, for example, could be segmented by business type – breweries, dry cleaners, car washes – and domestic customers by geographic area.

The benefits of this centralized operation are wide-ranging. The Customer Centre is able to handle the growing volume of calls with fewer staff than were required previously. On an average day about 150 CAs are answering calls and the availability of far more information on-screen enables them to resolve most queries during the call, thereby reducing the amount of follow-up action required. Another benefit is the ability to manage staff more efficiently, hour by hour, through the use of the multi-skilled agents and the availability of comprehensive statistics on call traffic. Training is also more cost-effective and centralization permits some degree of specialization, enabling the company to build a more highly skilled team. More complete and comprehensive management reporting from the new system, supporting better qualified decision making, has far-reaching consequences. Not only does it help with management of the Customer Centre, but it also provides valuable insight into the manner in which customers respond to various influences, including media reports and the company's own actions.

The primary motivator in making this major investment was not simply the prospect of cost savings. It was the ability to handle the growing number of enquiries at a time when Thames Water was becoming more proactive in encouraging customers to make contact. However, the ability to resolve customer enquiries quickly and efficiently, whether they relate to billing or not, has a direct influence on how quickly people pay their bills. One of the major benefits for the company is therefore improved cashflow. This will be further enhanced when the Customer Centre moves into telephone collection and debt recovery.

The most significant benefit that derives from centralized service operations, generally, is the wealth of information available to management. With the constant flow of communications between the company and its markets, channelled through one point, management can keep its finger on the business pulse. It can track the multitude of processes, identifying interactions and correlations, locate blockages and know instantly how well the company is responding to market needs, overall and at local level. Most important of all, the company acquires an in-depth knowledge of its markets and is thus able to become more responsive to changing needs.

However, the relentless striving to deliver ever-better customer service is creating unprecedented levels of expectation in the marketplace. It is a vicious circle in which it becomes increasingly difficult for companies to differentiate themselves through their service. One solution is to step aside from the actual process of conducting business and look at the wider needs of customers and prospects. This is the realm of customer care which is examined in the next chapter.

17
Customer care

Consumers and businesses are becoming more discerning. Increasingly they are looking for something 'special'. With less and less to differentiate one product or service from another, that something special must come from the suppliers. Although many companies strive to set themselves apart by delivering better service, it is becoming increasingly difficult to offer something significantly better than the competition, particularly in such industries as computer manufacturing. Also, in some sectors, e.g. fast moving consumer goods, there is in any case limited scope for improving customer service. Another approach is to take a broader view and ask how people would like to be treated as individuals, beyond the supplier–customer relationship. This is the domain of customer care, which can be defined as any action taken to enhance a relationship, which is not associated directly with a business transaction. The focus is primarily on retaining customers, although care initiatives can help to win new customers directly and through word of mouth.

17.1 What does caring mean?

What constitutes customer care varies between markets. After the purchase of a heavy duty machine press, for example, the customer could rightly expect the supplier to make regular contact during the months immediately after installation to ensure that the customer is satisfied and requires no additional support. It is an expected part of the after-sales service. After purchasing a washing machine, however, a call from the supplier would probably be viewed in a different light. The customer is more likely to think, 'These are nice people, fancy taking the trouble to ask if everything was OK. I should have asked if they supply beds.' The difference is clear. One customer expects the contact, the other does not and sees it as a 'caring' action. The demarcation between service and customer care is ultimately determined by what is commonplace in a particular market at the time.

Customer care is as much about attitude as it is about specific initiatives. A telephone enquiry to one company might elicit the response, 'No, sorry, that's not what we do.' That person calls another company and is told: 'No we're not involved in that area, but I think you'll find that Bloggs Cumbernauld in the High Street can help you.' The company does not know whether the caller might want to buy something from them at a later date, but the helpful response certainly registered and, either directly or through word of mouth, it could lead to a sale.

Case study 17.1

A striking example of customer care is an incident that occurred while telemarketing agency Brann Contact 24 was providing a service for Shell UK. The Shell Homeline 24 enables consumers to order domestic heating oil, servicing or emergency help by telephone 24 hours a day. In the winter of 1990, just before midnight on a Saturday evening, one of Brann Contact 24's operators answered a call on the Shell number from a Mrs Bamsey. That particular night the temperature was several degrees below zero and the lines were all busy with requests for emergency service. Mrs Bamsey, however, was a special case. Her boiler had stopped working and she was alone except for a small baby. She was in her mid-80s, and her son-in-law, due to collect the child some hours before, was stuck in a snowdrift miles away. The operator quickly recognized the seriousness of the situation: there was no other heating in the house and the neighbours were away on holiday. Using an emergency call-out directory, the operator soon got in touch with an engineer who was on call. But, like many others that night, he was snowed in. So she rang around until she found a non-emergency engineer, off call, further away, but on a road with better access. Then she contacted a colleague, another operator, who she knew was a nursing auxiliary, and called Mrs Bamsey back. She was able to give advice on caring for the baby there and then, and arranged to telephone every 30 minutes to check on the situation. In fact, the engineer was able to get to the house within the hour, and he had the boiler working again by 2 a.m. Neither Mrs Bamsey nor the baby was any the worse for the ordeal, but Mrs Bamsey had the comfort of knowing that, while she was waiting for the engineer, she could expect to receive a call every half an hour from someone who obviously 'cared'.

The whole purpose of customer care is to set an organization apart. Dictionaries define 'care' as: concern for, serious attention, heed, protection, to be solicitous, have thought or regard, to have a fondness or affection. This latter definition might seem inappropriate in a business setting, but it reflects the true ambition of customer care activities – to have people know, through words and actions, that they are important and that the company cares about them.

Apart from face-to-face contact, the telephone is the only way to convey the full spectrum of emotions that caring embodies. Caring requires the personal touch; not at every contact, but at the very least occasionally.

While customer care is very much about attitude, it needs to be planned as a programme of communications. Within this programme will be training specifically designed for people who have telephone contact with influential audiences, so that the caring attitude is reflected in every conversation. There is a fine line between being truly caring and being cloying and sycophantic.

Beyond the contact opportunities that arise in the course of trading and other *ad hoc* enquiries, there are many ways to initiate telephone contact with the objective (perhaps mixed with others) of showing that the company cares. Mostly these are directed at customers, although some may be directed wholly or partly at prospects. Some of these opportunities are listed in Table 17.1. The telephone may be used alone or in combination with other media like mail and press advertising. Obviously it is important that customers are not inundated with requests for a friendly chat. The objectives in many of these activities can be incorporated into the routine of normal customer contact. However, where there is no regular contact, the company can cycle certain initiatives so that every customer is contacted perhaps twice a year (depending on the market) for one reason or another.

Each of the initiatives listed in Table 17.1 is immediately productive in addition to reflecting the company's caring approach. Post-crisis comfort calls, for example, may be made following a crisis which has affected key customers. These calls serve to show that the company is aware that the crisis affected them, that it caused them difficulties, and that the company still regrets the incident. But they also enable the company to measure the impact of the crisis and the effectiveness of its crisis management plans, especially when compared with data gathered through one of the routine satisfaction surveys conducted prior to the incident.

The types of caring initiative used, and the way in which they are used, will vary depending on the business sector and the type of relationship that exists with the customer. In many cases, such as invitations to events and satisfaction surveys, the customer base may need to be segmented to enable an appropriate approach to be made to different groups.

Table 17.1 Some opportunities including the telephone in customer care initiatives

Welcome calls and courtesy calls
Ancillary information services
Carelines
Post-crisis comfort calls
Invitations to events
Customer satisfaction surveys
Product/service improvement surveys
New product/service testing
Ad hoc initiatives, e.g. arranging spent product collection for recycling, informing
    customers of the impact of legislative changes

17.2   Invitations to events

Customers are sometimes neglected when it comes to selecting audiences for events such as seminars and roadshows. Even when the primary purpose of an event is to inform and educate prospects as a part of sales promotion, the presence of customers can facilitate this process. The customers may not be in the market to buy again, or not yet, but there is no better advertisement for the company and its products or services than a satisfied customer. The mere act of inviting customers to an event like this is likely to increase their satisfaction by showing that, even without the prospect of a sale, they are valued.

17.3   Welcome and courtesy calls

Gaining a new customer is a significant event and inevitably is the result of some expenditure by the company. A welcome call to new customers, when their value warrants it, helps to consolidate the relationship built up prior to the sale and shows that the company is pleased to be doing business with them. Subsequent courtesy calls, designed to keep up to date with their changing circumstances, show continued interest and a willingness to help whenever possible.

Welcome calls serve to reassure customers that they have made the right purchase decision. If the product or service was not first rate, for example, would the company lay itself open to possible criticism? The company can check that purchases meet customers' requirements, that they are satisfied with them, and also ensure that they have all the information required to get full value, such as equipment operating instructions or how and where they can use their new credit card. Procedures for making payments, ordering consumables or arranging service calls can also be explained. Overall, the company is demonstrating that the customers' business is appreciated and it hopes they will enjoy their purchase. There can also be valuable by-products for the company. In the course of the conversation customers may offer additional information about themselves, their needs and preferences, without any prompting, and if they are feeling good about receiving a call they will probably be quite happy to answer a few questions.

Although welcome calls deliberately avoid giving any overt sales message, they can result in sales. With a credit card, for example, it might encourage earlier card usage and perhaps more frequent card usage (both of which can be tested). Someone who recently requested a mail order catalogue may take the opportunity of the welcome call to place a first order. Or a business equipment user, having found that the equipment is being used more often than expected, might want to place an order now for more consumables.

The viability of welcome calls depends on the value they generate. They are not restricted to high-value items and can be viable where consumables will be required (especially where these can be purchased from competitors) or where low-cost items are bought in large quantities, or perhaps where only one part of a large organization has so far bought from the company.

Courtesy calls are a method of keeping the company name in the minds of customers, while showing a caring interest. They serve to build the relationship, keep up to date with customers' needs and gather new information that may be relevant to fulfilling those needs. Like welcome calls, they can elicit orders or have other beneficial results, such as identifying small problems that customers could not be bothered to raise but which erode satisfaction with the supplier. Courtesy calls can also double as satisfaction surveys, examined later.

17.4 Information services

Information has value. If a company makes useful information available to its customers, outside that required for sales promotion, then customers will view it as a gift, and a caring act. Information can be provided on an *ad hoc* basis in response to general enquiries, but if relevant information is to be made available when required, the company has to ensure that it is kept up to date and is easily accessible, either directly by the customer or by company personnel answering enquiries. Automated information lines can give customers direct access to information at any time. This may be the best route when business is not routinely conducted by telephone and requests would therefore add unnecessarily to call traffic. The value of the information made available may be sufficiently high, either intrinsically or in terms of easy access, that customers will even be happy to pay, through a premium rate call, and still view the service as a sign that the company cares.

If business is normally conducted by telephone then information can be made available through the same channels.

Case study 17.2

Dental Linkline, a specialist supplier to UK dental practices, has increased turnover by more than 1500 per cent in seven years. It aims to become the best dental supply company in the UK. To succeed, the business has been structured to provide added value through a comprehensive customer service strategy (see page 175). But the service does not stop at the supply of goods. A single toll-free number is provided for all business transactions. Customers are also invited to call this number to obtain a wide range of information of professional interest, free of charge. Dental Linkline maintains lists of telephone numbers of manufacturers in the UK and overseas, with contact names, should dentists wish to raise specialist technical queries with them. Numbers are also provided for regional drug information offices throughout the

UK. Support even extends to broader interest information, such as British Dental Association local branch activities and opportunities for dental surgeons to work through Voluntary Service Overseas. The company also encourages customers to use the number to give feedback. Promotional literature invites suggestions on how the company can improve its service, and particularly on the product range stocked to meet dentists' needs.

17.5   Satisfaction surveys

Every company needs to know how well it is meeting market needs. High sales volumes alone are no measure of satisfaction. Only a tiny proportion of customers will usually make the effort to make contact and comment, either to complain or to congratulate. Satisfaction surveys provide the opportunity and encourage response.

Being open to criticism is one thing; inviting it is something completely different. A company which calls its customers and says, 'How do you feel about our performance? Is there anything we can do to help you more?', is seen as more benevolent that one which simply advertises an address, and possibly a telephone number, so that customers can get in touch if they want to complain. Most people will only make contact over major issues, good or bad. Yet many customers *will* have things they would like to say. They may want to congratulate the company on its speedy response to service requests, or they may raise points which, though not stopping them buying, are a niggling source of dissatisfaction. Most importantly, however, the dialogue provides the company with valuable information. The majority of comments may not be significant individually, but together they provide an insight into how the market views the company and its product or services, and may even draw comparisons with the competition. This alone can justify the cost; but there is also a chance of receiving comments which highlight opportunities either for incremental improvements or to create something totally new.

Satisfaction surveys can be used in many ways. BT's Telephone-Based Customer Satisfaction Measurement tool, for example, examined in Appendix 1 (page 269), has far-reaching implications for the management and development of call centre activities. A leading computer peripherals manufacturer routinely calls five people each week who have called its information centre and asks them about the handling of their enquiries. Their comments are converted into scores and plotted on a performance graph which is then analysed. Telephone surveys are also useful for talking with customers who otherwise would have no direct contact with the company, where they help to ensure that the customers have no cause for dissatisfaction.

Case study 17.3

Thames Water began a major research and customer satisfaction survey in March 1993, just months before its new Customer Centre went live (see page 190). A series of full-page advertisements in the regional daily press promoted Thames Water as a company dedicated to the interests of its customers and invited them to take part in the setting of its future priorities. The main thrust of the advertisements was Thames Water's massive investment programme – £4 billion, or £1 million a day, over ten years – and how it is benefiting customers. One, for example, described investments aimed at improving performance in five key areas – water shortages, drinking water quality, the environment, service to customers and value for money. The call to action read:

> We plan to do more in all of the areas we've mentioned – to give a better service not just to you, but to your children, and their children.
> Priorities, though, have to be set, and choices made. We'd like to know your views. Please write to us at ... or call us on ... All calls charged at local rate.

Another advertisement featured investment in the new Thames Water Ring Main, the most sophisticated water distribution system in the world, and filtration and water conservation technology. The call to action this time read:

> Naturally, this vast investment programme will impact on your water bill. But expenditure, unlike rainfall, is something that is under our control. We aim to ensure that the £1 million a day is well spent, and keep any increases to the absolute minimum. But we'd like to know your views.
> If you'd like to tell us where you believe our priorities should be set, please write to us at ... or you can call us on ... All calls charged at local rate.

The campaign pinpointed many areas of concern to consumers, not least the rising cost of water, but the main thrust was the positive action the company is taking on these issues. Combined with the invitation to take part in setting priorities, this was a powerful message that Thames Water cares about its customers. In addition, the feedback provided information of value in planning subsequent customer communications programmes.

Surveys need to be tailored to their purpose. There is no point in expecting customers to make negative comments without being expressly invited. Thus, if a company is looking for ways to improve product performance, for example, it needs to ask customers directly about specific aspects of product performance that could be improved, and perhaps whether they can suggest ways of making that improvement.

An extension of satisfaction surveys is to invite customers to take part in the testing of new products or services. The apparent esteem with which the company regards the customers' opinions is even greater than normal surveys. It can also be extremely valuable to the company to have the opinions of those who know the company and have experienced its other products or services.

17.6 Carelines

Telephone numbers first appeared on consumer goods packaging in the USA in the late 1970s, although it was another decade before European manufacturers seriously considered their use. Carelines are used primarily to offer consumers direct access to further information and advice about the product, although they can also serve other purposes. They are sometimes called 'customer care helplines' or just 'helplines'.

A survey of packaged goods in supermarkets in the UK, France, Germany and the USA, commissioned by London-based telemarketing consultancy The L&R Group, found that 83 per cent of packs in the USA carried a telephone number compared with 30 per cent in France, 15 per cent in Germany and just 8 per cent in the UK. *The Careline Report*, published in 1993, reveals that common reasons for consumers calling carelines include seeking advice on how to use a brand, availability, 'use by' dates, allergies and environmental issues. They are also used, inevitably, to make complaints and to respond to on-pack promotions.

It is vital to be clear about why a careline is being offered. The primary objective must be to reflect a caring image, by being seen to be easily accessible, open and supportive. If this objective is not fulfilled when people call, or is compromised in any way by other objectives, then the careline is unlikely to be perceived as such and will be unsuccessful. Other objectives can be met, such as getting feedback on new packaging or product formulation, or encouraging sales of more product by informing callers of other uses for the product, but they must not compromise the caring image. If callers get the slightest suspicion that the company is trying to sell to them, for example, the caring image is destroyed. A careline can lead to more sales of product or brand extensions, but this is achieved through informing customers about the brand and building trust and loyalty. For some products, helplines can fulfil clear sales promotion objectives, by directly supporting product usage, but this is done through caring for individuals' needs rather than trying to sell.

One of the main benefits of offering a careline is that it opens up a channel of direct communication with consumers. The company is seen to be open and easily accessible and not a monolithic organization that operates behind closed doors. For the company it offers the opportunity of direct contact, which often would not arise in any other way. The question then becomes: How can that relationship be nurtured to add value for the company and the consumer? The handling of the call sets the tone of the relationship; there may never again be such a good opportunity for dialogue with these consumers. As far as extending direct contact beyond the call, there is the option to send fulfilment materials. Recording callers' personal details is subject to restrictions under any prevailing data protection legislation. However, it is perfectly acceptable to ask callers to a careline if they would like to receive a recipe leaflet, for example, or other printed information. The fulfilment pack can then aim to establish an ongoing direct relationship. The consumer can be given the option to opt-out from receiving any further communications from the company. Those who do not opt out can then be targeted with a rolling programme of direct communications appropriate to their needs and their value. Name, address and telephone number may also be requested from some callers to enable a satisfaction survey to be conducted at a later date, or to follow up product complaints and other enquiries that cannot be answered immediately.

Other benefits of carelines include rapid feedback from the marketplace and the ability to capture *ad hoc* marketing intelligence that probably would not be available from structured market research. Kraft General Foods introduced an on-pack telephone number for its Maxwell House brand when it was relaunched in the UK in September 1992. The company was aware that any major product change is likely to raise comments from customers, and the relaunch included a new 'fresher tasting' product formulation, alongside the 'traditional' Maxwell House, as well as new pack design. Consumers were invited to call a toll-free number if they had any comments about 'the new fresher tasting Maxwell House'. The careline was seen as a method of getting feedback on the impact of the relaunch and of establishing a direct relationship with individual consumers.

Establishing a careline successfully requires extensive planning and encompasses many issues, from the selection of a telephone number (is it caring to charge for the call?) through to how the success of the careline will be measured (what are the success criteria?). The question of cost is obviously crucial. The number of calls a careline generates, and the resources required to handle them efficiently, can vary enormously. This often depends on how widely the telephone number is promoted (e.g. number of packs sold, whether the number appears on support literature or in advertising), what is being offered, the prominence and strength of the call to action, and so on. A decision has to be made about whether the careline operation is expected to generate measurable extra income or whether it will be accepted as a cost centre. This helps to determine the scale of promotion of the careline and consequently the resources required to support it. Some of the many issues to be considered are summarized in Table 17.2.

Table 17.2 Some considerations in establishing a careline

Objectives
- What are the objectives:
  - to be seen to be accessible and caring?
  - to reassure customers if they have queries?
  - to provide more product information?
  - to communicate directly with customers?
  - to support a new product or product change?
  - to encourage sales of more product or brand extensions?
  - to get fast feedback (on what and for what purpose)?

- Is the service expected to pay for itself?
- How many of the company's products/services will it cover?

Telephone number
- Will this be a free service for callers?
- Will one number be used to cover all the products served by the careline? What implications does this have for the information each operator will need to access?
- Will the number(s) be dedicated to the careline(s)?

Promotion
- What channels will be used to communicate the telephone number, e.g. on-pack, instruction leaflet, guarantee/service agreement?
- Will an address also be offered? If so, what will be the relative prominence of the telephone number/address?
- What type of call to action will be used, i.e. the 'offer' and the invitation to make contact?
- How will the service be launched and how large a launch is advisable?
- Will advertising of the number be extended (e.g. to press advertising) as part of the overall brand message?

Operations
- What volume of calls is likely and who will handle them?
- What capacity will be required to service calls efficiently?
- Will the operation be computerized and for what reasons?
- What administrative back-up will be required, e.g. for fulfilment, postal replies, handling complaints, product replacement, etc.?
- What internal systems will be required to ensure that queries not answered immediately are followed up?
- What new lines of internal communication will be required?

Information
- What range of enquiries could be expected and what answers will be required?
- How will operators access this information, e.g. a manual, a computerized script?
- How will the nature of enquiries be recorded?
- Who will deal with out-of-the-ordinary calls and what systems will be required to ensure they are followed up?
- Will fulfilment materials be used, and of what type?

- Will personal details of callers be captured and for what reason, e.g. for a database, fulfilment or follow-up, satisfaction surveys?

Staffing
- How many operators will be required and will they need to be specially recruited?
- What image should operators reflect?
- What training will be required and who will conduct it?
- Who will manage the operation?
- What would happen if customers used the careline during a crisis?

Evaluation
- What criteria will be used to measure success, e.g.
  - number of calls?
  - caller satisfaction levels? (How will this be measured?)
  - callers buying more brand extensions, or finding new uses for products and therefore buy more product, than those who do not call? (How will this be measured?)
  - the value of information gathered? (How will this be assessed?)
  - the perceived added value for the brand? (How will this be measured?)

- Are the promises made to consumers being fulfilled?

Case study 17.4

Unilever-owned Van den Bergh Foods was one of the first major FMCG manufacturers to offer UK consumers a careline – for Flora margarine, one of the UK's 10 top-selling grocery brands. The Flora careline was launched towards the end of 1991, after nearly 12 months of planning and development with London-based consultancy The L&R Group. By chance, the toll-free number first appeared on packs of I Can't Believe It's Not Butter!, a product Van den Bergh launched about four weeks before the new packs of Flora were due in the shops.

The careline is a dedicated unit at Van den Bergh. It has a manager and is permanently staffed by at least three operators. Several hundred consumers call the careline each week, about 20 times more than write to the company, although the offer of a free call has not decreased the number of written enquiries. The principal objectives in offering the careline were to set Flora apart by being an open and caring brand, and to open a channel of direct communication with customers to reassure them when they have any queries. In 1992, Flora commanded 23.4 per cent of the UK margarine and low fat spreads market (MLF), with production of over 15 million units a month, and the brand name also covers products such as cheese, cream and mayonnaise alternatives, oil and white cooking fat.

The L&R Group helped to plan, develop and manage the organization of the careline, including the recruitment of operators suited to the telephone customer care environment and advising on the selection of a unit manager. Operators received extensive training, conducted mainly by specialists from various disciplines within Van den Bergh while telephone training was provided by The L&R Group.

The launch of the careline was deliberately low-key to ensure that operators were well briefed, that staffing needs were confirmed and that the operational systems functioned well before encouraging large volumes of callers. It was vital that Van den Bergh could fulfil its promise of Flora being a 'caring' brand.

A vast range of enquiries are received, particularly on nutrition, product usage, stockist information, and triggered by promotional activities, but also extending to many other areas such as school projects and trader enquiries. One fact that has surprised Van den Bergh is the low level of people phoning with product complaints. Most enquiries can be answered immediately, but internal systems have been established to ensure that any requiring special attention are followed up quickly. Callers' personal details are only requested when follow-up is required.

One of the more unexpected benefits of the careline has been extremely fast feedback from consumers. An example is the launch of I Can't Believe It's Not Butter!, positioned as a spread with the flavour of butter but more appropriate for a healthy lifestyle. The on-pack message reads:

'FREEFONE' IF YOU HAVE ANY COMMENTS OR QUESTIONS ABOUT 'I CAN'T BELIEVE IT'S NOT BUTTER!' PLEASE CALL US FREE ON 0800 XXXXXX MONDAY TO FRIDAY, 9 A.M. TO 5 P.M. OR WRITE TO US AT ...

A large proportion of the first few hundred calls received on the careline were people asking if they could bake with the product, which Van den Bergh felt it had made clear on the packaging. Rapid feedback enabled the company to organize a pack reprint, making this clearer, within five or six weeks of the launch.

On-pack messages used to promote the careline vary from product to product, but are all variations on the same theme, inviting customers to call free with their questions, comments or suggestions. Promotion is a dynamic process. The message on packs of Flora was initially in the same colour as the ingredients, but a few weeks after launch it was highlighted in slightly larger red print to make it more noticeable to regular users. Awareness is boosted with periodic short-term use of the foil cover leaf on the two most popular sized packs of Flora, with a graphic of a telephone and a message beginning, 'The Flora Food Company is dedicated to your health, nutrition and enjoyment of good food'. Call volumes increase dramatically, by around 50 per cent, as a result.

Feedback from consumers also gives Van den Bergh marketing intelligence of a type that they would not necessarily receive through dedicated market research programmes. Where sufficient callers express similar views – although the figures may not be statistically significant – the company can take effective action based upon the information. As an example, the company talked to its trade customers after a considerable number of callers expressed difficulty in finding the Flora cream alternative in stores.

There are positive indications that consumers value this means of direct access. Some callers, for example, have used the careline because they have lost the reply address for a particular product promotion. On the negative side, there are periodic spates of nuisance calls, often coinciding with school holidays, but the company regards this as a small, if annoying, problem.

The introduction and apparent success of the careline caused considerable excitement and satisfaction within the company, but it was aware that this was no measure of how well the service was meeting its primary objective – of demonstrating Flora as a caring brand. Part of the initial plan was the intention to conduct customer satisfaction surveys to give a quantifiable measure of the quality of service being delivered. The first satisfaction survey was undertaken in July 1992 by a market research agency. For a while prior to this, callers has been asked if they would take part in the survey and, if so, leave their name and telephone number. The overall reaction from consumers in the survey was extremely positive, but Van den Bergh were actually seeking to identify negative reactions that would help to determine how the careline could be improved even further. Two of the findings, in particular, were a little surprising. First, while consumers were accustomed and willing to wait up to three to four weeks for a response to a written enquiry, they expected any follow-up to an enquiry on the careline to be made almost the following day. As a result, Van den Bergh began to explore their follow-up procedures to try to meet these expectations. Second, consumers enquiring about where to purchase a particular product expected the company to name a local store that would have it in stock. In reality, of course, it is impossible to *guarantee* that a particular store will have a certain product in stock at any particular time.

Van den Bergh intends to continue developing the careline service with guidance and advice from The L&R Group. It is looking at using the service for different purposes, such as inviting consumers to call for information on specific product uses, and intends to expand the product base on which the telephone number appears. The company regards the operation as highly successful, although it is constantly monitoring costs and efficiency. From the launch of the careline until early 1994, purchasers of Flora were invited to call between 8.00 a.m. and 8.00 p.m. In January 1994, Van den Bergh changed these hours to between 9.00 a.m. and 5.00 p.m., as it felt customers would be better served by concentrating staffing resources and increasing call-handling capacity during peak calling hours.

A very high proportion of careline expenditure is fixed costs, which means that the overall cost-efficiency will increase as the careline number is used on more products. However, there is already a heavy burden on operators with the amount of information they require to answer the wide variety of enquiries. At present, only a small proportion have to be referred, but with wider use of the careline number the volume of product information and related knowledge required will become increasingly difficult for operators to manage. There has been no need to computerize the operation on its current scale, although this could become a necessity as the service develops over the next two to three years.

It is apparent from this example that carelines are highly sophisticated marketing operations which require expertise and the commitment of resources to make them work. The promise has to be fulfilled. Establishing a careline is not something that should be undertaken simply because it is 'current practice'. There are many other ways in which organizations can demonstrate that they are caring.

Not all customer care initiatives require substantial investment. Even simple acts can be effective. First Direct, the telephone banking service (see page 90), has a two-page account application form which requests fairly detailed information. At the foot of the second page is a note reading: 'IF AT ANY STAGE OF COMPLETING THIS FORM YOU NEED ASSISTANCE PLEASE DO NOT HESITATE TO CALL 0800 222 000', which is the company's toll-free general enquiries number. This simple provision reflects a thoughtful, caring attitude on the part of First Direct. It also helps to minimize the number of incorrectly completed applications the company receives and the resulting administrative costs.

17.7 Social responsibilities

One area that has attracted growing attention in recent years is the ethical and social responsibility of businesses. This covers a wide spectrum of issues, including the welfare of local communities, trading policies and the environment. Many social and ethical issues are often of real concern only to a minority of people within a company's markets, and so any communications about them need to be well targeted. Publicizing an inbound telephone number is clearly a very cost-effective way to offer those who are concerned the opportunity to get more information or become involved. The oil giant Texaco, for example, established a pioneering initiative in the UK, in partnership with Bristol City Council, to encourage motorists to dispose of their used engine oil safely. Oil banks were set up at 14 Texaco service stations in the Bristol area and a city-wide poster and leaflet campaign urged motorists to dispose of their used oil and containers safely, simply and cleanly. The used oil is collected to be recycled as fuel oil for industrial use. Advertising promoted a helpline which motorists could call to get further information and answers to any questions they had about the scheme. The initiative has proved very successful and the company has had requests from several other local authorities who wish to provide oil banks.

There are many ways in which, given some thought, any company can show itself to be considerate and caring. The telephone can be used to inform, educate and address the issues which are of real importance to individuals in the marketplace. At the same time the company will want to gain maximum commercial benefit. The successful combination of these two objectives requires ingenuity and an understanding of what a caring, give-and-take relationship actually means.

18

Intelligence gathering and market research

Marketing intelligence helps organizations to learn and to adapt. Every organization needs to know where its markets are, what product or service features they need and want, the size of the potential markets, what channels are available to reach them, the impact of pricing strategies and advertising, the markets' perceptions and misconceptions, how products or services might be improved, and so on. This type of knowledge is essential for identifying and meeting market needs successfully, for advancing and growing within existing markets, and for tapping and creating new markets. It fuels decisions about where and how money will be spent to enable the organization to trade profitably in different markets. It provides guidance on getting the best return on investment and helps to avoid costly mistakes. Good-quality marketing intelligence is therefore crucial to an organization's profitable operation.

Today, an increasing amount of marketing intelligence can be bought-in. Regular detailed analysis of many existing and emerging markets is made available by specialist market intelligence agencies. In addition to this, a great deal of market information can be gathered by companies during their day-to-day trading activities and stored in a marketing database. Collectively this represents intelligence of a type not available elsewhere or to any other company. A good database can therefore provide a large proportion of the marketing intelligence required by any company.

With increasing competition, the growing sophistication of markets and marketing and the opening up of new markets globally, the need for marketing intelligence is growing. Acquiring it is expensive, whatever methods are used, and organizations need to consider their long-term needs and plan how intelligence can be gathered most cost-effectively. Exploiting all existing contact with different markets to gather relevant data obviously makes sense. Many marketing activities can yield valuable additional data, as a by-product of the main objective, provided this is planned. Ensuring that this data is captured and entered onto a database will reduce the overall cost to a company of acquiring the marketing intelligence it requires. In addition to day-to-day trading, there are many activities, such as customer satisfaction surveys and customer care initiatives, which can yield valuable information. Encouraging feedback from the marketplace and providing easy access, perhaps on a toll-free number, is one of the most cost-effective ways a company can keep itself informed.

However, there are many areas where neither a database nor *ad hoc* feedback is likely to provide knowledge, such as recall of advertising or opinions on proposed new distribution channels or retail sites. Also, while the intelligence from these sources might provide valuable insight, it may not provide the depth of understanding required or have the statistical validity a company would like before committing itself to a particular course of action. In these circumstances, dedicated market research is required.

18.1 A distinct discipline

Market research is a highly specialized discipline meriting professional training and qualification. There are many technical issues, such as sample selection and weighting techniques. There is some underlying conflict, in Europe at least, between telemarketing and market research professionals. This has arisen largely because of a small minority of unscrupulous companies which make sales calls under the guise of market research. The ability to conduct research successfully depends upon the willing cooperation of consumers and businesses. Anything which diminishes their confidence in market research, and therefore threatens their cooperation, is bad news for every commercial organization. There is concern among research professionals that consumers in particular will become less willing to participate in surveys as a result of both the growing amount of unsolicited calling generally and the confusion that can arise between market surveys and selling. Research must be distinguished clearly from telemarketing and it must be undertaken in a way that builds rather than erodes confidence. Various codes of practice for market research contain guidelines, summarized in Table 18.1, which help any company to do this.

A company's telemarketing resources, whether in-house or agency-based, do have an important contribution to make in gathering research data. However, it is important to recognize that many types of research project will require expertise that is not widely available outside professional research companies.

One research activity, market evaluation, was examined in Chapter 8. It is important to distinguish this from market research. Evaluation exercises yield information about potential customers and are often used to promote products or services at the same time as learning about the target market. Market research is very different. It deliberately avoids influencing contacts,

Table 18.1 Some guidelines, from market research codes of practice, for the conduct of telephone research

No activity is to be misrepresented as research.

Information gathered must not be used for any purpose other than research; in particular, where the words 'research' or 'survey' are used, the information gathered cannot be used for a sales approach.

Calls should be made at times considered reasonable in the target population, unless by prior arrangement.

When undertaking overseas research the conventions in each target country should be observed.

Participants must be assured of complete confidentiality.

It should be made clear at the outset that the call is for the purposes only of a research survey, and that the information will not be used in selling now or in the future.

Contacts should be told why they were selected and how their telephone number was acquired.

Contacts should be told how they can check (at no cost to themselves) that this is a legitimate research survey and raise any other queries about it.

Participants have the right to withdraw or refuse to cooperate at any stage and this must be respected. When people withdraw from a survey they have a right to have their questionnaire destroyed and to be informed in writing that this has been done.

Special care should be taken when interviewing children, e.g. asking for parental or guardian permission before a child under 14 is interviewed.

It is preferable that different staff are used for market research and telemarketing activities with any sales objective. Where the same people are used, they should be adequately skilled and briefed and the two types of project should be clearly separated operationally.

Research calls should be closed with a positive reminder of how the information will be used (i.e. what good will come of it) and a 'thank you' for the time and help given.

simply gathering responses to specific questions, and is generally more rigidly structured. Research provides an overall picture of certain aspects of a market, while evaluation provides knowledge of individual contacts that can be used to effect a sale. This is not to say that gathering knowledge of known individuals cannot be used for market research.

Case study 18.1

A leading food manufacturer used direct response television advertising in the UK to gather information for a database to be used for research. Health was the focus of the campaign – historically, the product featured had been promoted for its dietary benefits. Viewers were invited to call a toll-free number to obtain a free health information pack and be entered in a free prize draw.

The 30-second commercial was broadcast in three television regions – HTV, Anglia and TSW – in June 1992, using approximately 200 spots. Telemarketing agency Merit Direct had been appointed to handle the calls, build the database and conduct the subsequent telephone research. Staffing levels required for inbound call handling were estimated from viewing figures for each time slot in each region. Merit operators had been briefed and specially trained to use a professional but friendly, reassuring approach in order to obtain a range of personal information from callers. The food manufacturer was interested specifically in callers' eating habits, as they relate to the product benefits, and their associated health-related activities.

Approximately 9000 people called to obtain the information pack, which featured the product in the context of a healthy lifestyle. The majority of calls were received within 12 minutes of each broadcast, with housewives most often calling in the afternoons and men in the evenings. A school holiday occurred during the TV campaign which caused a noticeable rise in hoax calls. Merit used the information gathered to build a database from which it could identify patterns of associated lifestyle indicators for both users and non-users of the product. Subsequently, the agency made calls to a sample of consumers in both groups to determine whether the information pack had affected their eating habits, and how. The results provided the manufacturer with an insight into influences on the eating habits of consumers with different lifestyles, which would be used to help plan subsequent consumer campaigns. ·

Various types of direct response campaign, like sampling promotions for example, can be used to gather research data, provided that this is made a clear objective and the personal details gathered will not be used to make a sales approach.

18.2   Research methods

During the initial stages of planning market research a company should arrive at a definition of its objectives, together with the questions that need to be answered and the specific information that the research must provide. This will help to determine the research methods that are most viable (in terms of providing suitable data) and cost-effective. The main sources of research data are internal information resources (such as a database or other records), desk research (examining previous research and published sources) and field research. Internal and desk research are comparatively inexpensive, but they have the limitations mentioned earlier. Field research is conducted by interviewing a sample population and is therefore the most expensive method.

There are three main methods of conducting field interviews: face-to-face (street, doorstep or in-home), by telephone and by mail. Each of these methods has advantages and disadvantages which can vary according to the market and topic being researched. Face-to-face interviews in the home, for example, are more suited to detailed questioning than street or telephone interviews, and more suited to enquiring about some 'personal' issues, such as finance. Response rates are generally highest with face-to-face interviews, less with telephone and lowest with mail. Costs per interview, in time and money, are lowest by mail, higher by telephone and highest with face-to-face. The reliability of data gathered can also vary, being highest generally with in-home face-to-face interviewing. Accessibility and certainty of targeting may also be important issues. All of these factors must be considered in the light of what is being researched, and the nature of the sample population, in order to select the most appropriate interviewing method. Sometimes different methods will be combined, to take advantage of their respective benefits, as in the following example.

Case study 18.2

In 1989, the financial position of The Samaritans was relatively poor. As a charity, it relies on voluntary contributions and in terms of donations received it was relatively insignificant, despite having 186 branches nationwide, staffed by 22 000 volunteers, and receiving over 2.5 million calls for help every year. The Samaritans offers sympathetic, caring and confidential support at any time to anyone feeling suicidal or despairing.

At the time, there was little central coordination or management of branch fund raising. The Samaritans had only three central fund raising staff and the majority of fund-raising occurred at branch level, in no structured way It recognized the need for improved fund raising but was concerned to find out *why* fund raising was difficult and how best to increase funding. Did the public think, for example, that it was not in need of funds, or was less deserving than other charities? The Samaritans suspected that people might not think of it as a charity, and hence might not realize that it was dependent on voluntary donations. The positioning of The Samaritans was also in need of clarification; was it there for the suicidal, the pre-suicidal or, more widely, just as 'someone to talk to'? As a preface to any clarification of The Samaritans' role, it was essential to establish the public's perceptions to understand where and what type of changes were needed.

As part of a broader programme, The Samaritans' management decided to commission research to address the following questions:

1. Are people aware of The Samaritans as a charity and thus of its need for funds?
2. Are people aware of what The Samaritans is and what it does? Are some groups less aware than others?

A telephone omnibus survey (where each interview covers several topics for different companies) was felt to be the most appropriate and efficient method of interviewing for testing the first hypothesis, and face-to-face interviewing in the home for the more complex issues surrounding the second hypothesis. Research agency Audience Selection was chosen to conduct the telephone survey and NOP Market Research the face-to-face interviews.

Quantitative, rather than qualitative, research was commissioned to establish the public's attitudes with statistical validity. It was important to cover as wide a sample as possible, therefore both studies consisted of large samples systematically selected to be representative of the population. The research was designed to answer the following questions:

Telephone
- To what extent do people recognize The Samaritans as a charity?
- Is The Samaritans thought to be more, or less, desperate for money than other named charities?
- Is The Samaritans thought to be more, or less, deserving than other charities?
- Did receipt of a mailing from The Samaritans affect the replies?

Face-to-face
- Overall, to what extent are people aware of what The Samaritans does?
- Is The Samaritans seen more as a 'rescuing' organization than a 'preventing' one?
- Do people believe that national or local Government departments fund The Samaritans?

Research was conducted in November 1989, using a methodology similar to that used in the majority of UK market research. Audience Selection interviewed 1023 adults age 15+, as part of its regular phonebus (telephone omnibus) survey, between 10 and 12 November 1989. The survey was based on a representative sample of adults; telephone households were selected at random from telephone directories covering the whole of Great Britain, and set quota controls were imposed within region, by age within sex, and social class within sex. Interviews were supervised throughout the survey. NOP Market Research interviewed 1966 adults aged 15+ in their homes between 15 and 20 November 1989. Respondents were selected from the electoral register using a technique designed to give a sample representative of all adults in Great Britain.

The research findings confirmed some of The Samaritans' worst fears and put into perspective its fund-raising difficulties. The telephone survey, for example, revealed that awareness of The Samaritans as a charity needing public financial support was very low. Only 1.4 per cent of respondents spontaneously mentioned The Samaritans as a charity they could think of, and less than half the population realized it relied on public donations. The Samaritans was also seen to be less desperate for money from the public than other charities, although not less deserving. However, the level of 'don't knows' was higher than that for any other charity mentioned – a surprisingly large number of people just did not know how much The Samaritans was in need of money. The findings in the face-to-face survey were equally disturbing. For example, although 91 per cent of the population knew something about The Samaritans, many people had various misconceptions about its service. Half thought (or did not know either way) that The Samaritans takes soup and bread to down-and-outs.

The research had isolated specific problem areas. The need was not simply for more fund raising but for a programme of awareness of The Samaritans, and its need for money, in conjunction with concentrated targeting of fund-raising activities. The actions taken on the basis of this understanding were extensive, including reorganization of The Samaritans' management structure, definition of its positioning, greater integration of the fund-raising function and development of a fund-raising/education programme to give the organization a higher profile as a charity in need of donations.

The effect of the changes on fund raising were striking. Net funding increased by 73 per cent over the previous year, rising from £3.93 million in 1989/90 to £6.81 million in 1990/91. The research findings were key to effecting the changes that brought about this success and the campaign was recognized by the Association of Market Survey Organizations (AMSO), winning first prize in the 1991 AMSO Market Research Effectiveness Awards.

In the appropriate circumstances the telephone can be the most cost-effective way to conduct qualitative or quantitative research surveys in both consumer and business-to-business markets. Telephone surveys can be implemented quickly and closely monitored, for example, to identify any problems with the wording of questionnaires which might lead to ambiguity. Because feedback is immediate, and response analysis is available quickly when entered directly into a computer, any necessary changes can be made before the majority of the sample have been contacted.

Depending on the target population and what is known about them, it is often necessary to qualify people before asking them to participate. The telephone enables a company to contact large numbers of people, quickly and cost-effectively, until the quotas for people meeting the various qualification criteria are achieved. This must be handled carefully, however, to ensure that people who do not qualify do not feel rejected and resentful at having been disturbed.

Consumer surveys by mail often seek to encourage response by offering an incentive, such as free entry in a prize draw. This is less common in telephone surveys, which rely more upon the personal nature of the approach and the ability to answer immediately any questions contacts might ask. Good questionnaire design requires considerable skill. The opening is very important because it has to encourage the person to want to participate in the survey. Questions should fit into a conversational framework, as far as possible, so that they appear logical (and therefore self-explanatory) to the participant. They should also be as brief and as straightforward as practical. Objections to answering certain questions are handled as with any other telephone application, and interviewers should have available counters to the most likely objections. Among the most common reasons for objecting to answering survey questions are concerns over confidentially and poor interviewer manner.

Number availability

One problem in researching consumer markets by telephone is the unavailability of telephone numbers (see page 25). The geographic and demographic distribution of unlisted numbers tends to compound the problem of obtaining representative samples. One method used to help overcome the problem is to select a sample from directories and add 'one' to the number in order to generate a sample of both listed and unlisted numbers. Alternatively, the last digit can be replaced by a random one. However, because the distribution of unlisted numbers is not known, these methods under-represent unlisted numbers. The best alternative, currently, is random digit dialling (RDD) which, as the term implies, consists of creating telephone numbers randomly by computer within a framework of all possible numbers. This method has to take into account the country's numbering system, which can make the process more complex if it has a non-uniform structure (as historically in the UK). However, RDD does give all residential telephone numbers, listed and unlisted, equal probabilities of selection. Generating numbers in this way gives a high proportion of non-working and non-residential numbers and so various two-stage sampling methods are used. The first stage aims to eliminate blocks of numbers which look unpromising, i.e. where the proportion of working residential numbers is low. This works on the principal that numbers tend to be clustered according to type. The second stage then concentrates on the promising blocks.

The proportion of research interviews conducted by telephone is growing rapidly in Europe, although its use is not yet as widespread as in the USA, where it is the most common research tool (partly as a result of much lower long-distance call costs throughout the mainland). A great advantage of the telephone is its speed irrespective of geographical distance. It can be used to survey large, sparsely populated areas just as efficiently as urban conurbations. This quality is also being exploited more and more to conduct international research.

18.3 International research

The most common method of multi-country research is to conduct interviews locally in each country. Data is also often prepared locally and delivered to the commissioning company for collation and analysis.

Increasingly, however, international telephone surveys are being used. Research calls are made from a single, central facility using foreign nationals (or native speakers) to interview people in their home country, and interviews are monitored by multilingual supervisors. The main benefits of this approach are summarized in Table 18.2.

The single centre approach to international research raises a number of issues, such as sampling and cultural differences, which must be accommodated. Selecting a representative sample of people from European Union member countries would include covering Greece and Denmark, for example, but their influence on results may be insignificant overall while it would add considerably to the costs in terms of translation and administration. Many research projects could be limited to the European countries with the majority of the total population – France, Germany, Italy, Spain and the UK – without adversely affecting the validity of the results. In some instances, however, the sampling focus might be quite different. A survey of the olive oil market, for example, is more likely to include Greece and Portugal than Germany or the UK. So, while the majority of European research will probably focus on countries with the bulk of the population, it is important to understand the market being researched and how it affects sample selection across the target countries.

Another obvious problem is the cultural differences that exist between

Table 18.2 Some advantages of multi-country telephone research out of a central facility. (Courtesy of Research International)

There are economies of cost in set-up, project supervision and data preparation.

All interviewers receive the same briefing and the same ongoing support.

The respondent profile can be matched in each country.

Quality controls are guaranteed to be uniform.

Changes to questionnaires can be made quickly, easily and uniformly, across all countries, on an ongoing basis.

Work in each country can be progressed at the same rate and there is better control on the completion date.

No other method can match the speed of implementation and completion of a research project offered by telephone research from a central location.

countries, both in terms of contacts' willingness to participate and the manner in which interviews are conducted (see page 24).

18.4   Support technologies

Technology is becoming more important in telephone research, both as a means to reduce costs and to broaden the potential for exploiting the telephone as a research tool. A wide range of sophisticated software is available to guide interviewers through questionnaires, for example, prompting them with the next pertinent question dependent upon the last response given, and enabling the simple and quick capture of responses. Software for the analysis of responses has also become increasingly sophisticated. Two other areas where technology can play an important role are in automating the capture of responses and improving productivity with predictive dialling.

Automated response capture

With increasing segmentation of markets there is a growing need for more detailed information about numerically small but significant subgroups, which often are not adequately represented in large-scale surveys. Some of these groups are difficult to access, and gathering in-depth information, or tracking behaviour over time, requires considerable cooperation from subjects.

One method used is self-completion diaries. A disadvantage in tracking studies, however, is that there is no control over the accuracy of the daily entries. Subjects may forget to complete the diary on one or more days and rely on their memory to make the entry later. Also, it is not easy to introduce new questions, or topics, and data analysis is time-consuming because it is paper-based. An alternative method is to interview subjects, but potential disadvantages are the cost, if interviewers are used, and regular access to subjects. Inbound telephone, combined with automated data capture, provides a solution. In the USA, for example, interactive voice response systems are used to record data from market research panel members who call in on a regular basis and respond to questions voiced by the system.

In the UK, computer services company AT&T ISTEL offers another solution, the INTERview service. Selected subjects in the target group use interactive videotex terminals, placed in their homes or offices, to respond to on-screen questions. The terminals are connected via the subjects' telephone line to the nearest node on AT&T ISTEL's private telecommunications network and then to an AT&T ISTEL mainframe computer. Routeing calls via the private network helps to minimize call costs. Because subjects' responses are fed back to the computer instantaneously, results can be available within hours.

Case study 18.3

INTERview was developed by AT&T ISTEL with market research company Interactive Research, and can be used to monitor virtually any aspect of the daily lives of the target group. A population of typically 200 terminals is placed with selected members of the target group for, typically, about 28 days, during which time subjects are asked to answer usually no more than 10–15 minutes of questions a day at their own pace. Subjects are rewarded, although generally they are very willing to participate.

INTERview utilizes Alcatel videotex terminals, with screen and keyboard, which are the same as those used to access the Télétel ('Minitel') services in France. They are easy to use and require no training, although AT&T ISTEL provides panel members with a user guide and access to a telephone helpline. Each day, panel members follow a simple log-on procedure to gain access to the market research questionnaire held on the computer and then simply key in their responses to the questions appearing on screen. They can consider their responses, as there is no expectation from an interviewer, and personal questions can be answered without embarrassment. Individuals choose the time of day most convenient to them – between 6.00 p.m. (midday at weekends) and 3.00 a.m., taking advantage of cheap rate calls – to complete each day's questionnaire. If they miss a day, the system automatically presents that day's survey when they next log on.

Any form of question can be used, including open-ended questions requiring free-form text response, enabling the collection of both quantitative and qualitative data. All responses are validated on entry, through automatic quality checking, and the computer automatically routes individuals through the questionnaire. The service also allows the sending and receiving of personal messages, giving the system a more friendly aspect and encouraging high response rates.

At 3.00 a.m. each morning the system is automatically closed and the data consolidated, thus enabling results to be available within hours of the responses being obtained. New questions can be added or existing ones changed daily, if necessary, in response to earlier findings, to conduct further in-depth questioning, or to react to current events. INTERview also provides a panel management facility, which enables analysis of daily responses by individuals so that remedial action can be taken at an early stage if there is a poor respondent on the panel.

Quality of response compares favourably with conventional face-to-face or telephone interviewing, even among notoriously difficult respondents such as busy professionals. Media consumption results from INTERview panels correlate closely with industry standard research from the British Audience Research Bureau (BARB).

Response rates are good even over historically difficult periods to maintain any response, such as Christmas, New Year and Easter. In one project, for example, daily response rates measured over a month from March to April averaged 90 per cent for housewives and 85 per cent for other household members. The ease of use and novelty value of INTERview undoubtedly help to maintain high response levels.

Over a period of 28 days it is possible to hold five hours or more of interviewing with each panel member without it becoming too tedious. The flexibility of INTERview allows data to be collected across a wide range of subject areas from the same panel, providing single source data to facilitate cross-analysis and meaningful comparison. Substantial cost savings can be achieved compared with conventional research methods.

One user of the service has been London Weekend Television (LWT), the independent television contractor for the London area broadcasting at weekends to nearly 11 million people. Standard broadcasting industry research provided neither sufficient detail nor large enough sample sizes to meet its particular research requirements. LWT panels have included business people, 16–24 year olds, upmarket multi-income homes, and housewives with young children under 12.

The pharmaceutical industry has also used the service, setting up a panel of general medical practitioners to monitor patterns of drug prescription on a regular basis. A financial research agency used INTERview to access brokers to research topical issues within the industry.

It has also been used for omnibus surveys. A panel of 150 households in one television region were surveyed over a period from mid-November until the New Year. A wide variety of data was gathered, including purchases (groceries, drinks, Christmas gifts and toys), media consumption (TV, radio, newspapers, magazines, video, and advertisement tracking), and leisure activities (Christmas events, holidays, sports activities and entertainment). Companies participating in the survey included a building society, a major credit card issuer and a national high street pharmaceutical retailer, each of which gained a detailed picture of the consumers' behaviour over this period of high spending.

While the telephone is generally considered to be unsuitable for in-depth interviewing, the application of technology can make it viable and, as in the case of INTERview, provide market research data more cost-effectively than other methods.

Predictive dialling

Predictive dialling has been used by market research companies in the USA since the late 1980s and began to penetrate the UK market in 1993. Predictive dialling has particular benefits for telephone researchers, not seen generally in other application areas.

Marketing Research Services Inc. (MRSI) was one of the first USA market research companies to use predictive dialling, installing a system from Electronic Information Systems (EIS) Inc. in 1988. It is used in conjunction with Quantime CATI (computer-assisted telephone interviewing) software. The EIS dialler delivers the productivity benefits seen in all applications (see page 41), increasing the amount of time spent talking to contacts. In market research, however, a large proportion of operator time can be spent identifying qualified contacts before productive interviewing can begin. MRSI finds the EIS dialler particularly useful in 'low-incidence' studies, where many households must be dialled to find the small proportion who use a particular product or service. Only 5 per cent of the people contacted may meet the survey criteria, and only 30 per cent of those might agree to be interviewed. To obtain a sample of only 100 people would therefore entail speaking to about 6650 households. That involves a lot of diallings, and operator time, even before taking into account the calls not answered, unobtainable numbers and answering machines. MRSI also believes that the dialler helps to improve accuracy in sampling, where many more people than the sample size need to be contacted to identify those who meet the qualification criteria for a representative sample. The company initially automated dialling at 32 workstations. Productivity gains were apparent almost immediately and this number was soon doubled to 64, producing an overall increase of 200–300 per cent in the volume of contacts. The 64 operators could complete the same amount of work as 125 operators using manual dialling.

One of the leading UK mail order companies uses Davox predictive diallers, supplied by Datapoint UK, to conduct market research for all companies within its group. EIS entered the UK market in January 1993 and the market research company Taylor Nelson AGB was among its first clients.

With the growing importance placed on market knowledge, every organization needs a research strategy which shows how it will gather intelligence in the most cost-efficient way. The single most valuable source of marketing intelligence is undoubtedly direct contact with the marketplace. A research strategy should encompass all activities that provide opportunities for direct contact, particularly dialogue, so that they are fully exploited. Not only does this reduce the overall cost of acquiring essential intelligence, but it also enhances the organization's ability to respond to market changes.

19

Credit approval and cash collection

Credit approval and cash (or debt) collection are equally important in terms of a company's relationship with its customers and prospects. Allowing people credit beyond their means will almost inevitably lead to their defaulting on the repayment terms, putting themselves and the company in an awkward position. Equally, the refusal of credit will often lose a sale (although the prospect might reduce the order size or value to an acceptable credit limit) and can lose a customer. The speed of credit approval is also important in some situations. In retailing, for example, 'instant credit terms' can be a major selling point in a competitive market. The overall objective in granting credit is to balance the need to sell against the ability of the buyer to pay. However, people may default even when they have been set realistic credit limits – for example, owing to redundancy or a company losing a large order. Often the problem may be temporary. The majority of businesses, and an increasing number of consumers, delay payment as long as possible, often beyond the agreed credit period. Some people simply do not want to pay, while others cannot pay. Cash collection aims to manage all these different circumstances to achieve the best possible outcome for the company. Increasingly, trying to retain the customer's business is an important consideration in how debtors are handled.

19.1   Credit approval

As mentioned previously, the speed of credit approval can be a decisive factor in making or losing a sale. The telephone (or the telecommunications network) is used routinely in many situations to check the credit worthiness of prospective customers. Seeking approval for credit card purchases is perhaps the most commonplace example. A retailer simply calls the card provider, gives the relevant card information and the amount of the proposed purchase, and is told whether or not the individual has sufficient credit to cover the transaction. In many instances part or all of this process is automated. Terminals can be used to read the card details, key in the amount and transmit the information to the relevant approval agency. Many credit card providers are automating all or part of the approval process at their end too, using interactive voice response systems. These can guide the retailer in providing the necessary information, which is then used to search a database to check on credit availability. The system will then either state an authorization code and the amount authorized, or tell the retailer to refuse the transaction. Card details can be checked automatically against a 'black list' and the retailer alerted immediately if a card has been reported lost or stolen.

The credit worthiness of people placing orders over the telephone can also be checked quickly, using either the company's own computerized customer credit ratings or through a live link to a credit rating agency. Obviously to take advantage of the speed of the telephone for credit approvals it is essential to have the necessary information resource available to check credit ratings.

19.2   Cash collection

Probably of most significance today is the way in which the collection of outstanding debts is managed. No business can afford to risk losing an otherwise good customer through the mishandling of collections. On the other hand, monies outstanding after the agreed payment date are costing the supplier money and decreasing the profit margin on the original sale. All businesses must encourage their customers to keep to agreed terms. It is best done in a manner that retains the customers' goodwill *and* makes them pay. Obviously there can come a point, perhaps after repeated or continuous default, when the company no longer wants their business. In most situations, however, payment can be obtained without adversely affecting the business relationship.

Before a company considers trying to recover overdue payment from a customer it must be sure that the customer has accepted the goods or services supplied, has been billed in accordance with the agreement, and is aware of the credit terms under which the transaction was made. Simple precautions, such as ensuring that credit terms are clear, invoicing on time and sending regular statements, can reduce the amount of outstanding debt.

Assuming the money is owed and that no payment is forthcoming, a company must decide how quickly it will contact the customer to ask for the money in line with the credit terms. This can vary from business to business and customer to customer, from a few days to weeks. However, it is important to remember that delay in chasing overdue payments sets a precedent that the customer will be only too pleased to follow in the future. Early action helps to minimize subsequent delinquency.

The method of chasing payment is usually a combination of mail and telephone, unless regular face-to-face contact is maintained. The telephone has become the favoured medium for many businesses, some of whom do not use mail (apart from invoices and statements) in the early stages of collection. The telephone has several benefits. It is fast, it guarantees delivery of the message, it almost guarantees a response, and it is interactive. Being able to talk with the customer, or the customer's accounts department, allows reasons to be sought for the late payment which then form the basis of the company's response to the debt. This is not to say that the reasons for non-payment are easily discovered, but it gives the collector an opportunity to ensure that the supplier is in no way at fault and to gain some commitment from the debtor. The telephone also allows the conversation to be tailored instantly to the situation. When mail is used initially, it is a good idea to provide a telephone number and contact name to enable the debtor to call if certain queries are preventing or delaying payment. All invoices should, in any event, carry a telephone number to allow customers to call in case of queries.

There is no doubt that the telephone is an effective method of collecting overdue money more quickly. Dental Linkline is a specialist UK supply company whose sales operation has been based upon inbound telemarketing since late 1985 (see page 175). Rapid growth in turnover, averaging 49 per cent a year, put an extra burden on cashflow as the company bought in extra stocks to meet demand. It became increasingly important to have stricter credit controls. Invoices and a prepaid envelope for account payments are sent with goods, and customers can use the company's toll-free order line for any account queries. In 1990, the company began using outbound calls to chase overdue accounts, taking a low-key, friendly approach. The result, achieved during a severe recession, has been a reduction in average payment time from 49 days to 40 days. Account customers represent 98 per cent of sales. At current turnover, getting payment in nine days earlier has freed tens of thousands of pounds as extra working capital.

The importance of systems and procedures

There must be clear procedures for dealing with debtors and accurately maintained records are an essential basis for carrying out collections work. Obviously it is necessary to know who owes what and when it became due. This allows the chasing of appropriate payments, the tracking of payment behaviour, analysis of the age of debts and the identification of any trends (such as reasons for non-payment) as well as building a picture of the creditworthiness of individual customers. Computerized accounts enable sophisticated analysis of debts and debtors and provide valuable support for the collection team.

Whatever medium of communication is used in collections, the tone of the message delivered generally escalates, as the debt becomes more overdue, from a clear reminder that the customer should pay to the issue of a notice of legal proceedings to recover the debt. The telephone is the fastest and most flexible way to determine the reason for delayed payment and to respond appropriately to gain commitment to payment, minimizing the likelihood of escalation. It is more personal and less intimidating than a letter, and enables the approach to be tailored to the individual customer. Collections work requires highly skilled personnel who are able to deal spontaneously with diverse responses. It also requires excellent, tightly managed administrative support. There is no point in pursuing a company only to discover that it has been waiting for a credit note or completion of delivery. Internal communications are therefore vitally important. The collector must have the full facts of the situation at hand, including dates of previous contact, with whom, and what was said and agreed at that time. It is obviously useful to know the payment process within a client organization. It helps to identify the current status of an invoice and agree a practical time for payment (although many companies have emergency payment clearance mechanisms) and to contact the appropriate person(s) to effect payment.

One problem with telephone collection is that it is intangible. There is no automatic record of what was said by either side. Some companies follow up with a letter specifying the action that both sides agreed to during the call. If the customer has a query, then the collections department must ensure that its resolution is pursued internally with the relevant personnel. Outstanding queries can account for over half the debt to some businesses and their quick resolution is a significant factor in the success of collections. Company personnel dealing with customers should be reminded regularly about the importance of communicating information which affects collections, such as the issuing of credit notes, customer queries and the arrival of payments. Computerized account handling should make this type of information instantly available to the collector.

Boosting productivity

For businesses with large customer bases the cost of telephone collections can become very significant. However, when conducted by skilled personnel it is a cost-efficient method of collection and there are opportunities to improve efficiency through automation, as in the following example.

Case study 19.1

Bank of Scotland Card Services Division uses the telephone routinely to chase overdue payments at their card-processing centre at Dunfermline. It has proved to be the fastest and most efficient technique. Even so, unlike the mass mailings favoured by the industry in the past, telephone collection is labour intensive. As the bank became a major third party card processor, processing cards also for the Automobile Association, Chase Manhattan Bank, and the Halifax and National & Provincial Building Societies, the number of accounts grew over a four-year period from 400 000 to 2 million. These increased volumes meant that productivity became a crucial issue within the collections department.

Quality of customer service has always been a top priority of Bank of Scotland, and it was now serving not only its own customers but also third party partners and their customers. Any productivity increase had to be without risk to service levels. The solution chosen was to install an automatic predictive dialling system, manufactured in the USA by Davox and supplied by Datapoint (UK).

Prior to installation of the system, in 1990, collectors dialled numbers manually from an electronic list generated by the bank's collection system. Contact failure rate was high, at around 40 per cent, as many people called did not answer. Collectors also spent a significant amount of their time researching telephone numbers, where these had changed or were incomplete. Customers who could not be contacted by phone were sent a letter requesting payment and they, in turn, would write back. This process could take as long as 10 days, during which time payment may not have been collected and the debt could have worsened.

The Davox system would cut unproductive time dramatically, increasing the number of customers that collectors could talk to and therefore the amount collected. It would also reduce the customer record update time, using a 'smart' button facility. The nature of collections calls has not changed. Each case is treated on its merits. Some require a customer service-like approach or a simple reminder, while others need to be more demanding.

The system is linked to the bank's mainframe computer, holding card account records, and uses a filtering process to generate automatically a list of customers to be called. Selection parameters can be based upon any data fields within the records, such as particular balances, account ranges, product, or a code resulting from previous contact or action. This enables precise targeting of collection calls and appropriate briefing of collectors. Telephone numbers in account records are dialled automatically and only answered calls are connected to collectors. At the same time, the appropriate customer record, script and product name are displayed on the collector's screen. The product name enables collectors to introduce themselves appropriately. As a third party processor, clients insist upon calls made on their behalf being introduced with their name.

Flashing messages are generated automatically in situations that are out of the ordinary, such as first payment defaults, and require special handling by collectors. When the system is generating a calling list relating to more than one product, it can identify duplicate occurrences of the same telephone number so that only one call needs to be made to that customer.

The way in which the system handles negative call responses, such as 'no answer' or 'busy', is decided by the bank. The system can detect answering machines and can be set either to pass them to an operator, to leave a message, or re-dial later. When messages are left, a dedicated inbound telephone number is given for customers to return the call. Customer records with bad numbers, such as unobtainables or missing digits, are automatically coded and separated for number research.

The card-processing centre's calling hours are from 9.00 a.m. until 8.30 p.m. At those times of the day when a large proportion of customers called are usually available, the dialling rate is controlled by collectors. At other times it is set to autopaced dialling, where the system automatically adjusts the dialling rate in order to deliver the right number of answered calls to keep collectors busy.

A factor in the bank's choice of the Davox system was the 'smart' button facility, which enables operators to enter complex instructions at a single keystroke. At the simplest level, collectors can quickly log standard replies such as 'promised to pay' or 'left message'. This is not only quicker but also avoids the use of abbreviations which could confuse others. More significantly, the collections department sets up repayment programmes where cardholders place an offer to clear arrears by instalments. Before the system was installed, the collector had to carry out a number of operations to update the account record:

1. Place an appropriate status on the account record.
2. Change the work date.
3. Call up another screen.
4. Recalculate arrears.
5. Put a note on the account record.
6. Input the agreed repayment amount.

With the Davox system this is accomplished by a single keystroke followed by input of the agreed amount. The system offers 144 of these smart buttons.

One of the biggest headaches in collections is actually making contact with cardholders. The system's filtering process offers Bank of Scotland Card Services considerable productivity gains by automatically segregating and dialling batches of account holders when they are most likely to be available. The bank has found, for example, that female customers can be contacted best between 9.00 a.m. and 10.00 a.m. These accounts are filtered out, and dialled, automatically during that period. Another method used is to gear calls to coincide with the screening of popular television programmes, calling female customers during the soap operas and male customers during live sports programmes. The filtering parameters can be changed to take advantage of any trends identified from management reports generated by the system, thus the chances of contacting customers are always optimized. Other features of the system include automatic rescheduling of calls to a time when a customer is expected home, and automatic dialling of referral numbers given over the telephone.

Where both business and home numbers are available, the bank only calls business numbers after at least one pass through the calling file on home numbers, or when there is something wrong with the home number recorded. When business numbers are being dialled, all operators are logged on to the system so that they know every connection will be to a business number and can alter their approach accordingly.

The working environment is very important. Collectors may be talking to 40 or more customers per hour on matters that are at best delicate, so they require a noise-free area. Bank of Scotland Card Services have found that this is best achieved by providing individual booths. They have also reduced the length of shifts to four hours, as any longer time than that could result in extreme tiredness and declining quality of calls.

Introduction of the Davox system has achieved enormous productivity gains, and improved collection rates, as shown in Table 19.1. This has important knock-on effects. The higher volume of contacts made enables the collections department to sell the benefits of paying to a much more sophisticated degree, and to do it much earlier in the delinquency cycle. By speaking to new customers after a lapse of only one payment, they can educate them in the terms and conditions of the account and segregate the 'lazy' payers, the 'won't' pays and the 'can't' pays. This helps to reduce the flow rate from one delinquency band to another and ultimately to minimize bad debts.

Table 19.1 Productivity impact of an automatic predictive dialling system, with smart button update, in debt collection. (Courtesy of Bank of Scotland Card Services Division)

	Manual dialling from electronic list	Automatic predictive dialling and smart button update
Contacts per hour per operator	8	40
Average talk and update time	180 seconds	69 seconds
Increase in time spent talking to customers	–	+70–80%
Increase in operator productivity	–	+380%
Number of operators required	19	8
Increase in volume of calls returned	–	+100%
Increase in promises to pay received and kept	–	+200%

Such benefits have encouraged many organizations with large customer bases, particularly in the financial services sector, to use this technology to capitalize on the power of the telephone for collections. One of the UK's leading mail order companies also uses the Davox predictive dialler when chasing overdue payments. It has found that when a customer becomes a delinquent payer it is more often than not a temporary situation, perhaps the result of a change of lifestyle or a domestic problem. The cost of acquiring new customers in the mail order business is particularly high and the company feels that the telephone provides the most flexible method of attending to each individual's needs in terms of practical payment arrangements, and so on, to help retain their business. The company's attitude to customer retention within the cash collection activity was shown when there was major flooding in Wales in June 1992. Many people were made homeless by the flood and the company felt that it would be unfair to risk adding to their burden by calling and asking for money. When it was filtering customer lists for cash collection calls at this time it automatically removed those customers (based on their postcode) who might be affected by the flooding. This is indicative of the attitude growing within many organizations.

There is increasing realization that customer credit must be managed in a way that helps the company to retain its customers. The telephone, as a personal medium which allows every customer to be treated on merit, is proving valuable in helping to achieve this goal.

20
Crisis management

Critical situations can arise in any organization. Some business sectors – such as public transport, oil, water, fast moving consumer goods, pharmaceuticals – are particularly susceptible to causing great harm when things go seriously wrong, but even something as benign as disruption to normal services, or an industrial dispute, has potential to escalate and cause disproportionate commercial damage. In addition to any immediate loss in revenue (interrupted trading or production, loss of stock, etc.), and the cost of the operational response, a crisis situation has potential to damage the brand and company image (possibly affecting share prices) and consequently can result in loss of market share and long-term loss of revenues. The way in which an organization responds to a crisis, whatever it is, determines the extent of this damage. Communications lie at the heart of effective crisis management. The telephone now plays a major role in crisis communications, capitalizing on its speed and the ability to respond directly and personally to individuals' concerns. Telephone activity can begin within hours of a crisis arising and stands a much better chance than other media (except face-to-face meeting) of satisfying individuals' needs for information, help or reassurance. The message can be targeted, on inbound and outbound calls, to those most affected or concerned by the crisis, whether they be consumers, distributors and retail outlets, suppliers, employees, lobby groups, or anyone else with an interest.

20.1 A growing threat

Businesses are increasingly vulnerable to crises and to their damaging influence escalating out of proportion to the scale of the incident. Organizations are becoming operationally more complex, creating wider scope for things to go wrong as a result of either internal disruption or external forces. News travels faster and further than ever before, with the potential to inform markets world wide of a crisis within hours. Increasing diversity and competition in the media means that their appetite for a 'good' story no longer stops at the major corporations; even the small local business can become the focus of media attention. There is a growing threat of direct action and deliberate scare-mongering by groups seeking media coverage for their cause. Public expectations of openness and honesty from businesses are increasing and they have a growing appetite to hear about corporations that do not meet those expectations. A crisis can give rise to difficult and emotive issues and media coverage can compound consumer fears, fuel lobby group protestations and generally stir emotions among those affected. The tendency to 'trial by media' calls for an immediate response to try to control the messages being relayed to the marketplace. But while the media reach a mass audience, and are highly influential, the audiences affected by a crisis can be targeted more precisely, and with greater control of the message, by more direct means. Communications with the media are obviously of crucial importance, but they are only a part of the picture. Every organization has audiences whose opinions are important to its long-term interests. Response to a crisis should target all of those who are affected and who are influential, so that it can address their needs directly.

20.2 Contingency planning

In a crisis an organization will be judged most critically by its initial response. If it is perceived negatively, whether or not this is justified, it is extremely difficult to change these initial perceptions. At this stage there is a high risk of disproportionate damage and the organization must respond immediately to control perceptions. However, this is only possible if a crisis management plan is already in place. There are four main stages in planning and preparing to cope with a corporate crisis. First, identify the potential crisis; second, develop plans and procedures necessary for effective communication; third, train all the personnel involved in responding to a crisis; and, fourth, run a simulation exercise to ensure that the plans work effectively.

The potential for crisis

The first stage is often the most difficult. It involves not only identifying potential crisis situations but also evaluating the risk they present, the probability of their occurrence, and the issues they would raise. Crises can span a huge number of areas, such as an industrial accident, product failure or contamination, a pollution incident, staff held hostage or kidnapped, share price collapse, an industrial dispute, the theft of bearer bonds, or any one of potentially hundreds of different situations. Although each one of them requires a tailored response, situations will generally share many of the same procedures and use the same channels of communication.

Planning responses

The next stage involves planning how the organization will respond to any particular crisis. A crisis management committee should be elected to formulate, direct and manage communications during a crisis. It will include representatives from the range of corporate functions and possibly from external agencies such as advertising and PR. A senior, authoritative member of management is required to act as spokesperson for external communications, and this person may also have responsibility for giving final clearance for the release of information. Internal channels of communication should provide committee members with immediate access to the latest information on the situation to enable them to give appropriate advice when required. In addition to the management committee, there may be a host of other people involved in actually implementing communications (by mail, fax, telephone, etc.) depending on whether internal or external resources are used. A large organization may have a pool of between 40 and 60 people who support the internal PR team in dealing with external audiences during a crisis. When designating people for these roles it is important that they are selected from among personnel who would not be involved elsewhere in the operational response to a crisis.

Training

The third stage is training, which may cover a wide range of skills but will obviously concentrate on communication. Senior management on the crisis committee require training in media relations, particularly handling television and press conferences and media interviews. However, it is preferable to have a single media spokesperson during a crisis, to minimize the risk of conflicting messages being delivered. Members of the committee should also know how to liaise effectively with the emergency services, local and regulatory authorities and any other external bodies which may be involved in the response to a crisis. The crisis management plan will identify corporate and individual responsibilities with regard to complying with legislative and other regulations imposed by external bodies.

The biggest group of people requiring training is likely to be those involved in telephone activity, which is examined in more detail later. One of the most important aspects of response to a crisis is the attitude of those dealing with external audiences. While the methods of response will be defined in crisis procedures, it must be a human, caring response. The ultimate goal of training is therefore to enable people to understand the differing needs of the various external audiences and to respond appropriately.

Simulated response

The final stage of planning for a crisis is to perform simulation exercises, or 'practice runs'. These are designed both to test operational response and crisis communications and to ensure that those involved actually realize what a crisis is like – the pressures and demands of dealing with people who may be distressed, angry, confused or demanding action. A simulation enables plans to be amended, when necessary, and any additional training needs to be identified. Some organizations operate large-scale simulations of major incidents, involving customers, their relatives, the media and emergency services in role play. Crisis management plans must be reviewed regularly, perhaps yearly, to ensure that they accommodate changing needs, and refresher training should be provided at similarly regular intervals.

20.3 Message control

The crux of crisis management is message control. Although an organization needs to be open and honest in the face of a crisis, the release of information has to be controlled. The corporate position on all of the issues arising has to be consistent and it has to be consistently communicated to all the audiences concerned and across all the media used. The crisis plan will name the sources of information that will be used to formulate external communications, which may include external experts as well as company personnel.

The printed word, generally press releases, will usually form the basis of the information the organization wants to disclose and how it would like it to be conveyed. This information may be updated over time and expanded upon through certain channels, such as mail or a telephone hotline, but it is vital that nothing is disclosed without it having been approved and made easily available to the relevant interested parties. For example, disclosure to someone of information that has not been made available generally can quickly reach the media, which could respond by saying that the organization is not telling the full story.

Message targeting

The nature of the crisis will naturally determine the audiences that are affected or have a vested interest. The audiences that may be important are listed in Table 20.1, along with the main channels available to communicate with them and important issues in deciding the communications strategy for a particular crisis. The key consideration is the likely concerns of the relevant audiences and how they can be addressed most appropriately. Speed is essential and the crisis plan will include procedures for

Table 20.1 Some considerations in developing contact strategies in crisis communications

Audiences
- Who is likely to be 'concerned' about the crisis? For example:
  - buyers (including wholesale and retail), product/service users, prospects, suppliers, competitors, trade associations – and their representatives, e.g. lawyers
  - employees and their relatives, trades unions – and their representatives
  - environmental and health lobby groups, local and national pressure groups, academics, neighbours, local social groups
  - the parent organization, subsidiary/associated organizations, shareholders, the financial community
  - local and national government and its elected representatives, civil servants, regulatory bodies
  - the media.

- What are the numbers in each audience (known or estimated)?
- Are they known individually? If so, what contact details are available, e.g. address, telephone number?

The message
- What are the likely concerns of each audience and how best can they be resolved? Consider both the operational response (such as product recall), if any, and image management.
- Are there different priorities in contacting various audiences?
- Will members of each audience require a tailored response?
- How quickly do they need to be contacted?
- What elements are required to convey the messages, e.g. visual (still or motion), printed or spoken word?
- Will the messages change over time?

Communication channels
- What channels of communication (local, regional, national, international, consumer, trade) are available for contacting each of the audiences concerned? For example:
  - press, magazine, radio and television advertising and editorial
  - mail (post or hand-delivered)
  - telephone (inbound or outbound)
  - fax
  - outdoor advertising
  - leaflets (door drop, point of sale, street distribution)
  - personal visits.

- Considering all the relevant factors (message content and objectives; time-dependency; numbers affected, their location, accessibility, etc.), what are the best methods of communicating with the various audiences and, if necessary, keeping them informed?

implementing the communications plan immediately. Where press advertising is involved, for example, it will specify the titles available to reach the relevant audiences, lead times, costings, and so on. Contingency plans for telephone activity will include the resourcing of skilled staff, including how they can be contacted quickly out of normal working hours, telephone equipment and lines, and information management support.

The first communications response to a crisis will sometimes be a coordinated PR programme, including press releases to national newspapers, magazines, television and radio stations, together with journalist briefings or press conferences. In some situations, however, this may come only after key audiences have been contacted. In the case of an industrial accident, for example, relatives of the workforce (and not only those affected directly) will be among those contacted first. When a contamination scare necessitates product recall, the trade will be contacted, in person or by telephone and/or fax, before the news is released to the media. To ensure that communications can be implemented immediately, it is important that contact details (name, address, telephone and fax number) of all relevant, known contacts are kept up to date.

When a crisis affects only a select number of people from a particular audience it is vital that those people can be identified, if not personally then at least who they are likely to be. In the case of a product fault, for example, when only a particular batch from a certain production line is affected, it is necessary to trace the distribution of that batch. This will enable the company to identify and recall unsold risk stock, determine what has been sold and, if it is lucky, to whom. As risk stock has to be located quickly, the coding systems used (for the product, batch, production and distribution) have to provide a precise trail that can be analysed immediately to trace the whereabouts of all product from the batch. The warning of customers about faulty goods, asking for their return, is one of the areas where direct response advertising is used frequently. The importance of being able to identify immediately the people affected by a crisis cannot be over-stressed. Obviously it may be impossible to maintain details of end-user customers, for example, but knowledge of who they are likely to be will enable the organization to decide how they can be contacted quickly.

The telephone has an obvious role in contacting known individuals affected by a crisis, but sometimes outbound calling has to be used with care. Delivering potentially alarming or upsetting news by telephone should be avoided whenever possible, and in all situations the caller must ensure that the correct person has been reached before the message is delivered. Also, calls should be made at 'reasonable' hours if practical. Teleconferences (see page 250) are an increasingly important method for contacting specific audiences and addressing their concerns at once. Not only is this more efficient than contacting people individually, but it also demonstrates to all members of the audience that they are getting the same attention and the same messages as everyone else.

Probably the most valuable use of the telephone in crisis management is when those affected are not known individually. Direct response advertising, with a dedicated telephone number, enables a company to target those likely to be affected and invite people to call for further information. This method is used very widely for applications as diverse as informing people of the numbers on stolen cheques, the code numbers on a batch of faulty product and the impact of a local development. Providing a telephone number enables those affected to call and have their individual needs addressed. The company appears open and honest. This is obviously enhanced by providing a toll-free number. (Why should people pay for the call if it is the company's 'fault'?)

Achieving a consistent, accurate response

The interactive nature of a telephone conversation is a great advantage in dealing with diverse needs, but it also makes message control more difficult. Consistency in printed materials, such as press releases and advertising copy, is much easier to achieve than in a conversation. Handling inbound calls, in particular, requires expertise in fielding a wide range of enquiries and delivering a consistent, accurate and 'approved' response to each one. The following example illustrates how this can be achieved.

Case study 20.1

From early 1989, the UK food industry faced growing public anxiety raised by a barrage of often conflicting news stories concerning food poisoning. First there was a nationwide scare about salmonella in eggs, followed closely by reports on the dangers of listeria in pâté, chicken and other chilled foods. As time went on, stories on many other food safety issues emerged, including BSE ('mad cow disease'), Alar on apples, and food additives. It began to seem as if no food was safe to eat.

A growing number of consumers were showing their concern by either not buying certain produce or asking food retailers for advice and reassurance. It was whole product ranges that were under threat, not particular brands, and the amount of specialist knowledge required to answer consumers' questions was potentially vast.

For the first time, the six major UK grocery retailers joined forces to set up and fund the Food Safety Advisory Centre (FSAC). Their principal objective was to allay fears among the public by offering advice on food safety. The strategy was worked out in discussion between the six retailers (Asda, Gateway, Morrison's, J Sainsbury, Safeway and Tesco) and two PR agencies, Burson-Marsteller and City & Corporate Counsel. A key component was to be a toll-free telephone advice line, called Foodline, which would provide the focal point for direct communications with consumers. Telemarketing agency Telelab, specialist in crisis management, was chosen to provide this service.

A panel of independent experts was assembled to act as a technical resource for FSAC so that it could provide the public with the most advanced information available. The panel was drawn from the fields of microbiology, food safety and medicine, as well as representatives from the Institution of Environmental Health Officers and the National Consumer Council. In addition, there was a technical committee, comprising technical directors of the food retailers involved. These experts helped in the preparation of press releases and a question and answer document, the Issues Portfolio, for Telelab operators.

Foodline was launched on 20 February 1989 with a coordinated PR programme. Press releases were sent to national newspapers, magazines, and television and radio stations. A series of journalist briefings included a press conference where they saw Foodline in action. National press and radio carried stories, and television news showed Telelab operators dealing with enquiries. Leaflets and posters carrying the Foodline number were displayed prominently in the retailers' outlets and, in some instances, the number was even printed on supermarket checkout receipts.

Ensuring the accuracy and consistency of information provided by Foodline operators was a major task, because of the diversity of issues concerned. Regular press releases became the focal point for information. Careful planning and update briefings ensured that operators responded in line with the latest facts being released to the media, thus making certain that consumers received consistent, accurate data.

The Issues Portfolio provided Foodline operators with a message-controlled body of information in sufficient detail to handle all but the most technical of trade and consumer enquiries. A nutritionist was available, as part of the Telelab team, to handle more detailed calls. Members of the expert panel could also be contacted for advice on specialist enquiries that could not be answered immediately. As the range of enquiries was expected to be very diverse, and sometimes unusual, Telelab operators were briefed and trained even more rigorously than usual. The on-site nutritionist was also involved. When Foodline went live, on 20 February 1989, it was staffed with 20 operators.

Strict service levels had been set. Calls had to be answered after no more than two rings and the overriding objectives were to reassure and inform. Operators greeted callers and introduced themselves as the Food Safety Advisory Centre. The retailers' names were not mentioned unless requested by a caller. In many cases only simple reassurance and practical advice was needed. These calls lasted, on average, from two to three minutes. Other enquiries, especially those dealt with by the on-site nutritionist, led to calls lasting 30 minutes or longer. Callers whose enquiries required specialist knowledge were phoned back, usually within 24 hours, after consultation with a member of the expert panel, the team of retailers' technical directors, or other external source.

Information recorded during each call included the date and time, caller's name, address and telephone number, source of the Foodline number, topic of the call, whether it was referred to an expert, the response given to the caller, the nature of any follow-up required (with date and time to call), the outcome of any follow-up, and any further action required. This information was keyed directly into the computer to aid rapid analysis on an ongoing basis.

The results of calls, and the clarity of the information recorded, were checked continuously by the project manager. Accurate recording of what had been said helped to maintain continuity when a call had to be followed up by someone other than the initial operator. The project manager could also be assured that each caller had received a relevant and satisfactory reply. Call handling was monitored closely so that potential problems could be addressed quickly. Telelab operators and the on-site nutritionist were regularly re-briefed as new issues arose.

Being responsive to needs

The Issues portfolio was a dynamic document, updated on a daily, even hourly, basis. Issues for coverage were identified from analysis of public concerns and media enquiries, as well as information from market research and feedback from retailers about questions asked in-store. The portfolio was initially designed to deal with questions about listeria, salmonella and food storage and handling, but it soon grew to embrace a wide range of food-related topics (see Table 20.2). Feedback from the public was especially important. At the end of each day, analysis of enquiries highlighted the practical worries that were likely to arise. It could then be decided whether concern about a particular issue warranted drafting the appropriate question and answer for insertion in the portfolio.

Answers were drafted by, or in consultation with, the panel of experts, the on-site nutritionist and the team of technical directors. To obtain the most advanced information available, a large number of other sources were also consulted during the project, including the Microwave Association, the Ministry of Agriculture, Fisheries and Food, and the Canned Food Information Centre.

Initially, the Issues Portfolio was approximately 10 pages in length. By January 1990 it had expanded to almost 120 pages, indexed according to issue and

Table 20.2 Some of the issues on which Foodline operators provided consumers with advice and reassurance. (Courtesy of Telelab Limited)

Alar in apples	Listeria
Aluminium in food	Mercury in milk
Bread and flour	Mineral oil on dried
BSE	fruit
BST	Nitrates
Decaffeinated coffee	Organic produce
Dioxins	Other bacteria
E numbers	Pesticides
Fats and oils	Refrigeration
Food poisoning	Salmonella
Government food policy	Supermarket storage/
Home food storage/preparation/	preparation/cooking
cooking	Tecnazine on potatoes
Home hygiene	Toxoplasmosis
Irradiation	Wax on fruit

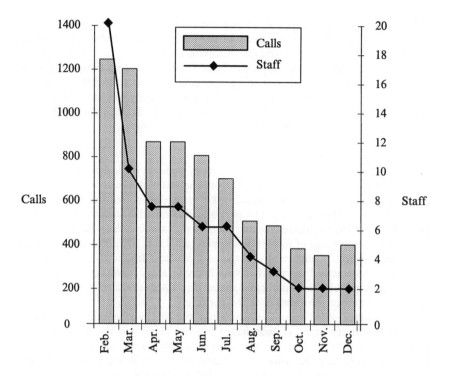

Figure 20.1 Foodline call volumes and corresponding staffing levels in 1989. (Courtesy of Telelab Limited)

cross-referenced for easy access. Special information was included, tailored to the needs of various special interest groups such as pregnant women and those with medical or dietary restrictions. All callers requesting medical advice were told to consult their general practitioner.

The portfolio was not computerized because the shape and extent of the document was changing so rapidly, and the wording had to be so tightly controlled, that it would have hindered unnecessarily the speed and flexibility with which Foodline was able to respond to shifts in public concern.

Foodline received an enormous variety of calls, on everything from food hygiene to environmental issues, from a diverse range of individuals. At one end of the scale, there were elderly people worried about the pork chops they had bought that morning in a corner shop. At the other, there were academics and food writers whose interest in particular food issues was of a more professional nature and required more detailed answers. Somewhere between these two fell trade enquiries, from independent retailers, for instance, worried that their display cabinets might not be adequately refrigerated. The vast majority of callers expressed real concern, but there were exceptions. Among these were a number of calls from representatives of pressure groups who used the Foodline regularly to express their views on issues often peripherally related to food. These callers were treated with the same politeness and respect as all others, and were supplied with relevant information and advice wherever possible.

Fulfilment did not have a large part to play in the early stages of the project, as the emphasis was on providing information there and then to allay practical worries. However, after three months, FSAC produced the *Good Food Safety Guide*, a four-page leaflet which provided advice on food safety 'At the Store' and 'At Home'. The only branding it carried was the retailers' names at the foot of the back page. Telelab mailed a copy of the leaflet to all enquirers, within 24 hours, as well as to the entire database of previous enquirers.

Because of the unpredictable nature of the response levels, Foodline began with 20 operators to ensure that sufficient call-handling capacity was available to maintain the strict service levels that had been set. However, as the project progressed, it soon became possible to make accurate quantitative predictions of call volumes and adjust staffing accordingly, as shown in Figure 20.1.

In January 1990, the Foodline operation transferred to PR agency City & Corporate Counsel. Four years after the launch, at February 1993, it was still receiving around 30–40 calls a week, generated by advertising through Citizens Advice Bureaux, Local Education Authorities and at point of sale in supermarkets.

Only the telephone enables an organization to address such a wide range of concerns, individually, with such a fast and accurate response. It is also highly cost-effective and ensures that resources are targeted where they are needed most and will do most good to protect brand and company image. Some of the other indications for incorporating the telephone into the crisis communications plan are listed in Table 20.3.

Staff: the key resource

Telelab estimates that with good training, thorough briefing, a well-written question and answer document followed by close supervision, an operator can handle around 90 per cent of the enquiries that arise on this type of crisis line. The vast majority require only immediate, practical advice. The other 10 per cent may require detailed knowledge of the subject that only a life-time of experience can provide, and the agency says that it is important to have the safety net of knowing that specialist back-up support is available if needed. Operators should never be allowed to pretend a level of knowledge they do not have. The role of experts was especially important with Foodline.

Rigorous selection and training of telephone staff for crisis communications is obviously important. They have to be consistently helpful, professional, polite and show genuine interest in every caller's enquiry and have the skills to deal sympathetically with anxious, irate or difficult callers, and with unusual enquiries. Telelab operators are trained to fit the style of

Table 20.3 Some indicators for considering the telephone for crisis communications

The communication is urgent.

Receipt of the message must be confirmed.

The issues are emotive.

The crisis has a significant personal impact on individuals.

Advice or instructions must be given on an individual basis.

Rapid feedback from those affected will be of help in handling the situation more effectively.

A relatively small number of high value contacts is affected.

Those affected are likely to have a wide range of different concerns.

The concerned audiences are very diverse.

Those affected are not known individually but must be communicated with personally.

The situation will change over time and many people may want to be kept informed.

their delivery (although *never* the content) to the caller. They are also trained to summarize the content of calls clearly. Any ambiguity or vagueness would be queried by the project manager, who checks the result of each call. This is important, because if the call has to be followed up by someone other than the initial operator, that person needs to know everything *relevant* that was said. The operator's response is also logged, to ensure that a follow-up caller has a record of the content of each conversation. The project manager can then also be assured that all callers have received relevant and satisfactory responses to their enquiries.

The primary objectives in handling consumer calls on a crisis line, says Telelab, are to *reassure* and to *inform*. One of the consequences is that calls should be answered quickly, on a dedicated line, with a salutation that includes the company name. Callers should never feel that they are being dealt with by an uninterested party or passed between internal departments. In order to ensure that all calls are answered quickly, crisis hotlines serving large audiences (e.g. consumers) are normally overstaffed initially, because it is difficult to predict the level of response. Where follow-up is required, the name, address and telephone number of the caller should be recorded, and there must be clear procedures to ensure that follow-up takes place when promised and meets the needs expressed by the caller.

Organizations with international operations have the problem of ensuring consistency of message across all their markets. The principles of crisis management are no different, but it is vital that all plans which exist to handle a crisis at a national level are geared to convey the same message internationally.

The telephone also has a role after a crisis has passed. The Foodline project resulted in a permanent information resource being made available to the public via the telephone, but it can also be used to help rebuild confidence in a brand and the company through 'normal' telemarketing activity specifically targeted at those most affected, such as trade customers.

20.4 Prepared for the inevitable

In some industries, such as the utilities, operational difficulties not infrequently lead to loss of service or supply and can generate massive response from disgruntled customers. The telephone may provide instant access for customers to report a problem and often to complain, but if their calls are not answered quickly and efficiently then their dissatisfaction will be heightened rather than quelled. There are usually insufficient operators available to cope with wholly unexpected crises, even in large call centres where staff can be diverted from other tasks. Automated call-handling technology can prove invaluable in these situations.

Case study 20.2

In 1991, Wisconsin Electric Power Company (WEPCO) in the USA installed an Aspect CallCenter ACD linked to a voice response unit (VRU). A VRU can be programmed very quickly with a message relating to a specific incident which can be played automatically to callers when all operators are busy, or to all callers. WEPCO's VRU proved its value when a major storm struck its service area, on 17 June 1992, throwing customers into darkness and creating a sudden surge of calls from people wanting to know what had happened. The average time to answer while the VRU was in operation was only 2 seconds. When the VRU had to be taken down, briefly, because of a problem with WEPCO's computer system, the average wait time jumped to 49 seconds. During this incident, the VRU handled 1584 calls while WEPCO representatives took an additional 5645. This compares with an average of 3800 calls received during the whole of a normal day.

Pre-emptive communications

The telephone can also be used in pre-emptive strategies, as in the following example.

Case study 20.3

The governing authority for an international airport, knowing it would be seeking planning permission in 1992 for a major development, decided to minimize opposition to its plans by announcing them, and inviting public comment, months ahead of submitting the planning application. By creating a channel of communication and inviting feedback, it hoped to take much of the heat out of a critical situation.

The airport authority recognized that its plans would be perceived in a negative way. It knew that opposition would come from many parties with an 'interest' in the planned development, including residents living within a 50-mile radius of the airport, relatives of older residents living nearby, competing airports, environmentalists, pollution pressure groups, the noise abatement lobby and transport authorities.

Infoplan International PR was briefed to organize a communications channel that would enable the public and representatives of various national, international and local bodies to debate the issues, ask for further information, or simply to air their grievances. The agency's crisis team was briefed over a period of five days, during which time 'questions and answers' were drafted on the 10 issues arising from the planned development likely to be of most concern to those affected. A crisis manager's manual was produced, containing the questions and answers, street maps of the entire catchment area, and information and statistics regarding the airport and its history. The agency prepared 10 of its dedicated crisis hotlines, which would be open 12 hours a day, 7 days a week.

About six months before applying for planning permission, the airport authority outlined its plans at a press conference and in a leaflet delivered to all residents within a 50-mile radius of the airport – all promoting the hotline number. The hotlines had been activated two days previously to enable the knowledge of the crisis team to be tested. Ten managers, and deputies, staffed the lines and handled 250 'angry' calls, made by an outside agency, covering every possible aspect of the subject.

The hotlines were opened to the outside world on the day of the press conference. The names and addresses of all callers were recorded to enable the airport authority, subsequently, to keep them up to date on the planning situation. The topic of each call was noted, briefly, as well as whether the caller was satisfied with the answers provided. Managers also noted the tone of voice and mood of each caller at the beginning and end of the conversation. The airport authority was sent copies of completed forms at the end of each day and wrote personal letters to callers who were not satisfied with the response they had received on the hotline. An average of 500 calls a day were received during the first week, rising to 600 a day in the following week as more of the one million leaflets were distributed. During a two-month period, over 18 000 calls were answered. When the application for planning permission was submitted, after an unexpected delay of a few months, it attracted far less animosity than expected from the public, and media coverage was far more positive than it had been when the original announcement was made.

The need to manage the perceptions of a brand and company in the marketplace is increasing. When the status quo is upset or threatened by a crisis, the company's response is a vital measure of protection for its brand and company image. Many insurance firms now review the crisis management provisions of companies before deciding their insurance premium. Preparation is itself insurance against the worst possible outcome in any crisis situation. The better prepared a business, the less damage it is likely to suffer. The power of the telephone to target those affected by a crisis, and personally offer information, advice or reassurance, means that it should be a key component in every crisis management plan.

21
Investor relations

Investors in a company are an important target for marketing communications. No matter how large or small the organization, it is important that shareholders, and those with loan investments, act in its best interests when making decisions about their investment. A wide range of intermediaries, such as brokers, financial analysts and advisers, can influence investment decisions and are therefore an equally important audience.

21.1 Highly valuable 'customers'

Investors and the financial community are little different to most market audiences; like any other customer or prospect they can be influenced in their decisions and in their recommendations to others. However, the stakes may be much higher, when there is a takeover bid for example, and there are stringent regulations governing the 'promotion' of stock investments.

If a company wishes to build a reputation as a 'good investment' it must establish a customer-oriented relationship with members of the relevant audiences, to earn their respect and support. All major companies have investor relations programmes, although in the UK it is only relatively recently that they have gone much beyond meeting their statutory obligations in communicating directly with investors. Compared with the early 1980s, however, the current climate is much more geared towards proactive marketing. Some companies, such as British Gas with its newspaper style review of annual results, are being much more creative in their communications strategies.

21.2 Opportunities to build relationships

The telephone is not yet used routinely for communicating with shareholders, although this is not to say that regular dialogue has no value. A sound knowledge of investors is invaluable, particularly when their support is required, and this can only be obtained through regular dialogue. A shareholder database, like a customer database, should provide sufficient information on individuals to enable precisely targeted communications when the need arises. The database should also facilitate planning of communications strategies to meet shareholders' changing needs.

Legal constraints

Telephone calls aimed at influencing investment decisions, directly or through intermediaries, are subject to strict regulations designed to protect individuals from being unintentionally or fraudulently misled. A general principal in these regulations is the provision of 'best advice', whereby the potential investor must be given all the facts necessary to make the best decision (i.e. completeness of disclosure). In the UK, there are additional regulations specifically covering telephone campaigns relating to takeovers, mergers and substantial acquisitions. For example, only previously published, currently accurate information may be used, and shareholders must not be pressurized but encouraged to consult their professional advisers.

The spontaneous nature of telephone conversations means that great care must be taken to ensure that telephone agents adhere to the regulations. Printed literature is used, invariably, to provide potential investors with any detailed information required, while the telephone can serve a variety of support roles.

Share offers

The most visible use of the telephone in UK investor relations has been as a response mechanism during the public offers of shares in such national industries as British Gas, BT and the water authorities. Multi-million pound direct response media campaigns, encouraging people to register their interest in buying shares, have generated massive response from the public. The telephone is used here purely as a response mechanism because, to comply with UK regulations, advertising must make it clear that investment decisions should be based upon the share issue prospectus and not the advertising.

These public share offers made shareholders of many people who otherwise would not have considered the investment, resulting in a large number of 'inexperienced' shareholders. This created an opportunity for companies to offer additional advice and support.

Shareholder support programmes

The massive direct response advertising campaign for the privatization of British Gas, in 1986, attracted hundreds of thousands of calls from potential small shareholders. The campaign was so successful that the issue was four times oversubscribed. British Gas has subsequently provided various types of support for its shareholders.

Case study 21.1

British Gas is the largest gas supply business in the western world, with a growing number of diverse business interests around the world and in the region of two million shareholders. The company set up a dedicated office in London, shortly after privatization, to provide shareholders with immediate, direct access to information and advice concerning their shareholding. The address and telephone number of the office were published prominently in UK telephone directories and on documentation sent to all shareholders.

Over 155 500 shareholders had contacted the office by March 1993, approximately 75 per cent of them by telephone. By this time, it had become apparent that the company's small shareholders were more familiar with the concept of share ownership and that much of the work being dealt with by the office could be transferred to the company's Registrars, National Westminster Bank plc, who are responsible for maintaining the share register.

From March 1993, shareholders would direct enquiries regarding their personal shareholding, such as arrangements for paying dividends and lost share certificates, to the Registrars either by letter or via their telephone enquiry service.

The Company Secretary's office within British Gas continues to provide a wide range of services to help small shareholders understand everything about their shares, and serves as a point of direct access for individuals to air their views and concerns specifically on matters of company policy. The office reports regularly to British Gas senior management on the issues raised with them.

The shareholder communications programme is designed to meet the changing needs and preferences of shareholders. One of the channels that has been used is the Shareholder Newsline, a 24-hour recorded information service accessed by dialling a standard London telephone number. Launched in March 1989, it provided the latest information on recent company events and developments. The service had received 10 737 calls by the time it was superseded by other channels, in March 1993, as part of the ongoing development of the communications programme.

Rights issues

The telephone is the ideal communications channel when a company must contact its shareholders quickly to obtain their views, provide information and perhaps answer questions. Tactical telephone campaigns are therefore not uncommon (see Table 21.1).

Table 21.1 Opportunities for using the telephone in investor relations

Audiences	Issues and opportunities
Shareholders (private	Takeovers, mergers, acquisitions
and institutional)	Flotations
Investment advisers	Rights issues
Financial analysts	Stock market suspensions
Brokers	Re-rating of share price
Portfolio managers	Eliciting proxy votes
Financial press	Encouraging attendance at emergency general meetings
High-potential investors	Tracing lost shareholders, e.g. prior to a rights issue
	Company results and other announcements
	Ongoing reporting and opinion research

Case study 21.2

During the summer of 1987, the management of a specialist UK engineering company decided to raise additional capital to fund the development of a rotary engine, which was to be used for military drones and industrial purposes as well as in a newly designed motorcycle.

The aim was to raise £3.77 million by a rights issue of shares in the company. Current shareholders were mailed an attractively designed prospectus containing all the documents they would need to take up their rights and to subscribe to further shares if they wished.

The response from the shareholders was slow. It became important for the company to contact its shareholders quickly, to generate an immediate reply before the approaching deadline date when the offer would be opened to the public.

Telemarketing agency Programmes was contracted to spend 200 hours contacting the company's shareholders throughout Britain. The purpose of each call was to check whether the shareholders had received all the documents sent to them, explain their rights under the terms of the issue, and invite them to take up their rights and the additional share offer.

Many of the company's shareholders were over 50 years old. The majority of them particularly appreciated being contacted directly by phone, as they found it easier to understand a personal explanation of the offer rather than the prospectus.

Of the 1395 shareholders contacted by phone, 68 per cent decided to take up their rights. Of these, 457 people took up further shares. The rights issue was a success and the target sum of £3.77 million raised enabled the company to continue engine development and, subsequently, to launch the new motorcycle.

The take-up of shares in a rights issue demonstrates the importance of establishing an ongoing relationship with shareholders. If the company wants them to take up their rights, and provide the funds required, then they need to earn investors' loyalty. As regulations governing the promotion of

Table 21.2 Telephone contact strategy during a takeover bid in the UK. (Courtesy of The Decisions Group)

Day	Stage of bid	Action
	Bid announcement	Initial strategy discussed and formulated
0	Offer document posted	
1	Shareholders able to accept bid	Telephone research of shareholder reaction to bid
14	Deadline for defence	Analyse shareholder register
21	First closing date and disclosure of acceptances	
30	All defence documents presented may withdraw	Commence outbound calling; open inbound helpline
42	Shareholders who have accepted offer are known	
46	Final bid (predator purchases more than 30%)	Recall 'undecided' shareholders, latest calling completed by day 57
57		
60	Bid declared unconditional or it will lapse	

investments make it impossible to use last-minute persuasive tactics, the company must rely to some extent upon its past performance in developing the relationship.

Takeover bids

Where speed is vital, such as under the time constraints on takeover bids (see Table 21.2), the telephone is invaluable.

Case Study 21.3

A national UK supermarket chain was in the initial stages of a bid to take over a smaller Yorkshire-based chain. The bidder's merchant bank needed to find out what would motivate the primarily local private shareholders of the Yorkshire company to accept the offer, and it approached telemarketing agency Programmes for assistance.

Together, they devised a two-stage campaign that would not only directly affect the outcome of the bid, but would also enable the supermarket chain to plan its subsequent strategy more effectively.

In the first stage, Programmes called shareholders of the Yorkshire company to gain feedback and information. The objectives of the call were to check that the shareholders had received the offer documents, to ascertain the local issues that were likely to stop the offer being accepted, and to gauge the general response to the offer.

Programmes discovered that many of the shareholders wanted a better offer for their shares and had decided to wait before making up their minds. These shareholders were noted for calling in the next stage.

As a result of the feedback obtained, the national chain increased its bid and mailed the shareholders with details of the revised offer. Programmes then carried out stage two, calling undecided shareholders identified at the first stage to find out whether the improved offer had made a difference, to clarify the revised offer, and to encourage the shareholders to take action before the agreed deadline.

Of the shareholders who had not made up their minds at the first stage, 11.6 per cent of those called the second time (stage two) stated a preference. As a result, the Yorkshire company lost 2.8 per cent of its support and the national chain gained 5.5 per cent. At the end of stage two, 50.3 per cent of the Yorkshire company's shareholders had said 'yes' to accepting the bid offer. The national supermarket chain successfully used the merger to spread into the Yorkshire area while retaining the goodwill of the local shareholders.

Courting the advisers

Most companies do not have regular dialogue with their individual shareholders, but only with the large institutional investors. To build confidence among the smaller shareholders they rely largely upon the financial community to act as mediators and influencers. They are the principal targets for investor relations programmes.

The impact of the most recent recession has demanded even more of these programmes. Companies have had to explain to the financial community their strategic decisions, on issues such as disposals, redundancies and corporate restructuring, and reassure them about the business's future. The volatile nature of the world's economies and the pressures on profitability have created additional uncertainties. The need for regular dialogue has never been greater.

Many USA companies use the telephone routinely to communicate with the financial community. Investor relations departments, if companies have one, are usually small, which means that time-consuming face-to-face meetings are often impossible, and the telephone is the best alternative.

Communication with analysts and portfolio managers is almost exclusively by telephone, backed by mailing of information when necessary. One objective is research, where companies ask them about their clients and business to learn how to improve communications.

Brokers are also called regularly. They rely heavily upon the telephone, using it to keep in touch with their clients and for cold-calling prospects. It is their normal method of doing business. Although companies are restricted in their statements about their stock, they can alert brokers to new developments, get important feedback on the market, or simply call to tell them to expect important mail.

TELECONFERENCING

One of the fastest growing uses of the telephone in USA investor relations is the teleconference. Many thousands now take place every quarter, when companies link up simultaneously with all the significant members of the financial community to talk with them by telephone about the quarterly results. Participants are alerted to the date and time of the conference and when it arrives they simply enter the organizing company's identification code and they have a live link with the proceedings.

The technology is sophisticated. Individuals may participate in listen-only mode, while others can be allowed a two-way link; when they want to raise a point with the company representatives they simply key a code into their telephone and are automatically placed in a queue. Some companies, e.g. AT&T during its acquisition of NCR, may have up to 1500 people participating in a single teleconference, which can be organized within a matter of hours. The growth of teleconferencing has been driven largely by the USA financial community, who see it as a very efficient way to do business.

21.3 A planned programme of communications

Not surprisingly, some of the USA telecommunications giants, such as AT&T and GTE, are among the most enthusiastic users of the telephone in their investor relations programmes.

Case study 21.4

GTE Corporation is the world's fourth largest publicly owned telecommunications company, with annual revenues of $20 billion (1992). Its shareholders, numbering approximately 540 000, have equity in the Corporation worth just over $10 billion. Direct communications with shareholders, through mail and inbound telephone, is handled by GTE Shareholder Services in North Quincy, Massachusetts, which maintains the shareholder databases. It offers a toll-free number for shareholders' enquiries on issues such as stock ownership, dividend reinvestment and share transfers.

GTE's Investor Relations Department, in Stamford, Connecticut, focuses primarily on institutional investments and runs the communications programme targeting the financial community. The department is small, with three investor relations professionals, and the telephone is used routinely as a marketing communications channel. Face-to-face meetings would be preferable but, with a limited resource, it is sometimes impractical in a market which is large in number and distributed across several financial centres in the domestic market and many abroad.

Although the department has two secretaries screening incoming calls, responding to the random arrival of enquiries is fairly taxing. The communications programme is therefore designed partly to minimize the volume of inbound calls and at the same time to build relationships with members of the financial community. As an example, at the time of GTE's quarterly earnings release, the department calls those investment analysts who have been identified as the key target audience. Given this opportunity to talk with GTE, the analysts are less likely to need to call the department. Equally important, they appreciate not having to chase information and regard the call as a valuable service which distinguishes GTE's investor relations programme from those of other companies.

When looking for new investors, the department uses the telephone to make initial contact to determine if there is interest in a personal meeting. Then, once contact has been established, the telephone is used to maintain regular, systematic communication in order to develop the personal relationship. It is GTE's way of telling the financial community that they are important to the company.

GTE also regularly uses conference calls – for example, if the company decides not to hold a meeting for reasons of cost or time. Analysts will be alerted, by mail or fax, that the call is being held on a certain date at a specified time. Somewhere between 90 and 120 analysts will 'gather' on a normal quarterly conference call.

Conference lines are also used to provide live monitoring of presentations and question and answer sessions at key meetings. Analysts in distant markets who cannot attend will be notified that they can monitor the conference by dialling the conference line, so that at least they can listen to the meeting as it is taking place.

Apart from incoming enquiries, the department has little telephone contact directly with shareholders. However, at proxy time, it does make outbound calls to GTE's largest shareholders, to ensure that they understand the proxy issues, to gauge their reactions and, if they are voting against company management, to reinforce management's point of view (subject to USA regulations on shareholder communications).

GTE's Investor Relations Department strives to have a face-to-face 'selling' relationship where possible. Use of the telephone is driven largely by necessity. Even so, in independent surveys, the company is rated highly for the personal attention it gives to the financial community. To help build an even closer bond with these all-important markets, GTE recruited another investor relations professional, in the second half of 1993, to concentrate on face-to-face meetings.

The USA is an exceptional market, in that the geographical spread of the financial communities makes regular face-to-face meetings more difficult. In most other countries the target audiences in the home market tend to be concentrated in one or two financial centres. Also, large-scale tele-conferencing facilities are not yet widely available, although they will have undoubted value for companies wanting a relatively inexpensive way to maintain a regular dialogue with key sectors of the financial community.

Technology may be the answer to improved direct communications with individual shareholders, perhaps not by voice but by some other interactive medium linked over the telecommunications network. Small shareholders have grown in number and their collective voting power is significant. Ideally, a company would have the same style of relationship with its shareholders as it should have with its customers. The shareholder database would be segmented according to criteria such as number and type of shares held, level of past and pledged support, personal needs (on investment return, and so on) and preferences on such topics as corporate direction and strategy. It would drive a communications programme designed to attract investment and build loyalty among the shareholder base to ensure that any investment decisions they take are in the best interests of the business. The telephone can contribute to this process, as well as in building bridges with the financial community.

22
Campaigning and fund raising

Encouraging people to give their committed support to a cause, whether by donation, purchase of goods or action, requires marketing communications as sophisticated as those used in the wider world to get people to buy products or services. It is often a more difficult task, however, since in most cases people do not get anything tangible in return for their support. Also, there is usually a more limited universe of 'customers' for the non-profit organization, so it is crucial to achieve their full value. The issue of costs is also likely to figure more prominently in the minds of fund raisers, since all costs directly reduce the monies available to support the organization's activities. The telephone is becoming an increasingly popular element in the marketing mix of non-profit organizations, for soliciting support directly and for capturing the interest of supporters attracted by advertising. It is being used by organizations as diverse as charities, universities, museums, zoos and national sports teams.

Telephone communication has most of the benefits of face-to-face meeting (e.g. street collections) but is faster, less expensive and can reach many more people. It is highly flexible, targeted and provides a rapid return. A wide range of objectives – raising funds or awareness, upgrading donors to committed supporters, recruiting members or volunteers, campaigning, and so on – can be achieved on either inbound or outbound calls. However, the telephone does have disadvantages if it is not used properly. Outbound calls, for example, can easily generate complaints and telephone calls are remembered very well – positively *and* negatively. A common failing, particularly on inbound calls, is not capitalizing on the opportunity to develop the relationship. Handling calls from direct response advertising is often little more than taking donor and donation details. The power of the telephone in building a relationship is one of its key benefits, and its effective use requires the same sort of expertise as any other area. Telephone fund-raising staff, for example, need to know about donor relationships and their cultivation, how to listen to and answer the questions people ask, and how to make sure that every telephone call ends positively. Ideally they will also have commitment and enthusiasm for the cause. One reason why the telephone is so effective is that commitment to a particular cause is generally a very personal issue and people enjoy contact with others who are like-minded. Non-profit organizations are becoming more sophisticated in segmenting and targeting supporters and prospects, and about knowing when to mail and when to call, but generally they have not yet achieved the sophistication seen in most other business sectors. Ever-increasing competition for funds and support demands that they use every means available to identify prospects, win their support, and build and nurture these relationships to maintain a loyal base of long-term supporters.

The use of the telephone for campaigning and fund raising is most highly developed in the USA, where inbound and outbound calling have both been used extensively for many years. Many organizations, including charities and universities, have large in-house telephone operations dedicated to raising funds and support, sometimes using sophisticated technology such as predictive dialling. Inbound calling has also been used widely elsewhere, but outbound calling was not exploited more widely in Europe until the early 1990s. There are some crucial differences in approach, however, which are examined later.

22.1   Inbound

Bearing in mind the emphasis on relationship-building in campaigning and fund raising, the role of inbound calls can span many of the applications seen in other business sectors, including direct response solicitation, promotions, catalogue sales, donor service and care, and research. Direct response to advertisements soliciting support, usually a donation, is the most widely used application, although it is not always used to best effect. Like other sectors, non-profit organizations need to exploit this opportunity to maximize the long-term potential of each caller. Their support needs to be nurtured. At the same time, there is an immediate opportunity to increase the value of their support, for example by up-selling from a single donation to a regular banker's order or direct debit. The organization has to be 'sold' and shown as worthy of individuals' long-term support. Obviously a life-long commitment cannot be won in a single call, but this first contact is the most crucial. It should lay the foundation for an ongoing relationship. However, direct response campaigns can be used very effectively without any focus at this early stage on potential long-term relationships.

Efficient response handling

The emphasis on cost-efficiency means that some organizations use a coupon in direct response advertising, whenever possible, in preference to the telephone, or give the coupon more prominence. Maintaining call-handling resources is just too costly where the volume of calls will not be sufficient to use these resources efficiently. Very large, high-profile campaigns, on the other hand, sometimes have the problem of providing sufficient telephone resources to ensure that donations are not lost through failure to answer calls. One solution is automated call handling. In the case of the National Society for the Prevention of Cruelty to Children (NSPCC) in the UK, for example, live operator and automated call handling is combined (see page 168). The automated facility takes the overflow of calls when all operators are busy. It also provides callers with access to information on the NSPCC, which serves a promotional function to help encourage long-term support.

Many major appeals would lose a considerable proportion of donations if automated call handling was not used, or would have to pay for massive operator resources which might be under-utilized.

Case study 22.1

When the first pictures emerged of the famine in Somalia, it was clear that help was needed urgently. This lead to the Africa in Crisis appeal, coordinated by the UK's Disasters Emergency Committee (DEC). The DEC is the body through which Britain's aid agencies coordinate their fund raising in response to major overseas disasters. It launched the nationwide Africa in Crisis appeal within one month.

The appeal was aired on 3 September 1992 on national independent television, BBC television and BBC Radio 4, and was followed up by advertisements in quality national daily newspapers. The appeal was active for a period of one month and a premium rate telephone number was promoted for all credit card donations. British Red Cross, where the Secretariat of the DEC was located at the time, had bought a single premium rate number some time before which would be used for all DEC appeals.

The call volumes on the night of the television and radio appeal were unpredictable but almost inevitably would be huge. Although BT (the UK's principal network provider) gave a 150-operator site for the appeal, free of charge, it was likely that even this would not be sufficient to handle all the calls with offers of money. The DEC therefore appointed agency Greenland Interactive (formerly Legion) to provide an automated credit card donation service, with 400 lines. This would take calls when all BT operators were busy on the night of the appeal, and all calls in response to the national newspaper advertising campaign over the following month.

Callers connected to the automated service were asked to give details of their donation, their credit card number, name, address and daytime telephone number. On the night of the appeal, all 550 lines, both staffed and automated, were saturated until about 11.30 p.m. Operators handled 9500 calls on the night, while the automated system handled approximately 22 700 over the duration of the appeal. The average duration of calls handled by the automated system was 90–100 seconds, compared with around 60–70 seconds for a live operator. The appeal ultimately generated in excess of £1 million.

Other support technologies

Technology can support campaigning and fund raising in other ways, as the following example illustrates.

Case study 22.2

World Vision U.S. is a charitable organization providing international emergency relief, community development and child sponsorship in 91 countries. The organization's call centre, based in Monrovia, California, operates 24 hours a day, 365 days a year. About 80 per cent of new donors contact the organization through the centre, which uses an Aspect CallCenter linked via Application Bridge (Aspect's intelligent ACD/computer interface) to a computer running Brock Control Systems software.

The centre has 60 operator positions and handles nearly 600 000 calls each year, most of them generated by an extensive appeals programme using television, radio and print media. At times, this creates peaks of calls that cannot be answered immediately and callers waiting for an answer are greeted by a recorded message reaffirming their importance to the organization's mission. If a caller is still waiting after one minute, the CallCenter's voice system offers them the option to leave a message for an operator to return their call later. This option reduced abandoned call rates dramatically in the first year, from 18 per cent to 8 per cent. World Vision estimates that this 10 per cent reduction represents more than US$2.5 million in contributions that previously could have been lost.

Half of World Vision's appeals are to Hispanic communities and the organization uses two telephone numbers, one each for English and Spanish campaigns. The CallCenter automatically routes callers to an appropriate operator group according to the number dialled, using dialed number information service (DNIS). Around 60 per cent of World Vision's operators are bilingual, providing greater flexibility in staffing.

Existing donors are identified when they call using automatic number identification (ANI). By matching their telephone number against the donor database, their file can be sent to an operator's screen as the call is connected. This facility is particularly useful in conjunction with World Vision's Automatic Child Reservation system, which enables operators to match a child of a particular age, sex and country to a donor during the call. Sponsors are given the immediate satisfaction of knowing who their donation is helping. With the Application Bridge and ANI, when a sponsor calls again the operator can personalize the conversation with relevant details of the children being sponsored.

To enable calls from people without donor accounts to be handled more efficiently, World Vision has been considering subscribing to an ANI reverse-matching service which would provide on-screen information about the subscriber to the number from which a call is being made. This would be transparent to the caller but would help operators to ensure that address details are recorded accurately and thus cut down on returned mail and lost sponsorships.

Case study 22.3

Ross Perot, candidate in the 1992 USA Presidential campaign, has used this technology to great effect to build a database of people calling as a result of his talk show appearances and presentations in bought air time. The system automatically identifies and records the details of those who call on the toll-free number given. It has helped Perot to create a vast database of potential voters and campaign workers. At the beginning of 1993 he started promoting his new organization, United We Stand, America, in a similar way, encouraging people who supported his ideals to call and join the organization for a $15 subscription. The money is used to buy further air time and attract more supporters, continually adding to the database that will prove its worth during Perot's 1996 candidacy.

Inbound activity does not have to be high-tech to be effective. In fact, smaller-volume operations allow an organization to focus more easily on establishing and building a relationship with individual callers and on maximizing their immediate value. Catalogues of 'branded' merchandize, for example, are an increasingly popular means of raising funds and awareness, and skilled operators can raise the average order value substantially.

Choice of number

Some interesting issues arise when considering the choice between offering toll-free and premium rate calls in campaigning and fund raising. In the wider commercial world it is now generally accepted that the offer of toll-free calls, in preference to even standard charge, is more acceptable and productive in the long-term for the majority of applications. In the case of non-profit organizations, however, an important additional question arises. Obviously in many situations there is a commitment to donate money, which to some extent justifies the use of premium rate calls to raise additional funds. In some situations, however, the loss of those additional revenues, and the cost to the organization of paying for calls, may be preferable to help develop a stronger relationship. An organization has to consider the benefit it will gain in the long term from the use of toll-free access. It may not always be applicable when contact is being initiated (although toll-free can increase the volume of responses – as well hoax calls), but for subsequent contact there is a case to be made for offering committed supporters a toll-free number to maintain contact.

The use of inbound telephone in campaigning and fund raising is subject to the same sort of factors acting in other applications, which were examined in Chapter 15 (page 147). While an increasing number of organizations are using inbound applications to nurture relationships, the power of the telephone to influence people to give support is seen most clearly in the development of outbound calling. Some of the comments made about outbound campaigns apply equally to inbound calls.

22.2 Outbound

The success rates in outbound telephone fund raising in the USA have declined as the volume of calls has risen. It is used so widely that people can feel inundated by calls. Those in the USA who give to one charity will often give to several, each of which may call the supporter on a routine basis. In addition, there will be calls from other charities trying to establish a relationship. Faced with a barrage of calls, people will often simply say 'no' to these new callers, or say 'yes' just to close the call and then not convert their pledge to a donation. So, although outbound telephone remains a powerful fund-raising tool, conversion rates in the USA have declined. In Europe, however, receiving a call from a charity is still a relatively new phenomenon, and the success rates can be staggering.

One UK charity used direct response television advertising for fund raising, but was only breaking even. It decided to try to convert 'television' donors into more significant or committed supporters by mailing them, but the conversion rates were relatively poor. Then the charity tested the effect of calling donors. A pledge rate of over 59 per cent was achieved, with an average gift value of over £100. It is a simple truth that some people are just not direct mail responsive. It makes sense, when people are identified as non-responsive to mail, to call them rather than send them mail repeatedly.

Minimizing complaints

Targeting – who is called and about what – is one of the most significant factors in success. The telephone works best when a relationship already exists, or when contacts have a known interest in the organization or its area of work. Cold calling, generally, is unlikely to be cost-effective and will probably generate a significant number of complaints.

The issue of complaints is important in Europe, which does not have the telephone culture of the USA. Because of this, the approach has to be tailored for the European market. The most significant difference is the pre-call letter, which forewarns supporters that they will receive a call during the next few days. It states the purpose of the call, with background information, and in most situations offers the individual the opportunity to opt out of receiving the call, for which a reply device, often both mail and telephone, is provided. To maximize the value of those who decide to opt out, it is also wise to say in the letter that, if they feel they do not wish to receive the call, the organization hopes that they will consider making a contribution using the envelope enclosed.

One UK charity identified past donors who had not responded to regular mailings in at least two, often three years, and sent an opt-out letter prior to calling them. Of those mailed, 17.5 per cent opted out with a donation. Providing an oppotunity to opt out does have a financial impact, however, since some of those who opt out without a donation might have given when called, and those who opt out with a contribution might have given a higher gift. However, the opt-out approach has all but eliminated complaints and also saves the cost of calling people who are just not interested.

Other ways in which outbound fund-raising calls have been tailored for the European market include offering an opportunity to opt out during the call and softening the 'ask', for example: 'Would you consider a gift?', or 'Is this something you are able to do?'

One UK organization, concerned that calling donors may alienate them, decided to conduct a test to measure the impact of a call on future giving. The test sample were supporters who had not donated in at least three years, but who had been mailed regularly. Three groups would be tracked: those who said 'no' to a donation during the call; those who pledged a donation; and a third, control group, who were not called. An opt-out letter was sent to the first two groups before calling. After the calls were made, supporters in each group were mailed in the organization's usual mailing cycle. Of those who pledged support during the telephone call, 24 per cent gave additional gifts over the next 18 months, even though they had not responded to mailing in the previous three years. Of the people who were not called, 5 per cent made a gift over the 18-month tracking period. However, the most surprising result was that 14 per cent of those who had said 'no' during the call responded to mailings with a donation. So, while this group did not, and perhaps could not, give when phoned, a significant proportion of them (almost three times as many as those not called) felt positive enough about the organization to respond with a gift. It is important to remember that these are people with whom the organization had a relationship, and they were building on those relationships.

Another tactic used to minimize complaints is the non-monetary last request. One of the possible reasons for complaining about receiving a fund-raising call is that people may feel bad or guilty about not being able to say 'yes', and they are likely to resent being put in that position. By enabling people to say 'yes' to something at the end of the call, the probability of their resenting the call is reduced. There are many different options for a non-monetary last request, and it may depend on the nature of the campaign. People can be asked to contact their Member of Parliament, for example, or asked a few survey questions to find out about their opinions on the direction of the organization or its fund-raising programmes. The survey is a valuable option. Not only are people likely to feel good because they have shared information that can help the organization, but it may also reveal how best they can be approached for support in the future.

Encouraging committed support

Another difference between the USA and European markets, which acts in favour of European campaigns, is the method of making payments. In the UK, for example, many people use direct debits and standing orders routinely in business transactions, and on the Continent they use banker's orders and direct debits. In the USA, however, these methods of payment are a more recent phenomenon and are not yet used widely. This means that in Europe it should be easier to encourage people to give committed support through regular payments, since the methods of making regular payments are commonly used in other situations.

The opportunity for an interactive dialogue on the telephone means that people can be encouraged to give committed support. Convincing people to give what seems like a smaller amount – but on an ongoing, open-ended basis – greatly increases their value to the organization. A monthly standing order for only £5 becomes £60 in the first year, without any attempt at subsequent upgrading; and the life of a standing order can be many years.

The structure of outbound campaigns

There are often four elements in an outbound campaign soliciting support: initial research, a test, the main campaign and follow-up research calls. Research among a small sample from each of the groups to be called helps to decide how best to win their support. The questions asked would be designed to learn about attitudes to the organization, for example, and what might motivate contacts to make a contribution at this time. This information is used to start drafting scripts and preparing responses to objections, but can also be of use in planning direct mail campaigns and other fund-raising activities. The test campaign, to a small representative sample of the target audience, is conducted once initial scripts have been finalized. Testing serves to confirm the viability of the campaign (or not) and to identify possible improvements in the approach. When a campaign is rolled out, regular debriefing of callers, as with any telemarketing campaign, helps to refine the campaign to achieve optimum results.

Call monitoring is also used to identify reactions to calls as well as to monitor the performance of callers. It is critically important that callers should hear things properly as well as communicate properly. For example, if they think they are getting pledges but are not, it is likely to generate complaints when people receive a pledge form asking them to fulfil a promise they did not make. Follow-up calls to a sample of the target audience also help to analyse the performance of callers as well as the campaign. People are asked about such things as how they felt about the call, whether the caller was polite and well-informed, and so on. When campaigns have been well planned, this research will generally show that most people are pleased to have received the call. Again, it is important to remember that these are people who have a relationship with, and who care about, the organization. Follow-up calls may also be made to thank donors for large sums, or sums over a predetermined amount.

The length of calls depends partly on how involved a person is with the organization. Normally a call should be fairly brief, but obviously it is important to gain people's interest, and one route to this is to learn what they are concerned about and what questions they may have, and to address these issues. Thus, to some extent the length of a call and the detail of the conversation will depend on the individual contact, but callers should be knowledgeable and prepared for a potentially involved conversation. The message being delivered, however, should be fairly simple and focused.

The timing of successive communications is important, as in any other application. Telephone follow-up to a pre-call letter, for example, generally should be made within three to five days and, when donations are pledged, pledge packs should be sent to supporters as quickly as possible (ideally being despatched the same day). Follow-up to unfulfilled pledges may be made by mail or telephone, depending on their value, up to about four weeks after the initial pledge. A special pledge pack may be sent to those who are undecided about making a donation, which obviously is designed to sway their decision in favour of the organization. Another mailing may be sent to individuals who could not be contacted by telephone, explaining the situation and soliciting a donation, so that maximum value is gained from the contact list. An example contact strategy is shown in Figure 22.1.

Cost-saving technology

Technology is being used to improve the cost-efficiency of outbound as well as inbound calling. Predictive dialling, for example, is used very effectively in the USA, enabling an organization to dial a large number of people to identify the small proportion who are at home during the day to take the

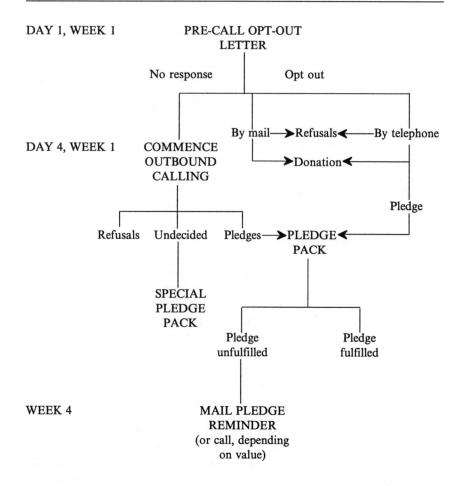

Figure 22.1 Example contact strategy for outbound telephone fund raising

call. Recorded message-playing is also used, particularly in political campaigning but also to relay testimonials from personalities promoting an organization and its aims. These types of call were often made automatically, by computer. However, to avoid occupying lines that people may need to use in an emergency, there are increasing restrictions on this type of call and they are now more likely to be introduced by an operator (giving people an opportunity to refuse the recording). While this is a relatively inexpensive method of broadcasting a message to a well-targeted audience, it does not have the same impact, or flexibility, as a person-to-person call.

Types of outbound application

Some specific applications of live outbound calling, and the results that can be achieved, are outlined below. There is considerable overlap between these applications, some of which may be combined in a single campaign. It is important to view these in the context of relationship building and therefore to see calls as a means to promote the organization, and build commitment to its cause and activities, at the same time as soliciting donations.

DONOR ACQUISITION

Soliciting donations from people who have not given before is most effective when they have some relationship with the organization. In the UK, for example, calling people who have bought merchandise through catalogues has produced pledge rates of 70 per cent in some instances, and rates of over 65 per cent among those who have purchased charity Christmas cards. In a donor acquisition campaign on behalf of a USA Olympic team, prior to the 1992 Olympics in Barcelona, Facter Fox International called subscribers to a magazine devoted to the team's sport. Of the 15 090 subscribers contacted, none of whom had previously donated to the organization, 59.9 per cent (9039) pledged their support with an average gift of over US$27.00. In another example, as part of an ongoing member acquisition programme, a USA activist organization identified signatories of petitions in support of women's rights as good prospects. None of the prospects sourced had previously donated to the organization. The telephone campaign, undertaken by Facter Fox International, had two objectives: to acquire new members with a donation, and to obtain names and telephone numbers from prospects of friends who they considered would, if asked, join the organization. All prospects, whether or not they promised a donation, were asked for referral names. The results are shown in Table 22.1.

Table 22.1 Results of a member acquisition campaign for a US activist organization. (Courtesy of Facter Fox International)

	Membership pledge rate (%)	Average pledge value ($)
Prospects	36.27	30.93
25% referrals from pledgers	56.76	39.05
16% referrals from non-pledgers	52.38	31.82

Referral campaigns, like the example above, have worked very well in the USA for activist organizations (although not, for example, for museums and zoos). In some instances they can yield around one referral for every two people contacted. Individuals are asked if they know anyone who shares their interest and, if so, to give that person's name and telephone number. These people are contacted and asked the same questions, yielding more names and thus creating a cascade of new contacts. Interestingly, the third generation contacts (given by the first set of people referred) tend to represent better value than the people who recommended them.

One reason why member-gets-member campaigns work well is possibly that contacts do not suggest other people who they know cannot afford to give. When this method is used in the UK, addresses are requested for referral names to enable an opt-out letter to be sent.

DONOR UPGRADE

It is generally much more cost-efficient to 'sell' to existing supporters, like existing customers, than to identify and win new ones. The idea of donor upgrade is to increase the value and commitment of existing supporters. The likely potential to upgrade, and whether it is worth while using the telephone, can be assessed by calculating donor value from past 'donation' history, as in the following example.

Case study 22.4

Scope (formerly The Spastics Society) is a leading UK charity, working for the disabled. In March 1992, the Chapter One Group undertook a donor upgrade campaign to raise funds for the charity's Conductive Education Assessment Centre, the first to be established outside Hungary. Scope has a large donor base arising from a wide variety of fund-raising activities, including sponsorship and donor acquisition campaigns, house-to-house collections, shops, events and legacy marketing.

Past supporters were approached in two ways, according to the sum of their donations over the previous two years. Those who had given £100 or more, as single or frequent gifts, were approached using a combination of mail and telemarketing. A more expensive but more personal approach was seen to be justified for these supporters, who numbered 7150. A further 600 000, all donors of smaller sums, were mailed.

No telephone numbers were held on the donor database, so Chapter One Group sourced numbers for the top 7150 supporters using telephone directories and the PhoneBase service, which provided access to BT's computerized directory enquiry database. Numbers were found for 66 per cent (4719) of these supporters. The 34 per cent (2431) for whom a number was not available were sent a mailing about the campaign, which invited them to become a 'Pioneer' with a donation of £100 or more. The mail pack was very similar to that sent to the 600 000, although higher donation levels were suggested. Both mail packs included a personalized letter, a donation form with a credit card donation hotline number, and a reply envelope.

All people to be telephoned were sent a personalized pre-call letter, which briefly introduced the new centre and explained the need for donor support. It indicated that a telephone call may follow the letter to give more information and ask for their support. A telephone number was provided for supporters to call if they wished to opt out of receiving the call. Only telephone response was offered, both to speed the process and to provide the opportunity for a dialogue with the supporter. Those who called to opt out were offered additional information about the campaign and a donation was requested if appropriate. A dedicated inbound line was provided for this service, with an answering machine taking calls received outside office hours. Pre-call letters were sent first class, staggered on a daily basis to match the required level of calling. Calling began to each group on the evening of the fourth day after posting.

Any queries or complaints raised by people called were faxed to the charity the following day for follow-up action, or to prepare them for a call from the supporter. Supporters who promised a donation, or agreed to consider donating, were sent a follow-up pack by first-class post the following day. This consisted of a letter thanking them for their support, a reply envelope, a donation form with details of the campaign objectives, and an outer window envelope.

The thank-you letter and the donation form, which formed the addressing medium, were hand personalized. The amount promised was written on the donation form where appropriate. The purpose of hand addressing was to prolong the personalization of the dialogue and hopefully remind the supporter of the personal telephone call. Supporters who could not be contacted during the calling period, which lasted just over three weeks, were subsequently sent a mailing inviting them to

Table 22.2 Results of a donor upgrade telephone campaign by the Chapter One Group. (Courtesy of Scope (formerly The Spastics Society))

Major supporters	Number	Telephoned	Mailed
Total number	7150		
With numbers (66%)	4719		
Without numbers (34%)	2431		2431
With numbers (66%)			
Contacts made (82.3%)	3884	3884	
Not contacted (17.7%)	835		835
Conversion rate		36.61%	14.00%
Average donation		£66.11	£48.51
Total raised		£94 000	£22 180

become 'Pioneers'. These amounted to 17.7 per cent (835) of the supporters for whom telephone numbers were available.

All donation forms and reply envelopes had a specific code to enable tracking. Returned donations were sent to the fulfilment and response centre in Liverpool, and copies of the donation forms were sent to Chapter One Group. On this occasion, supporters who did not send the promised donation were not followed up. The majority of donations were received by post, with only a small proportion using the credit card hotline. The results of the telephone campaign, which exceeded agency estimates, are shown in Table 22.2. The overall *net* income from the campaign was nearly £121 000. Using only mail achieved a response rate of 14 per cent, compared with 36.61 per cent for telephone contact, and an average donation of £48.51, compared with £66.11 by telephone.

Upgrading to committed giving, in the form of standing orders, direct debits or banker's orders, is potentially a very cost-efficient method of increasing the value of donors (see earlier in this chapter). The tax laws of different countries can also be exploited to gain maximum value in donor upgrade and other fund-raising campaigns, at the same time as adding value for the donor. Gift Aid, for example, is a scheme set up by the UK Government enabling charities to reclaim income tax paid by donors (at the basic rate of 25 per cent) on one-off gifts over a certain limit (£250 at the time of writing). A gift of £400, for example, would be worth £533 to the charity under this scheme, and donors have the satisfaction of knowing that the tax they have paid already will be going to a favoured charity. Deeds of covenant are another form of tax-beneficial giving.

COVENANT RENEWAL

A deed of covenant in the UK refers to an agreement by the donor to make a gift of the same amount each year for more than three years (although, by agreement of both parties, a covenant can be cancelled and renewed at a new amount in the interim period). As with Gift Aid, the charity can reclaim the income tax (at the basic rate) already paid by the donor and thus increase the real value of the donation. Covenant renewal campaigns involve calling supporters prior to expiry of their current agreement to encourage and negotiate renewal.

MEMBERSHIP RENEWAL

Members who fail to respond to direct mail appeals in the renewal cycle, which may consist of three or four letters, are often responsive to a telephone call, and reducing the donor attrition rate must be a key concern.

In a 'last pass' donor renewal campaign for a UK environmental organization, Facter Fox International called past supporters who had made donations in the ranges £35–50 and £51–75. The results are shown in Table 22.3. A total of £64 000 was pledged by 1250 supporters, with a subsequent conversion rate of over 85 per cent. In addition, one supporter made a gift of £10 000. In 1992, Facter Fox International undertook the first ever telephone fund-raising appeal in Switzerland for an environmental organization. A pre-call letter was mailed to past supporters, informing them that they may be called and giving a telephone number to use if they wished to opt out. Of the 1772 supporters contacted by telephone, 975 (55.02 per cent) pledged a total of 101 098 Swiss francs. Contacts were encouraged to make their donation by banker's order, a method which previously had not been used for making donations in Switzerland. The results are shown in Table 22.4. Of the specified pledges, 37.33 per cent were made by banker's order. The overall pledge per contact was 57.05 Swiss francs, i.e. average for all contacts.

Membership renewal can also be combined with other objectives, such as donor upgrade (for example, by asking supporters to match the cost of subscription with an additional donation).

Table 22.3 Results of a donor renewal telephone campaign for a UK environmental organization. (Courtesy of Facter Fox International)

Previous donation	Pledge rate (banker's orders)	Average pledge (1st year BO value)
£35–£50	67% (60% +)	£63.26 (£86.64)
£51–£75	81% (67% +)	£100.61 (£130.56)

Table 22.4 Results of a fund-raising appeal for a Swiss environmental organization. (Courtesy of Facter Fox International)

	Conversion rate (%)	Number of supporters pledging	Average pledge value (SF)	Total pledged (SF)
Banker's orders	20.54	364	181.12*	65 928
One-off pledges	34.48	611	57.56	35 170
Overall	55.02	975	103.69	101 098

*First-year value

LAPSED DONOR REACTIVATION

The telephone can be cost-effective in reactivating lapsed donors, provided that calls are targeted carefully. The previous level of donation is important; and the highest value, most recently lapsed donors are the best prospects (see the case of the UK environmental organization above, for example).

SPONSORSHIP

An increasingly diverse range of sponsorship programmes are being devised to add value for donors by offering something more tangible for their support (sponsoring a Third World child, for example, or adopting a whale or part of the rain forest). A typical contact strategy might use advertising to stimulate interest and solicit response, and then a mailed information pack to encourage donation. One or two reminder letters might then be sent, after timed intervals, to those who have not responded with a donation. Introducing telemarketing into this contact strategy, calling non-respondents a few days after they receive the first reminder, can increase the sponsor recruitment rate by more than one-third.

The success of telephone campaigning and fund raising, like other applications, depends upon delivering the right message to the right people at the right time. The only way to do this effectively is to learn about individual supporters and to exploit that knowledge in communicating with them and in recruiting others like them. With increasing competition in the non-profit sector, as in other markets, there is growing emphasis on retaining supporters, by nurturing relationships, to maximize their lifetime value. The telephone has an important role to play as an integral part of the communications programme, and many non-profit organizations could benefit from studying the way businesses in some other sectors are using the telephone to build a loyal customer base.

Appendix 1
BT's Telephone-Based Customer Satisfaction Measurement

Telephone-Based Customer Satisfaction Measurement (TBCSM) is a tool to help measure the effectiveness of a call centre operation, a telemarketing application and the performance of individual agents. It also provides valuable information on customer expectations, the key qualities they are looking for in a telephone service, and the probable impact of each call on their immediate and future behaviour. In other words, TBCSM can monitor effectiveness from the customers' perspective and help the company to use that feedback constructively for continuous improvement.

TBCSM was developed at BT's Customer Communications Centre (CCC) in Bristol, one of the world's leading call centres. CCC, incorporating BT's commercial telemarketing operation (*Connections in Business*), is a unique centre of integrated expertise for BT and acts as a role model call centre for other organizations.

A1.1 The methodology

TBCSM is an outbound telephone research programme that is conducted no longer than 24 hours following the interaction between company and customer. The methodology and questionnaire were designed by Dr Guy Fielding of Queen Margaret College, Edinburgh, an academic with a worldwide reputation in Communications Studies, and Jon Reynolds from BT's CCC. Using independent researchers (an important element of the technique), the following areas are covered:

- Service compared to expectations
- Service provider performance and behaviour
- Overall satisfaction and service reliability
- Company reputation and future behaviour.

The questionnaire is designed to provoke recall of events within the original interaction to ensure that feedback is specific and scores are more accurate. There is a core set of questions but others, specific to a type of call or application, can be introduced. This means that the technique can be used to deliver specific and actionable feedback on any type of telemarketing activity.

The research framework (Figure A1.1) is designed to enable mapping of the effect of the interaction on customer perceptions and its immediate, and likely future, consequences.

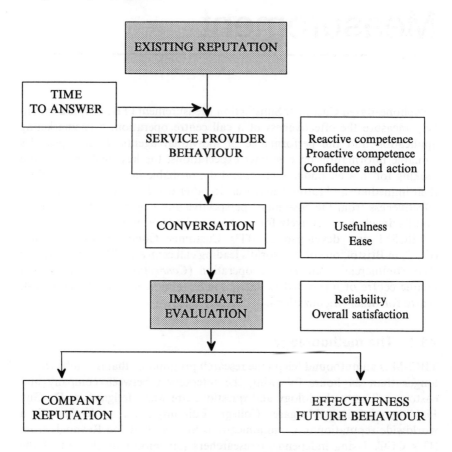

Figure A1.1 Telephone-Based Customer Satisfaction Measurement research framework

A1.2 Results

Results from the research are best monitored and tracked over time, although valuable information can be obtained through an *ad hoc* survey. CCC began by measuring a number of key customer satisfaction areas which are part of the Centre's monthly performance indicators. These include overall satisfaction (graded on a scale 0–10) and service compared to expectations.

The key measures of satisfaction derive from customers' experience and perceptions of service provider behaviour. Three areas of their performance are measured: *reactive competence* (responding to customer needs), *proactive competence* (encouraging customers to express their needs and preferences, and responding to them), and *confidence and action* (creating confidence – in the service, in the information given, and that any further actions required will be carried out).

Results can be enhanced further by using data from the original interaction. This could include call type, application, product or service ordered, individual agent, time of day, time to answer, call length, task completion, call attempts, etc. As an example, CCC have measured the impact on customer satisfaction of the time to answer. The effects identified by CCC are summarized in Table A1.1. With the higher range of time to answer, where call abandonment and repeat attempts are increasing, customers are increasingly likely to consider using an alternative service provider.

The results of TBCSM have been found to have applications in scripting, performance appraisal, motivation and training, and identifying commercial opportunities. At CCC, for example, recognition and incentive programmes (to reward individual and team behaviour) are now based on the research results.

Initially, CCC have used TBCSM to enhance their own call centre operations. As a research service, however, it is already available to other organizations on a commercial basis through BT's own telemarketing agency, *Connections in Business*.

Table A1.1 Effect of time to answer on customer satisfaction

Time to answer	Effect
10–12 seconds (up to 4 rings)	Multiplies satisfaction
12–30 seconds (up to 10 rings)	Neutral/causes dissatisfaction
30 + seconds (over 10 rings)	Multiplies dissatisfaction

Appendix 2
Extracts from
Teleculture 2000

Teleculture 2000: The Growth and Acceptance of the Use of the Telephone in Sales, Marketing and Customer Service, was published in July 1994, the result of extensive research by the Henley Centre for Forecasting. It is the first study of its type in the UK. The research was sponsored by a Consortium consisting of Abbey National, Audi UK Ltd, Brann Contact 24, BT, The Direct Marketing Association, Forte Hotels, IBM UK Ltd, Midland Electricity, Mitel Telecom, Next Directory, Private Patients Plan, and Prudential.

The limited extracts reproduced here, by kind permission of the Henley Centre, are designed to provide an insight into opportunities for exploiting what the authors of the report call 'telebusiness'. Although the research was conducted in the UK, this study is directly relevant to all countries where telemarketing is still undergoing rapid development. This applies particularly to the European markets.

Copies of the full report are available from The Henley Centre, 9 Bridewell Place, London EC4V 6AY, priced £1100. For more information call +44 (0)171 353 9961, or fax +44 (0)171 353 2899.

❝❝ A2.1   Introduction

This report looks at both the current and the potential use of the telephone in dealings between businesses and their customers. The study was supported by some of Britain's leading companies, all of which believe that the telephone has a major role to play in their future marketing, sales and customer service activity.

One of the principal reasons why the telephone is not more widely used is that the level and quality of service offered by many businesses is poor. BT has recently released figures to show that three in every four calls to businesses do not achieve their objective on the first attempt, either because lines are engaged or because the caller can not get through to the right person. Clearly, most UK businesses still fail to see telephone communication with customers as a strategic priority. Consequently, most have not invested enough resources to provide a professional service.

Despite growing interest and media coverage, few senior managers accept that the much-vaunted potential of direct communications is relevant to them in 1994. Yet, it is no longer appropriate to talk about direct distribution channels and communication as if it were still 'on the horizon'. 'Low-tech', telephone-based solutions are already available. We believe there are growing consumer segments who are happy, or would even prefer, to do business by telephone if offered the right services in the right way – as a number of examples of 'innovators' in this area demonstrate.

A2.2 The new consumer environment – ripe for telebusiness?

There is widespread use of the telephone by consumers to call businesses. BMRB's Target Group Index (TGI) figures suggest that about 30 per cent of people call a shop or business each week from home. To put this in context, however, BT estimates that the average residential line is used for such purposes for just 30 seconds a week, compared to six full minutes a week in the US.

Based on the qualitative discussion, in which many participants talked about making calls from work as consumers not related to their work, we decided to include these calls in the quantitative survey since we felt that this would give a more realistic picture of overall usage.

Figure A2.1 shows that as many as 67 per cent of the sample had used the telephone to get service or repairs for household goods, although only 19 per cent claimed to do this as often as monthly. The proportion claiming to use the telephone to query invoices and bills was 62 per cent (but with only 10 per cent saying they did this monthly), while those who used the phone to order entertainment and leisure services did so with the greatest frequency with more than 60 per cent doing it at least once a month.

In terms of receipt of calls at home (outbound calling), 56 per cent of our sample claimed to have received a call in the last six months at home.

The business person as teleconsumer

There has always been a tendency to think of business decision makers as being qualitatively different from consumers – as motivated by exclusively corporate goals and bound by strict professional codes. Yet they too hold personal attitudes to media and communications. Among them, in fact, the telephone has been enormously successful.

Outbound calling has been an accepted part of business communications for many years. There is some evidence that growth in this area, and in the use of the telephone to conduct market research, is making it less and less productive as more and more calls are screened out. Yet it remains true that the results, once the target has been reached, are still impressively good.

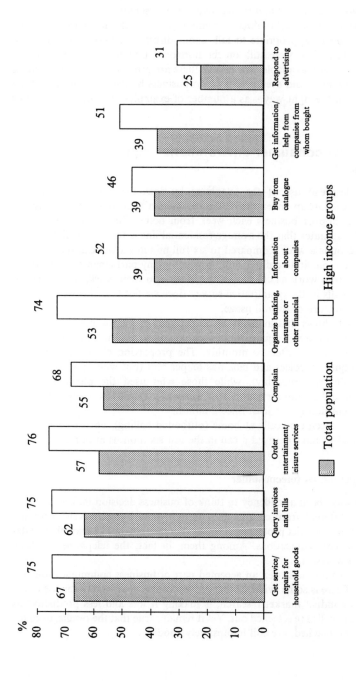

Figure A2.1 Use of the telephone for telebusiness

A2.3   Consumer attitudes to telebusiness

When will consumers use the telephone? The three Rs

The three Rs stand for *relevance, relationship* and *reputation*, all of which are critical in the successful use of the telephone in sales, marketing and customer service.

RELEVANCE

Over the past few years, our research at the Henley Centre has suggested that traditional socio-demographic segmentation techniques have lost some of their power to explain the extent and nature of consumer behaviour. The Henley Centre has increasingly focused on attitudinal patterns such as how confident, interested and knowledgeable different consumers are about different markets. *How relevant is a particular market/activity to the particular consumer?*

We found this to be very important in our consumer research into telebusiness. Interest and confidence emerged top among many other factors of preparedness to use the telephone to buy different goods and services. In every single market, people who are both interested in and confident about a product or service are very significantly more likely to say they are prepared to buy it over the telephone than the population as a whole.

RELATIONSHIP

In both inbound and outbound calling, an established relationship with a company is an important factor in the acceptability of using the telephone. Here, we concentrate on outbound calling, since the general perception is that consumers are specially negative about this.

Despite the overall negative attitude to cold calling (although there is a gradual softening of opposition), as many as 58 per cent of people were very happy, and 36 per cent fairly happy, to receive a call to follow up a complaint; 50 per cent were also very happy, and 39 per cent fairly happy, to receive a 'checking' call one month after the purchase of a good or service. Even the 36 per cent of the sample who said that there was never really a convenient time to get calls of this kind at home, were reasonably positive about these sorts of telephone contacts.

The existence of a *relationship* came out as being essential from the consumer perspective alongside the *relevance* of the call.

REPUTATION

Consumers also introduced a new criterion, that of *reputation* for quality – 53 per cent said that they would be happier to buy from a company that had a reputation for good quality. In the consumer discussion groups, most people were not interested in buying groceries by telephone, but several said this *would* be conceivable if the grocer was Marks and Spencer since they could be certain of the quality of produce. This adds a new dimension to an issue we have addressed over the years in 'Planning for Social Change' (our proprietary research and analysis programme) – that is, the role of corporate branding.

In looking at what consumers need to reassure them sufficiently to engage in a remote buying process, where the biggest stated disadvantage is that they cannot see what they are buying (79 per cent), trust, relationship and quality are essential prerequisites.

Getting the telephone offer right: the three Cs

The three 'Cs' – which stand for *convenience, cordiality* and *consistency* – are the factors which emerged as being particularly important in terms of people's actual experience and expectations of telephone operations.

CONVENIENCE

Given the increasing time pressures for many in British society, it is not surprising that convenience is seen as a key benefit of telebusiness. In particular, speed is seen as the main component of this. When we asked consumers what they see as the main advantages of telebusiness, the top three factors were: you can get immediate answers; it saves time; and it is usually a quicker way of getting hold of what you want. All these factors relate to speed of service. In addition, speed in answering is a vital determinant of a good call, far more important than any other factor.

Speed of response thus seems to act as a threshold factor – the first hurdle that has to be passed if other elements of the interaction are to be appreciated to make a significant impression on the caller.

CORDIALITY

Once the demand for speed is satisfied, other factors play a part – in particular, the quality of the human contact and the knowledge and professionalism of the individual answering the call. It is appreciated when the operators are friendly and warm, and, of course, if they are helpful.

CONSISTENCY

Finally, we found that while expectations of service by telephone are generally low, a single badly handled call can have an extremely damaging effect on the customer relationship, with as many as 68 per cent strongly agreeing that they would prefer not to do business with a company again (see Figure A2.2).

Reinforcing the importance of efficient call handling, the likelihood of calling back if unable to get through varies significantly with the reason for calling and how essential the call is. At one end of the scale, 65 per cent would always call

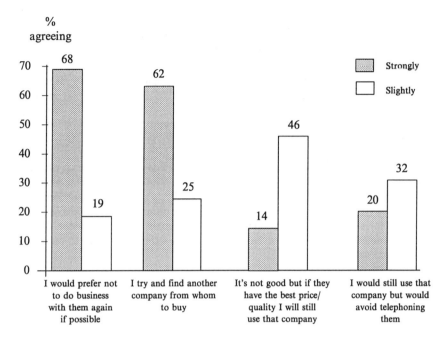

Figure A2.2   Effects of a badly handled call

back if they could not get through to a venue, such as a hotel or restaurant or theatre; at the other only 14 per cent would always call again in response to an advertisement. Perhaps the most surprising of the answers was that just 31 per cent of people who were ringing to order from a catalogue said they would always call back if unsuccessful.

The key segments in the teleculture

Taking all the strands of our analysis together, we can identify some key groups of consumers who are more prone to using the telephone for sales, marketing and customer service. Cluster analysis – a computer statistical analysis technique – revealed four distinct groups of people with a common pattern of attitudes.

Telephiles – 47 per cent of the market: This group of people are generally very positive about the telephone and about telebusiness. They are confident telephone users who enjoy using the phone and are high users. They are positive about its role as an easy and convenient way of getting information and service and relatively positive about receiving outbound calls from businesses.

Telephobes – 16 per cent of the market: These people are the opposite of telephiles. They are unfavourably disposed towards the telephone and towards telebusiness. They are the least confident group when it comes to using the telephone and are the lowest users of the telephone at home and at work. They are the least likely to be prepared to buy or to have bought over the phone.

Functionals – 15 per cent of the market: These people do not enjoy using the telephone, but are very confident about using it and are prepared to use it socially, at work and for telebusiness. They are relatively well disposed to receiving outbound calls and almost as positive as the telephiles to the idea of businesses building a relationship with customers.

Protectionists – 22 per cent of the market: The protectionists are people who are generally positive about using the telephone, but who do not want a two-way relationship with businesses. They are generally positive - second only to telephiles - about the principle of telebusiness, and, although they are less likely to use it in this way than telephiles or functionals, they are more active teleconsumers than telephobes. However, they are strongly opposed to receiving outbound calls.

(Here, the report suggests how companies might manage different aspects of telephone contact with members of each of these groups in order to make it a more positive experience for them.)

A2.4 The current telebusiness market

The size of the market

Our survey suggests that considerable human and financial resources have been devoted to the telebusiness industry. Members of our business sample have an average of forty-seven staff whose principal job is dealing with customers or potential customers on the phone; each also spends an average of £600 000 a year on telebusiness operations. Our research leads us to the following estimates of market size (all companies with 100+ employees):

Total calls received	4.5 billion
Total calls made	2.6 billion
Total staff employed	800 000
Telebusiness spend	£10.4 billion

The role and organization of telebusiness

We estimate that 66 per cent of all UK businesses with more than 100 employees employ staff who spend more than half of their time on the telephone in communication with customers.

Even more telling is the fact that as many as 34 per cent of medium-to-large businesses do *not* have dedicated staff to deal with customers on the telephone.

This raises the first of many questions as to how these companies view customer relationships and their potential value over time.

There is evidence that most companies undertake very varied types of telephone contact with their customers, ranging across applications such as complaint handling, outbound retail stocking, account management, order taking, response handling, lead generation, outbound appointment setting and welcome calls.

From the qualitative interviews, we formed two hypotheses about the level of development of different types of companies. One was that the types of distribution channels a company uses would affect its use and organization of telephone contact, as would the absolute size of its end-user marketplace. Companies using direct marketing or direct distribution channels to large audiences, for example, would necessarily have to be well-organized in handling *inbound* telephone contact. Other firms using salesforces to reach discrete business segments were more likely to use *outbound* telemarketing in sales support applications such as appointment setting and lead generation.

The second hypothesis concerned the presence or absence of dedicated teams in areas other than customer service – that is, in either sales or marketing. Paradoxically, those companies which only have teams in a customer service function were generally the least developed in terms of organization and employment of sophisticated technology to support a high quality of service.

Among those firms which organize telephone contact, the most common location for dedicated staff is customer service, both in terms of receiving and making calls. The second most common is sales, and trailing third is marketing. The ranking indicates the lack of development of the market, given that all the most advanced applications and practitioners are in the telemarketing field.

Linked to this is the way in which telephone contact with customers is measured. The picture we found suggests that most UK businesses do not quantify telephone customer contact in the service area as stringently as more advanced practitioners, who see it as part of overall sales and marketing and more specifically linked to direct marketing. Many companies measure how many calls are made and taken; but few record what happens during the call – mainly because they still lack the systems to perform these tasks in an integrated manner.

A2.5 Factors driving a change in business attitudes

In this section, we consider some of the major aspects of the economic and business environment in the 1990s which are likely to focus attention on the benefits of using the telephone.

The economic environment

A number of macro-economic factors point to unspectacular economic growth over the next five years. These, combined with the impact on consumer psyches of the length and breadth of the recession, lead us to believe that the next few years will see relatively modest increases in consumer spending.

The drive to cut costs

The continuing drive to cut costs is likely to focus corporate attention on the role of the telephone in their operations. For example, one of the principal reasons that outbound calling was adopted by business-to-business marketers in the early to mid-1980s has been the rise in the cost of running salesforces.

If the late 1980s was the time in which business direct marketing and direct distribution became established, a prolonged recession and a growing pressure on all types of businesses to cut costs set the keynote for the 1990s. In banking, the spiralling cost of maintaining extensive retail networks, along with reduced margins in more competitive markets, have prompted the adoption of distribution alternatives.

The more advanced companies which have adopted the direct distribution approach have also shown how costs can further be cut and margins improved without sacrificing the level of service provided to customers. Our qualitative interviews highlighted the fact that companies which had taken steps to centralize were the most advanced in terms of their understanding of the importance of customer relationships, their commitment to total quality in customer care, and their use of state-of-the-art technology.

Widespread scepticism still exists about how far the telephone can be used to replace more traditional forms of distribution. Consequently, there is little apparent understanding among UK businesses as to what is required to maximize the benefits of customer contact by telephone.

Increasing competition and the need to gain competitive advantage

Another factor driving a reassessment of the role of the telephone is the potential for non-price differentiation in an increasingly competitive environment.

On a second front, the competitive battle for 'ownership' of the consumer between retailers and manufacturers in the grocery sector, and in others too, has also had a great impact. Today, we see the growth of customer care telephone lines on packaged goods, as manufacturers try to develop their links and relationships with consumers.

Development of the telecommunications infrastructure

Another vital context is the dramatic and sweeping changes that are taking place in two areas of the telecommunications field – market de-regulation and the spread and adoption of new technologies.

Underlying the development of new services has been the upgrading of the UK network to digital exchanges. Digital technology now gives BT and its competitors the flexibility, accuracy and power to provide value-added services to businesses and consumers alike – at highly attractive rates. Digitalization of UK telecoms provides companies with the technology to offer relatively complex interactive services and cable continues to spread across the country.

These developments are likely to promote the concept of the telephone as an interactive, sophisticated medium and will help to accelerate the emergence of a society adept in telecommunications.

The advent of the Single European Market has also created a better environment for telecoms companies to compete internationally. The planned standardization of European and international Freefone numbers has engineered an unprecedented cooperation between the main national carriers, and will doubtless provide an impetus to pan-European marketing campaigns and the development of centralized call-handling facilities.

Fragmenting media use and the declining power of traditional advertising

There are a number of trends in print and broadcast media use which suggest that traditional advertising may begin to lose some of its effectiveness in the second half of the 1990s and beyond.

First, the proliferation of media outlets and the increasing fragmentation of media audiences mean that it will simply be harder for advertisers to reach the same size of audience (although there remain some very considerable mass audiences).

Second, greater media choice will make it increasingly difficult to target consumer groups through traditional media. The traditional ways in which media audiences are segmented – age, sex, class, income group – have less and less purchase on consumer habits. This will make it increasingly difficult for advertisers to target audiences and will raise concern about the cost of wastage.

Third, there is already a claimed degree of irritation with the volume of advertising. Two-thirds of respondents in the Centre's 1993 'Media futures' survey agreed that they found the number of advertisements on television irritating, while half said the same of advertising in newspapers. Not surprisingly, there is also a high level of advertising avoidance.

Given these three changes, it is scarcely surprising that advertisers are relatively down-beat about their expected expenditure on conventional media. They identify direct marketing as an increasingly powerful communication tool in the more fragmented context of the late 1990s.

Changing attitudes and 'top-down' commitment

The final factor driving change in business perceptions of telebusiness is a mixture of increasing orientation towards customers, focus on customer loyalty, a commitment to getting more out of the existing customer base, and interest in various measures such as life-time value. This changed emphasis in commercial objectives is of crucial importance to the role of the telephone in sales, marketing and service. Television is seen as the pre-eminent medium in areas such as raising awareness, repositioning brands and launching new products. It is seen to be less effective in the areas which are likely to be the focus of commercial concern in the second half of the 1990s – building long-term brand loyalty, directly increasing sales, targeting consumers and providing value for money.

The suggestion is that 'customer care' has important bottom-line implications.

Yet, it remains difficult to prove. However, there are growing numbers of senior managers who are prepared to make a commitment to investing in new telephone-based customer care systems. Some commentators describe this as an 'act of faith'. In other instances research has shown that it represents a good return on investment.

A2.6 The constraints on growth

If much of what we have said so far in this report paints a truly positive picture for growth in the use of the telephone in sales, marketing and customer service, there are a few causes for concern. All revolve around business attitudes to the use of the telephone and, in particular, corporate ignorance of its potential and of the relative degree of consumer receptiveness towards it.

Negative attitudes and ignorance – telephone on the periphery

Our corporate research, both qualitative and quantitative, revealed a rather negative set of attitudes towards telebusiness and a lack of necessary investment in it. However, these attitudes are easily explained by a number of historical factors prevalent in the UK marketplace.

A major issue is the lack of interest among companies in the prospects for independent channels of distribution. While many manufacturers and service providers are now aware of the potential for such new channels, most are worried about upsetting the existing distribution network.

Interestingly, not all retailers are happy with this. Argos, for example, now insists that all small electrical appliances sold through its catalogue are supported with customer help line numbers run by manufacturers. On the other hand, however, many manufacturers see their 'customers' as the distributors: end users are merely 'the consumers' – a category which reflects the distance at which the relationship with end users is conducted.

The final and most resounding negative was the view, quite widely held, that customers in many areas are not necessarily happy to use the telephone and are wary about providing personal data. This implies that customers do not want to embark on a relationship with suppliers. Yet, while we have seen this is true for a minority of consumers, it is certainly not the case for the majority.

A missed opportunity? A mismatch between business and consumer views

Not surprisingly, given the low levels of professional organization and these widely held negative views, there are several points on which the consumer and business research findings are inconsistent. At a general level, the story is one of disappointment and lack of service from the consumers' point of view. Clearly, in this area of marketing, as in all others, the secret of success lies in understanding and meeting consumer needs.

In our research, we found that businesses failed to meet consumer needs in three ways. First, when asked what were the three most important benefits of using the telephone in dealings with business, 74 per cent opted for the ability to get immediate answers, and 71 per cent time-saving. Yet as many as 55 per cent of all companies put all calls through their switchboards. Thus, in the majority of instances, callers do not experience the benefits they most appreciate.

Second, while about one in two consumers would prefer to use a Freefone 0800 number, rising to three in four among regular users of 0800, only 18 per cent of businesses actually offer either a Freefone or local rate number.

The third failure of businesses involves queuing systems. The 40 per cent of our sample of companies who provide these were most likely to give a voice message followed by music or voice only. This was the least favoured system among consumers. By contrast, only 12 per cent of firms provide a system that tells callers where they are in the queue.

The need for professional advice (and knowing where to get it)

While agencies and a growing number of specialist telemarketing consultants are vitally important in leading the market with new technology, new applications and techniques, their impact is only really felt at the very top end of the market. As the amount of telephone activity conducted by businesses expands, so these companies have diminishing influence and market share – which creates problems for the future. The American telephone operation management techniques which have been adopted by the UK market, largely through agencies, are very specific – like the basic disciplines of direct marketing. If these techniques are not more widely disseminated and made available to the larger market of small and medium companies, they are unlikely to be able to deliver the quality and the results that could be achieved.

A reticence to invest, test and research

Related to lack of knowledge and insufficient use of specialist skills is a more general concern: the timidity of UK businesses to invest in new techniques, particularly given continuing economic uncertainty and the relentless pressures of cost and competition. For though these pressures will all make telephone communications more important, many UK businesses are still grappling with quite different problems — and in particular, outmoded company structures. Such structures result in inflexible decision making; separate functional units are responsible for different parts of the customer relationship, so there is little overall coordination. All this creates deep-seated barriers to being 'close to the customer', and thus to using telephone communications with the market.

Equally, the investment required to set up a telephone operation is substantial, even if, because the cost of technology is falling, obstacles to entry are now considerably lower than they were five years ago. Returns are rarely realized in the short term; anyway, real returns tend to relate to long-term customer loyalty and the contribution this makes to greater profitability over time.

There is also concern about the acceptability of many of the new technologies to the consumer, particularly with interactive computerized voice and electronic media. However, we have seen that advanced technologies are already considered acceptable to a significant minority of consumers, providing that there are discernible benefits and that there is the option of speaking to a live operator if required. So, for firms looking at computerized alternatives, costs are likely to be outweighed by rewards.

UK business betrays a lack of appreciation of the potential benefits of telephone-based operations. It is reticent about investing, unconfident and weak in testing and monitoring, and hesitant about technology. All this holds back the take-up of telebusiness in Britain.

A2.7 The future potential for telebusiness in the UK

Making the most of the opportunities

We can see no inherent reasons why, for a wide variety of goods and services, British consumers will avoid using telephone-based services more in the future. In terms of attitudes, and in terms of the situations in which they already use the telephone to contact businesses, they differ from their American counterparts in degree, not in kind. At the same time, consumer demands for improved quality, better price and service remain buoyant.

One of the key issues for British businesses is how they can deliver, cost-effectively and competitively, what sophisticated consumers actually want. In a climate of growing concern over the cost of maintaining extensive retail outlets and the threat posed to manufacturers by the 'own label' offerings of the major retail chains, telephone-based channels have a chance to come into their own as a low-cost, effective route to meeting consumer needs.

Corporate innovators in telebusiness have already benefited from the willingness to use the telephone, which we have identified in this report. Indeed, in many ways, the telebusiness services British consumers will want over the short to medium term will be determined by those corporate innovators.

Of course, one of our key findings has been that some consumers resist dealing with businesses over the telephone. But that only confirms how important it is to be able to identify *and target appropriately* consumers around the four segments we have discussed. At one level, staff could be trained to assess the 'type' of caller. First Direct already does something like this in training its staff to gauge the mood of the caller. We believe, however, that further research by business would allow them to link certain behaviour patterns to particular segments. Alternatively, simple attitudinal questions could be added to scripts, forms or questionnaires – for example, 'would you be happy for us to call you at home?' Collecting such information and analysing and applying it across a database would provide a very powerful targeting tool for more focused communications activity.

Companies should invest in sophisticated consumer research to understand better the qualitative requirements of their customers. Increasingly, companies should extend their research into the types of communications that customers want.

Fast forward to the future

That telephone communication will continue to expand between customers and companies is indisputable. Because consumers arc also confident with this medium, more than other aspects of IT, it will dominate until the millennium, even though other interactive technologies will begin to grow in significance before that date.

From our research, we have seen that the telephone is an acceptable way for consumers to access information and service from companies. We have seen that, across several markets and to confident consumers, it has potential for distributing a wide range of products. We have also seen some potential for controlled calling to customers. But until British business decision makers wake up to these facts and invest in the technology, skills and services required to satisfy consumer needs, the market will not grow as rapidly as it should. The few and the brave, and only them, will reap the enormous potential rewards available. 🟊🟊

Appendix 3
Use of the telephone in TV advertising

In 1993/94, BT and Channel 4 Television commissioned quantitative and qualitative research into direct response television (DRTV) advertising. This was the first study of its kind in the UK. The objectives were:

- to identify what makes DRTV work effectively and to determine guidelines on how to maximize the efficiency of response, and
- to understand what motivates viewers to respond to a DRTV commercial.

The following outline of the research project and its findings is published by kind permission of BT and Channel 4 Television.

A3.1 Outline research methodology

The quantitative research was carried out by Broadcast Monitor, AGB and BT. It involved monitoring all TV commercials shown:

- on two channels (ITV, Channel 4)
- in four regions – London, Yorkshire, Scotland, North West – representing 50 per cent of TV viewers
- during the last two weeks of three months – September, October, November – in 1993
- between 12 p.m. and 12 a.m.

AGB Television Information Systems developed the research methodology, which was designed to provide a reporting system enabling continuous tracking of DRTV advertising. During the research period, Broadcast Monitor identified all commercials with a telephone number and recorded the following data for each one:

- channel and region
- day/date/time
- duration
- programme environment

- manufacturer/supplier
- brand
- telephone number
- duration of phone number on screen
- call to action.

A total of 8547 commercials with a telephone number were shown during the monitoring period (advertising 91 products and giving 70 different telephone numbers). Of these, only 5500 were 'true' DRTV commercials in the opinion of the researchers (i.e. where the telephone number is there for a purpose) and so these were also analysed independently (referred to later as 'Selected DRTV').

BT collected call response data for those commercials carrying certain types of telephone number, i.e. 0800 (toll free), 0345 (local call charge) and 0891 (premium rate). Only incremental calls were measured. This means that any background activity immediately before the commercial was shown (perhaps as a result of other media activity) was taken as the base level; only calls above this level after the commercial had been broadcast were attributed to being as a result of the commercial. Call response data was matched with each DRTV screening and then response levels were compared with 'opportunities to see'.

The qualitative research was conducted by the Psychology Department of Leeds University, using focus group interviews with known responders and non-responders to DRTV commercials. This research was designed to begin to explore consumer attitudes and reactions to DRTV advertising.

A3.2 Summary of research findings

The qualitative research revealed that all commercials carry certain values for viewers:

- *Informativeness*, i.e. How much am I being told about this product?
- *Relevance*, i.e. Could this product have any relevance to my life?
- *Involvement*, i.e. Am I just sitting on the sidelines or should I get involved with the advertisement for this product?
- *Quality*, i.e. Are the standards of what I am looking at high enough for me?
- *Expense*, i.e. What level of financial involvement do I want with this proposition?

Some of these values are more relevant to DRTV advertising than others.

The objective of DRTV

People viewing a TV commercial are somewhere between traffic light changes, between the state of mind where they have no intention of responding ('red') and being ready to respond ('green'). An individual can be at any point between these two states at any time. The objective of direct response advertising is therefore to move people to the green light.

Action values

The research showed that, for DRTV commercials, the action values of *relevance, quality* and *expense* are most important in moving people towards the green light (i.e. in creating preparedness to respond). The values of *informativeness* and *involvement* contain attributes of relaxing, enjoying and unwinding, and are associated more with non-direct response commercials.

A direct response commercial must stimulate viewers and motivate and prepare them for action, i.e. it should tell them that this message is different and it will require a response. The way in which the values of *relevance, quality* and *expense* come through in a commercial will move the viewer either positively or negatively – towards the green light (prepared to respond) or towards the red light (unprepared to respond).

Relevance becomes a positive value if it makes the viewer think about the product personally. *Quality* becomes a positive factor if the commercial builds the viewer's trust in the company, quality of service and reliability of the product. *Expense* becomes a positive factor if viewers fully understand the cost to them of responding, and their fears of hard-selling, unwanted direct mail, etc., after they respond are minimized. One effective way of making *expense* a positive factor is to convince viewers that they will make savings by taking action.

Once viewers reach the green light they are ready to respond; all they need is a well-displayed and positioned phone number. The quantitative research helps us to understand how to maximize the number of green light viewers who pick up the phone.

Creating an efficient response

The response efficiency of a DRTV commercial can be defined as 'the number of calls generated as a percentage of the number of viewers'. It is usually expressed as an index against the average. The two key factors affecting the response efficiency of a DRTV commercial are the timing of the broadcast and the creative elements of the commercial.

Index

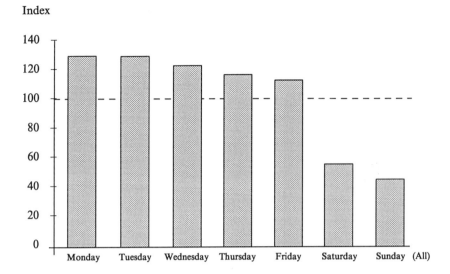

Figure A3.1 DRTV response efficiency by day of the week

BROADCAST TIMING

Mondays were found to generate the most efficient response, with a very gradual decline in response efficiency as the week progresses (Figure A3.1). By the weekend, however, especially Sunday, the response could be up to 3 times *less* efficient than a Monday.

As regards the time of day, slots between 12 p.m. and 2 p.m. result in the most efficient response, followed by 2 p.m. to 4 p.m. (Figure A3.2). Commercials broadcast later in the evening, i.e. 6 p.m.–9 p.m. and 9 p.m.–12 p.m., are 5–6 times *less* efficient.

Positioning relative to a programme was also found to be important, with end breaks being 1.8 times more efficient than centre breaks.

Collectively, these findings provide guidelines for the broadcast timing of DRTV advertising.

CREATIVE ELEMENTS

In general, the longer the duration of the commercial the better the response efficiency. Comparing 10 second and 90 second commercials, 90 seconds therefore generates the most efficient response. However, when you take into account the differing costs of the slots, then both the 10 and 90 second commercials come out as giving the most efficient response (Figure A3.3).

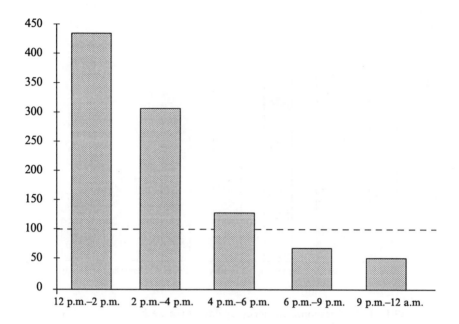

Figure A3.2   DRTV response efficiency by day part

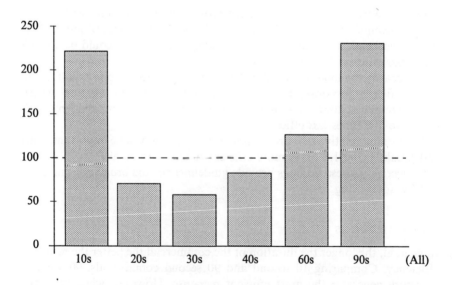

Figure A3.3   DRTV commercial response efficiency by duration, weighted by cost factor

commercials lasting 20 or 30 seconds are up to 4 times *less* efficient, possibly because these time lengths are traditionally associated with brand and awareness advertising.

In terms of how long the phone number is displayed on the screen, the response efficiency is 4 times greater when it is shown for more than 10 seconds (1–5 seconds, response efficiency index = 50; 6–10 seconds, index = 83; 11+ seconds, index = 402). Adding a voiceover of the telephone number increases response efficiency threefold (a response efficiency index of 142 versus 44).

Handling response

The timing of response obviously impacts on the ability to handle calls efficiently. The research showed that the majority of calls are made within the first 15 minutes after the commercial is shown, with most of those arriving in the first 3 minutes (Figure A3.4). 'True' direct response commercials were found to produce the highest response. The best response rate was 0.23 per cent, i.e. 2300 calls per million viewers. The top ten average response rate was 0.038 per cent.

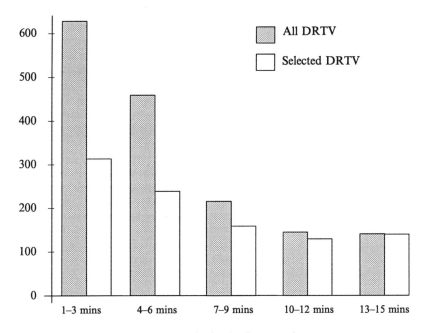

Figure A3.4   DRTV response profile in the first 15 minutes

To summarize the key findings of the research, when you are looking at using DRTV, consider:

- how you will motivate the viewer to take action and respond to your commercial;
- the timing of the commercial, i.e. the TV slots you buy;
- the length of the commercial and the duration of phone number display;
- the likely response rate and levels, and how you will handle the calls.

Index